Corpus Linguistics for Online Communication

Corpus Linguistics for Online Communication provides an instructive and practical guide to conducting research using methods in corpus linguistics in studies of various forms of online communication. Offering practical exercises and drawing on original data taken from online interactions, this book:

- introduces the basics of corpus linguistics, including what is involved in designing and building a corpus;
- reviews cutting-edge studies of online communication using corpus linguistics, foregrounding different analytical components to facilitate studies in professional discourse, online learning, public understanding of health issues and dating apps;
- showcases both freely-available corpora and the innovative tools that students and researchers can access to carry out their own research.

Corpus Linguistics for Online Communication supports researchers and students in generating high quality, applied research and is essential reading for those studying and researching in this area.

Luke Curtis Collins is a Senior Research Associate at Lancaster University, U.K.

Routledge Corpus Linguistics Guides provide accessible and practical introductions to using corpus linguistic methods in key sub-fields within linguistics. Corpus linguistics is one of the most dynamic and rapidly developing areas in the field of language studies, and use of corpora is an important part of modern linguistic research. Books in this series provide the ideal guide for students and researchers using corpus data for research and study in a variety of subject areas.

Series consultant: Michael McCarthy
Michael McCarthy is Emeritus Professor of Applied Linguistics at the University of Nottingham, UK, Adjunct Professor of Applied Linguistics at the University of Limerick, Ireland and Visiting Professor in Applied Linguistics at Newcastle University, UK. He is co-editor of the Routledge Handbook of Corpus Linguistics, editor of the Routledge Domains of Discourse series and co-editor of the Routledge Applied Corpus Linguistics series.

Series consultant: Anne O'Keeffe
Anne O'Keeffe is Senior Lecturer in Applied Linguistics and Director of the Inter-Varietal Applied Corpus Studies (IVACS) Research Centre at Mary Immaculate College, University of Limerick, Ireland. She is co-editor of the Routledge Handbook of Corpus Linguistics and co-editor of the Routledge Applied Corpus Linguistics series.

Series co-founder: Ronald Carter
Ronald Carter (1947–2018) was Research Professor of Modern English Language in the School of English at the University of Nottingham, UK. He was also the co-editor of the Routledge Applied Corpus Linguistics series, Routledge Introductions to Applied Linguistics series and Routledge English Language Introductions series.

Other titles in this series

Corpus Linguistics for Grammar
Christian Jones and Daniel Waller

Corpus Linguistics for ELT
Ivor Timmis

Corpus Linguistics for Translation and Contrastive Studies
Mikhail Mikhailov and Robert Cooper

Corpus Linguistics for Vocabulary
Pawel Szudarski

Corpus Linguistics for Pragmatics
Christoph Rühlemann

Corpus Linguistics for Online Communication
Luke Curtis Collins

More information about this series can be found at www.routledge.com/series/RCLG

Corpus Linguistics for Online Communication

A Guide for Research

Luke Curtis Collins

Routledge
Taylor & Francis Group
LONDON AND NEW YORK

First published 2019
by Routledge
2 Park Square, Milton Park, Abingdon, Oxon OX14 4RN

and by Routledge
52 Vanderbilt Avenue, New York, NY 10017

Routledge is an imprint of the Taylor & Francis Group, an informa business

© 2019 Luke Curtis Collins

The right of Luke Curtis Collins to be identified as author of this work has been asserted by him in accordance with Sections 77 and 78 of the Copyright, Designs and Patents Act 1988.

All rights reserved. No part of this book may be reprinted or reproduced or utilised in any form or by any electronic, mechanical or other means, now known or hereafter invented, including photocopying and recording, or in any information storage or retrieval system, without permission in writing from the publishers.

Trademark notice: Product or corporate names may be trademarks or registered trademarks, and are used only for identification and explanation without intent to infringe.

British Library Cataloguing-in-Publication Data
A catalogue record for this book is available from the British Library.

Library of Congress Cataloging-in-Publication Data
Names: Collins, Luke, author.
Title: Corpus linguistics for online communication: a guide
for research/Luke Curtis Collins.
Description: Milton Park, Abingdon, Oxon; New York, NY: Routledge, 2019. |
Series: Routledge corpus linguistics guides |
Includes bibliographical references and index.
Identifiers: LCCN 2018048756 | ISBN 9781138718838 (hardback) |
ISBN 9781138718968 (pbk) | ISBN 9780429057090 (e-book)
Subjects: LCSH: Communication–Data processing.
Classification: LCC P96.D36 C65 2019 | DDC 410.1/88–dc23
LC record available at https://lccn.loc.gov/2018048756

ISBN: 978-1-138-71883-8 (hbk)
ISBN: 978-1-138-71896-8 (pbk)
ISBN: 978-0-429-05709-0 (ebk)

Typeset in Baskerville
by Deanta Global Publishing Services, Chennai, India

Printed and bound in Great Britain by
TJ International Ltd, Padstow, Cornwall

Contents

List of figures		vi
List of tables		vii
Abbreviations		viii
Acknowledgements		x

	Introduction	1
1	What is corpus linguistics?	8
2	Designing and building corpora	29
3	Analysing corpora	51
4	Online communication: Corpus approaches	76
5	Business and organisational communication online: The Dukki Facebook corpus	97
6	Online learning platforms: The Nottingham Online Business Learner English (NOBLE) corpus	122
7	Online user comments: A corpus of the responses to news on antimicrobial resistance (AMR)	149
8	Dating apps: A Tinder corpus	170
9	Corpus linguistics in perspective	189
	Appendix	195
	Glossary	196
	Task commentaries	200
	Index	204

Figures

1.1	Corpora available at corpus.byu.edu	17
2.1	Features of a webpage for boilerplate removal (Author's own)	40
3.1	The collocation network for 'table' and 'tennis' displayed in GraphColl	60
4.1	A rendering of the 'distracted boyfriend' meme	85
4.2	Labelling strategies of the 'distracted boyfriend' meme	86
5.1	Distribution of Dukki Facebook posts across 2017	105
5.2	Categories of images posted on the Dukki Facebook page	107
5.3	Collocates of 'we' in the Dukki Facebook corpus	112
6.1	Learner comments that have been copied and pasted to a word processor	130
6.2	Number of comments per unit by year across the NOBLE corpus	133
6.3	Number of words in the comments data per unit by year across the NOBLE corpus	133
6.4	Relative frequency of 'face' by learning unit and year	138
6.5	Relative frequency of 'social face' by learning unit and year	139
6.6	Collocation network for 'social' as extended from 'face'	139
6.7	Collocation network for 'social face'	140

Tables

3.1	Categories of pronouns in CLAWS	57
3.2	Most frequent words across texts	67
3.3	Keywords in *Harry Potter* when compared with BNC1994	67
5.1	Examples of studies of 'enregisterment'	104
5.2	The most-frequently used non-standard words in the Dukki Facebook corpus	108
5.3	Keywords in the Dukki Facebook corpus compared with BNC1994	111
5.4	Concordance lines for 'me' followed by 'ducks' in the Dukki Facebook corpus	114
6.1	Number of comments and number of words in the NOBLE corpus	132
6.2	Keyword list for the NOBLE corpus	134
6.3	Keyword lists for the NOBLE corpus by year	135
6.4	Collocates of 'face' in the NOBLE corpus	137
6.5	'Face' terms across the BNC1994, COCA and the NOBLE corpus	138
6.6	Concordances of 'social (identity) face' that include 'distinction'/'difference'	141
6.7	Learner activity in terms of number of comments	143
6.8	Keywords for new comments (Level 1) and replies (Level 2) compared with the BNC1994 Written Sampler	143
6.9	A comparison of keywords for Level 1 and Level 2 comments	144
7.1	Highest number of articles including the search terms 'AMR'/'antibiotic resistant'/'antibiotic resistance' by publication	155
7.2	'AMR' articles with the highest number of user comments	156
7.3	Key semantic categories and constituent tokens for the *MailOnline* article	157
7.4	Key semantic categories and constituent tokens for *The Guardian* article	158
7.5	Top semantic categories for the *MailOnline* comments thread	161
7.6	Top semantic categories for *The Guardian* comments thread	163
8.1	Respondents by gender and sexual orientation	179
8.2	Most frequent 3-grams in the Tinder corpus	182

Abbreviations

ACE	Australian Corpus of English
AMR	Antimicrobial Resistance
ANC	American National Corpus
API	Application Programming Interface
BE06	British English 2006 Corpus
BNC1994	British National Corpus (original)
BNC2014	British National Corpus (data collected 2012–2016)
BYU	Brigham Young University
CA	Conversation Analysis
CADS	Corpus-Assisted Discourse Studies
CAMDA	Corpus-Assisted Multimodal Discourse Analysis
CANBEC	Cambridge and Nottingham Business English Corpus
CANELC	Cambridge and Nottingham E-Language Corpus
CDA	Critical Discourse Analysis. Also, CDS: Critical Discourse Studies
CLAWS	Constituent Likelihood Automatic Word-tagging System
CLiC	Corpus Linguistics in Context
CMC	Computer-Mediated Communication
CMD	Computer-Mediated Discourse
COCA	Corpus of Contemporary American English
COHA	Corpus of Historical American English
CorCenCC	Corpws Cenedlaethol Cymraeg Cyfoes, the National Corpus of Contemporary Welsh
CORE	Corpus of Online Registers of English
FLOB	Freiburg-LOB Corpus of British English
FROWN	Freiburg-Brown Corpus of American English
GDPR	General Data Protection Regulation
GIF	Graphics Interchange Format
GloWBE	Corpus of Global Web-Based English
HERMES	100-million-word Twitter Corpus
HTML	Hyper Text Markup Language
HTTP	Hyper Text Transfer Protocol
ICAME	International Computer Archive of Modern and Medieval English

ICE	International Corpus of English
KWIC	Key Word in Context
LBRTD	Location-Based Real-Time Dating
LiPP	Linguistic Profiling for Professionals
LL	Log-likelihood
LOB	Lancaster-Oslo/Bergen Corpus
MD	Multi-Dimensional (analysis)
MICASE	Michigan Corpus of Academic Spoken English
MOOC	Massive Open Online Course
NLP	Natural Language Processing
NOBLE	Nottingham Online Business Learner English Corpus
PII	Personally Identifiable Information
SMS	Short Messaging Service: colloquially known as text messaging
UCREL	University Centre for Computer Corpus Research on Language
URI/URL	Uniform Resource Identifier/Uniform Resource Locator
USAS	UCREL Semantic Analysis System
VARD	Variant Detection tool
WaC	Web as Corpus
WHO	World Health Organization
XML	eXtensible Markup Language

Acknowledgements

I would first like to thank all of the research participants who volunteered to take part in the studies reported here and to those who helped in the recruitment stages. Special thanks go to Heidi Hargreaves and Ian Jones at Dukki Gifts & Souvenirs and to the Linguistic Profiling for Professionals (LiPP) team behind the MOOC 'How to Read Your Boss'.

I am grateful to Paweł Szudarski, Louise Mullany, Gavin Brookes, Norbert Schmitt and Mike Sharples, with whom I have consulted in one way or another about this work. I would also like to thank Anne O'Keeffe and Michael McCarthy for their feedback, and the editorial team at Routledge, particularly Lizzie Cox, for their support.

Finally, I would like to thank Emily James for providing artwork and encouragement throughout.

Introduction

> It was not the linguistic climate but the technological one that stimulated the development of corpora.
>
> (Tognini Bonelli, 2010: 15)

The advancement of research has often gone hand in hand with the advancement of technology and this is as true with respect to the development of **corpus linguistics** as with any other field. Definitions of 'corpus linguistics' often cite the 'machine' at the heart of the process that facilitates our systematic exploration of large sets of language data (the '**corpus**', plural: 'corpora'). For example, Biber and Reppen (2015: 1) tell us that studies in corpus linguistics typically "make extensive use of computers for analysis, employing both automatic and interactive techniques". McEnery and Hardie (2012: 1) provide the following general definition of corpus linguistics to account for the different procedures that are carried out within the area: "dealing with some set of machine-readable texts which is deemed an appropriate basis on which to study a specific set of research questions".

Similarly, in extolling the virtues of corpus linguistics, researchers tend to foreground the qualities afforded by its computational processes. Adolphs (2006: 7–8), in summarising the advantages of using electronic text analysis (wherein she cites her own preference for focusing on corpus linguistics techniques), suggests the following benefits:

- Using electronic text analysis is a more replicable process and can be verified by other researchers.
- Electronic text analysis allows us to extract information about language that does not tend to be open to intuitive inspection.
- The use of software tools allows us to manipulate language data in various ways to suit a particular research purpose, leading to more accurate and consistent results in a very short amount of time.
- Sorting the data in an accessible way allows us to identify patterns that we might not be able to describe purely on an intuitive basis.

Certainly, these latter points attest to the computer being 'better' than the manual researcher at counting and sorting data, in a more consistent way and much more quickly. It is the computational processes that are said to ensure consistency and minimise the impacts of human error and subjective bias as captured in the purported benefits of electronic text analysis introduced above. Indeed, in addition to the utilisation of computers, Biber and Reppen (2015: 1) report that corpus linguistics approaches "are empirical, analysing actual patterns of use in natural texts" and "are based on analysis of a large and principled collection of natural texts". Our analysis, therefore, is predicated on 'real' language use and the computer supports us in saying something meaningful about language that is based on evidence.

Corpus linguistics resides within a broader field of computational linguistics, which has overlapped with developments that have brought together language studies and computer programs in other disciplines, such as Natural Language Processing (NLP) in computer sciences and computational psycholinguistics in psychology (for an overview of the development of these fields, see Jurafsky and Martin, 2008: 9–14). Many of the processes that characterise NLP are fundamental to corpus linguistics, which in turn has contributed significantly to developments in NLP, as corpora offer "unparalleled sources of quantitative data" (McEnery, 2003: 459). The development of tools in NLP, such as machine translation and speech recognition, has been informed by the types of questions that have emerged from, and to some extent been answered by, studies in corpus linguistics.

Computational linguistics has seen theoretical developments in language and cognitive science, alongside systems of mathematical modelling, and technological advances in computer sciences and electronic engineering. Arguably, one of the main drives behind computational linguistics is to facilitate 'conversation' between humans and computers, but the early efforts in the 1950s to carry out machine translation simply highlighted how complex language processing is (Grisham, 1986). It then became apparent that in order to support machines in using language, it would have to be modelled in some way. In the 1960s, Joseph Weizenbaum published details on a program called ELIZA[1] (Weizenbaum, 1966) that we might now recognise as a Chatbot and which used relatively simple pattern matching to formulate seemingly appropriate conversational responses. For example, were you to type, 'You are x', you would get the response, 'What makes you think I am x?'. This system for recognising key phrases and returning preprogrammed responses has been the basis of most subsequent Chatbot interfaces and is now manifest in customer service chat relays online, even supported by Facebook Messenger and WhatsApp. When combined with speech recognition, such programming has led to the creation of dialogue systems on smartphone devices, such as Apple Inc.'s 'Siri' and the intelligent personal assistant of the Amazon Echo speaker system, known as 'Alexa'. Such software recognises speech commands when delivered using salient keywords and carries out a relevant programming task, whilst also offering an appropriate audible ('spoken') response.

The creation of computerised corpora is generally thought to have begun with the Brown Corpus, at around the same time as Weizenbaum's work. Henry Kučera and W. Nelson Francis compiled this corpus of around 500 texts published in the U.S.A. in 1961, amounting to approximately 1 million words of data. A counterpart British-English corpus known as the Lancaster-Oslo/Bergen Corpus (LOB) of British English was compiled based on the same criteria and this process was replicated in 1991 to generate the Freiburg-Brown Corpus of American English (FROWN) and the Freiburg-LOB Corpus of British English (FLOB). The expansion of what has become known as the 'Brown family' has ensured that the original corpus has remained a significant point of reference.

It was in the early 1990s when the processing power of desktop computers made available texts and language data on a previously unimaginable scale, marking what has been termed the 'First Serendipity' (Tognini Bonelli, 2010: 17). Sinclair (1991: 4), recognising that "the ability to examine large text corpora in a systematic manner allow[ed] access to a quality of evidence that ha[d] not been available before", was one of the drivers of the expansion of corpus linguistics. It was arguably at this point that corpus linguistics switched from a research area that suffered with insufficient data, to one that was so rich with data that it was the methodologies that needed to be swiftly developed in order to capitalise on what was available. Tognini Bonelli (2010: 17) recalls a "theoretical and qualitative revolution" during this period, whereby the computer developed from being a tool that enabled the processing of language data along existing theoretical models, to a means through which new methods were now available and the very way in which we asked questions of the data – the very object of the data – had shifted.

Simultaneously, the 1990s saw the development of the World Wide Web, which was originally proposed by Tim Berners-Lee in 1989 while he was working as a software engineer at CERN (http://info.cern.ch/Proposal.html). Over the next two years, Berners-Lee would establish the core technologies of the Web: Hyper Text Markup Language (HTML); Uniform Resource Identifier (URI), now commonly known as URL (Uniform Resource Locator); and Hypertext Transfer Protocol (HTTP). In 1991, the World Wide Web was made public. Since then, one of the key terms used to mark developments in Web technologies and functions is 'Web 2.0' (DiNucci, 1999: 32), an informal label for a phase of Web applications that are characterised by user-generated content, interaction, and interoperability and epitomised in the expansion of social media. The term was coined principally to distinguish these observed developments from the early stages of the Web (retrospectively, Web 1.0) that, in contrast, were much more static and while supporting information sharing, were limited in facilitating user interaction. Now, we are beginning to see the dimensions of 'Web 3.0', the Semantic Web, which relies on a significant integration of tools from computational linguistics.

If in Web 2.0, the 'social Web' supported users talking to users, then Web 3.0 is about "machines talking to machines" (Berners-Lee et al., 2001). In this model, Web contents are conceptualised, first and foremost, as data that can automatically be processed and, to some extent, interpreted by machines. Although recognising that it had not yet arrived, Berners-Lee has frequently and publicly discussed this vision for the Web (see for example, Berners-Lee et al., 2001), which is contingent upon the development of automated reasoning systems that not only tag data for what it is, but offer some deduction of what it *means*. For example, in conventional HTML, the use of 'means' in the previous sentence might be tagged for use of italics (<i>). Semantic HTML would generate a tag that denotes some form of inference, such as <em> for emphasis. This of course relies on some degree of interpretation of the text, perhaps in relation to the surrounding text and not least of all because the use of italics can serve various purposes. In the last few years we have seen the development of vocabularies that have the capacity to carry out this automatic semantic analysis of online data (e.g. http://schema.org/) and its use in millions of websites (Guha, 2013).

Web users will be familiar with the concept of targeted advertising, the combination of a search query with geolocation tools to ensure nearby results and how social media will not only indicate what is 'Trending', but also arrange this under general news categories such as 'Politics', 'Entertainment' and 'Sport'. These features are the result of developments in computational linguistics, such as topic modelling, which quantitively evaluates the prominent themes in texts on the basis of the use of particular terms. Businesses are using sentiment analysis to canvass customer reviews in order to capture a general sense of the positive and negative responses submitted in online platforms (Pang and Lee, 2008). In 2011, Michel et al. (2011) published a report of their work in 'culturomics', capitalising on Google's digitisation of 130 million books to investigate cultural trends as evidenced in changing language and grammar between 1800 and 2000. Each of these examples combines the potential and the demands of the Web and Big Data, as well as an extrapolation of fundamental tools in corpus linguistics.

As much as digital technologies have generated new avenues for communication and as much as users have, in turn, driven technological developments to enable new forms of expression, corpus linguists have worked with computer tools and processes to redefine what we can know about language use and how we come to know it. This also corresponds with the practical combination of 'automatic' and 'interactive' techniques corpus linguists use to integrate the computer into their research (Biber and Reppen, 2015: 1), as well as in the very design of the computational tools that support that work where manual correction is still (very occasionally) required. Beginning in the 1990s, the swift advancement of computer technology, most notably the advent of the World Wide Web, has propelled both human interaction and corpus linguistics. These parallel developments – both in terms of function and chronology – have prompted this practical guide. The motivation for this book was to consider how corpus linguistics has developed, and is developing, to support our exploration of those innovative forms of online communication.

About this book

It is the aim of this book to offer a demonstration of how to conduct corpus linguistics research in an online context. Developments in Web communication and corpus linguistics are swift and so this text is intended as a guide to the implementation of the latest methods in corpus analysis as well as an examination of emergent forms of communication found in online spaces. As such, readers will find practical tasks throughout that provide opportunities to try out the methods that are introduced and to critically reflect upon their own research objectives and study design. The commentaries that accompany these tasks will offer some guidance as to how to process and interpret the results of those tasks, though the reader will no doubt develop their own skills and ideas that will extend beyond the parameters of the material introduced here.

While there are some very useful introductions to corpus linguistics that discuss the theoretical considerations (McEnery and Hardie, 2012); showcase a breadth of applications (O'Keeffe and McCarthy, 2010); and offer in-depth practical guidance (Weisser, 2016), this book focuses specifically on the opportunities and challenges of working with online data. There are numerous examples of studies in corpus linguistics exploring online data that have shown what insights can be generated from its implementation in this context and the work that is reported here has benefitted from the outcomes of such work. Here, the reader has the opportunity to explore the methods and processes that are involved in corpus analyses of Web data at a level of detail often not permitted in journal articles and book chapters. Readers are presented with a number of case studies that offer transparency and specificity, as demonstrations of what they will encounter in their own work and which apply a range of tools and analytical measures to different online contexts.

Chapter 1 offers a very general introduction to the field of corpus linguistics, based on what studies in corpus linguistics typically involve and how it is defined in relation to other forms of language analysis. Readers will also be introduced to some of the widely used and freely available corpus query interfaces, which support searches of commonly cited corpora. Chapters 2 and 3 detail the fundamentals to designing, compiling and analysing corpora, discussing key practical considerations and introducing analytical terms. Chapter 3 also introduces some of the corpus analysis tools that readers can download, to carry out their own corpus analysis.

Chapter 4 focuses on studies of online communication and reviews some of the wider discussions of what it is that is interesting and unique about communication on the Web. Chapters 5–8 each present a case study of a specialised corpus of online data and guide the reader through the practical and analytical aspects of these individual research projects. Chapter 5 examines the Facebook page of an independent business, to consider how corpus analysis offers insights into the construction of a brand identity. Chapter 6 introduces a corpus of learner comments, collected through an online course on the topic of business communication in order to consider how corpus analysis helps us to generate evidence of learning. Chapter 7 explores user comments following news articles on the topic of antimicrobial resistance, demonstrating some of the ways in which the public debates complex global health issues. In Chapter 8, the topic of self-promotion in dating apps is explored through a corpus of Tinder profiles.

Chapter 9 considers corpus linguistics from a wider perspective, highlighting some of the methodological challenges for applied linguistics more broadly and reviewing some of the innovations that reflect the cutting edge of corpus linguistics research. This chapter then summarises what has been discussed and encourages the reader to consider further areas of exploration.

Corpus Linguistics for Online Communication presents a breadth of topics relating to online communication and as such, can be read in its entirety as a coherent practical guide. However, you can also treat the case study chapters as individual studies and focus on those parts of the book that best relate to your skills and interests. Each chapter ends with a list of references that offer an ideal expansion on what is introduced here and there is a glossary of key terms, which appear in **bold** when they are first introduced in the text.

Note

1 An ELIZA interface is still available at: http://psych.fullerton.edu/mbirnbaum/psych101/Eliza.htm.

References

Adolphs, S. (2006). *Introducing Electronic Text Analysis: A Practical Guide for Language and Literary Studies*. London: Routledge.

Berners-Lee, T., Hendler, J. and Lassila, O. (2001). The semantic web. *Scientific American*, 284, 5, 35–43.

Biber, D. and Reppen, R. (2015). Introduction, in D. Biber and R. Reppen (eds) *The Cambridge Handbook of Corpus Linguistics*. Cambridge: Cambridge University Press, 1–8.

DiNucci, D. (1999). Fragmented future. *Print*, 53, 4, 32, 221–222.

Grisham, R. (1986). *Computational Linguistics: An Introduction*. Cambridge: Cambridge University Press.

Guha, R. V. (2013). Light at the End of the Tunnel. *The 12th International Semantic Web Conference*. 21–25 October 2013, Sydney, Australia. Available at: http://iswc2013.semanticweb.org/content/keynote-ramanathan-v-guha.html, accessed 6 April 2018.

Jurafsky, D. and Martin, J. H. (2008). *Speech and Language Processing: An Introduction to Natural Language Processing, Computational Linguistics, and Speech Recognition*. London: Prentice-Hall International.

McEnery, T. (2003). Corpus linguistics, in R. Mitkov (ed.) *The Oxford Handbook of Computational Linguistics*. Oxford: Oxford University Press, 448–463.

McEnery, T. and Hardie, A. (2012). *Corpus Linguistics: Method, Theory and Practice*. Cambridge: Cambridge University Press.

Michel, J.-B., Shen, Y. K., Aiden, A. P., Veres, A., Gray, M. K., The Google Books Team, Pickett, J. P., Hoiberg, D., Clancy, D., Norvig, P., Orwant, J., Pinker, S., Nowak, M. A. and Aiden, E. L. (2011). Quantitative analysis of culture using millions of digitized books. *Science*, 331, 6014, 176–182.

O'Keeffe, A. and McCarthy, M. (eds) (2010). *The Routledge Handbook of Corpus Linguistics*. London: Routledge.

Pang, B. and Lee, L. (2008). Opinion mining and sentiment analysis. *Foundations and Trends in Information Retrieval*, 2, 1–2, 1–135.

Sinclair, J. (1991). *Corpus, Concordance, Collocation*. Oxford: Oxford University Press.

Tognini Bonelli, E. (2010). Theoretical overview of the evolution of corpus linguistics, in A. O'Keeffe and M. McCarthy (eds) *The Routledge Handbook of Corpus Linguistics*. London and New York: Routledge, 14–27.

Weisser, M. (2016). *Practical Corpus Linguistics: An Introduction to Corpus-Based Language Analysis*. Oxford: Blackwell.

Weizenbaum, J. (1966). ELIZA – A computer program for the study of natural language communication between man and machine. *Communications of the ACM*, 9, 1, 36–45.

Chapter 1

What is corpus linguistics?

1.1 Features of corpus analysis

Corpus linguistics is concerned with understanding how people use language in various contexts and incorporates computational tools to identify recurring patterns in 'natural' or authentic language use. However, as McEnery and Hardie (2012: 1) observe, "corpus linguistics is not a monolithic, consensually agreed set of methods and procedures for the exploration of language" and what they propose to call 'corpus methods in linguistics' offers a critical resource that can be implemented across and beyond the field of linguistics.

Corpus linguistics is founded on a frequency-based view of language that determines significance from the recurring patterns evidenced in observations of 'real' language data. As Tognini Bonelli (2010: 19) remarks, "The significant elements in a corpus become the patterns of repetition and patterns of co-selection. In other words, in corpus linguistics it is the frequency of occurrence that takes pride of place". This measure of frequency can be in relation to the occurrence of particular features, or it might be the co-occurrence of one feature with another. Furthermore, this might be a measure of a distributional frequency, i.e. regular occurrence across a number of texts within a corpus. The underlying assumption is that the regularity of a formal pattern (i.e. the regular use of a particular form) reflects some functional difference, that language users are regularly opting for one form of expression over another and that this indicates something of its meaning.

We have looked at the role of the computer in our analysis, not least of all in being able to process much more data than a team of manual researchers would be able to – and considerably faster. It is the capacity to process large amounts of data that helps to identify patterns that may be beyond our intuition and which may escape our reading, even if we were given the time to analyse the same amount of data. As manual readers, we are susceptible to giving disproportionate value to some words over others. For example, politically loaded words like 'anti-Semitism' or 'terrorism' may stand out to us more than an unusually frequent use of functional words, such as 'but' or 'you'. Nevertheless, the frequent use of 'you' might attest to a deliberate form of direct address in a piece of marketing discourse; the regular use of 'but' might reflect the counterclaims that typify a debate. The computer does not hold the same biases as we do and will count each word 'equally' (so long as we program it to do so), which allows us to construct our reading on the basis of what is there in the text, though of course we can also conduct searchers for the features we are particularly interested in. Corpus analysis can also support us in validating observations that we have made based on smaller datasets; as Baker and McEnery (2015: 10) assert: "Being able to draw conclusions based on extremely large samples of data adds validity to claims, even if they confirm what we suspected, while providing a quantitative summary gives substance to what may have been a suspicion". The corpus, then, is a resource for evidence-building, that can support our claims but equally, challenge assumptions made about language use that are not reflected in the data.

As much as corpus linguistics foregrounds frequency, corpus linguists emphasise the importance of recognising the context(s) in which language has been produced. Corpus retrieval tools allow the researcher to search for a term and view the **co-text**: the words or features surrounding a particular term that help to determine its meaning. In the most immediate sense, this is enabled by one of the most recognisable and fundamental forms of corpus analysis: Key Word in Context (**KWIC**). This presentation format allows the analyst to view each occurrence of a search term – the **node** word – as a series of **concordance lines**, providing a **span** of the original surrounding text. This process is known as **concordancing** and the presentation of KWIC allows us to read the data both 'horizontally', to recover some of the context in which it is used; but also 'vertically', to elicit a sense of the patterns of how the term is used across texts.

Below is a series of concordance lines for the term 'viral' from the British National Corpus (BNC) 2014:

```
 1  S2FQ  the crowd mm to to create a        viral  story mm and the reason why it is
 2  S55M  this video that went kind of       viral  and was like really controversial
 3  S5B4  bably and try and make it go       viral  yeah er locally viral yeah yeah
 4  S5B4  it go viral yeah er locally        viral  yeah yeah yeah that's what I mean
 5  S5B4  not not like on the internet       viral  but yeah if you do the Wechat
 6  S72E  yeah and make it you know          viral  in whatever way and yeah yeah
 7  S784  because he's the ultimate          viral  guy no no but yeah but he's he he
 8  S784  it's ridiculous the amount of      viral  content they have and like yeah
 9  S784  erm talks on how they get          viral  content and it's interesting like
10  SASC  Twitter that went completely       viral  today er what? by surprise well
11  SASC  and it kind of instantly went      viral  to like forty thousand people
12  SF3V  he's hang- yeah he went            viral  little while back it was oh did
13  SG7X  like your photo it's gone          viral  round the world is it? oh I see yes
14  SGSY  so powerful that's why             viral  videos are so powerful is because
15  SUVL  cos a lot of people get            viral  tonsillitis that's just when you
16  SUVL  UNCLEARWORD if you were            viral  ? --UNCLEARWORD just have to put
17  SUVL  uni but it might have been         viral  I think I just got on with it
18  SXCB  bird or something it went          viral  a woodpecker it was a woodpecker
19  SYED  media thing that could go          viral  viral oh my god cos we said you
20  SYED  thing that could go viral          viral  oh my god cos we said you should
```

Each line represents the next occurrence of the node word ('viral') and these can be sorted in various ways: in the order in which they appear in the text (which is often the default), but also alphabetically by the word that appears, for example, to the immediate left or right of the node word. This helps to identify recurring patterns in how the word is used. For example, we can see in the above 20 concordance lines that the word 'viral' is often preceded by forms of the verb 'to go' (go/gone/went), referring to the process by which social media content becomes widely disseminated in a short space of time. This, of course, is a metaphorical extension of the meaning relating to viruses and how they are transmitted, which we can also see here in reference to 'viral tonsillitis' (line 15). While this is only a small sample from the larger corpus, we can also begin to observe that more frequently, 'viral' is used in relation to social media content than illness. Not only can we quantify this with respect to the entire corpus, but we can also compare this with occurrences from the original BNC, which was collected throughout the 1980s and early-1990s, to see how this has changed over time.

Task 1.1

Go to the BNC search interface available at https://corpus.byu.edu/bnc/ and type 'viral' into the search box. This will show you how many occurrences there are in the BNC and by clicking on VIRAL you will be able to view the concordance lines.

- What types of words tend to follow the use of 'viral'? Are they mostly in reference to illness?
- Can you find any examples of a figurative use of 'viral', in the way that social media content has been described as 'going viral' in the examples above?

The search interface offered by BYU also indicates what category of text the concordance line has been taken from (e.g. newsp_tabloid for a tabloid newspaper, ac_medicine for an academic paper in the field of medicine, fict_prose for a text of fictional prose).

- Do you notice any patterns for how 'viral' is used that relate to the type of text in which it appears?

You will find a commentary on this task at the end of the book.

Corpus linguists will also often document other important aspects of the circumstances in which the text has been produced to inform their reading. For example, they might document the identity of the speaker/author (e.g. in terms of age, gender, class); the mode of communication (spoken conversation, academic journal, social media post); or, for example, the purpose and topic of the communication. This type of **metadata** can help us to explore questions in relation to who is using the term and in what contexts. In the concordance lines presented above each line is labelled with an alphanumeric code, which will refer to the text from which the example has been taken. This provides some initial indication of the extent to which the node word occurs across a range of texts. Concordance lines present us with a lot of condensed information and are therefore a useful way of identifying patterns of language use that we can examine in closer detail, drawing more from the context of the original text.

In some of the instances from the concordance lines provided above it may still be unclear what is being communicated. Most concordance tools will allow the user to extend the span of the co-text and even directly link to the full text. Even then, the analyst may still have questions about the circumstances in which the text has been produced, for what purposes and for whom. One of the concerns that has been expressed in relation to corpus linguistics is that in favouring an exploration of broader patterns, some of the nuance of less pervasive uses could be overlooked. As Tognini Bonelli (2010: 19–20) observes, "The type of information gathered from a corpus is evaluated as meaningful in so far as it can be generalised to the language as a whole, but with no direct connection with a specific instance". Egbert and Schnur (2018) use the analogy of 'missing the trees for the forest' to convey one of the potential drawbacks of relying solely on corpus linguistic methods, which is based on an understanding of the difference between the 'corpus' and the 'text(s)'. They explain: "In order for discourse analysts to learn about language use within a discourse community, their focus must be on the actual texts created by individual members of that discourse community, rather than on a contrived data set" (Egbert and Schnur, 2018: 159).

It is certainly worth remembering that the producer of the text will have an awareness for the internal structure of what they have generated but little or no awareness of the other texts that researchers include in the sampling design of their corpus. Texts are self-contained and function as a cohesive unit, which is significant in terms of understanding how certain information is foregrounded; we would likely want to distinguish an occurrence of a language feature that appears in a headline from another singular instance that appears in a paragraph further down. Partington (2008) reminds us to be cautious about the 'recontextualisation' of corpus data and encourages researchers to familiarise themselves as best they can with the texts that make up a corpus in order to get some sense of their original context. This is not always possible of course, particularly if the researcher is using a corpus they have not themselves collected. We may be relying on minimal (or no) metadata, which is also a reminder of the significance of the value of the appropriate **markup** and **annotation** of corpora. These terms, which refer to how information can be added to a corpus, are explored in the next chapter.

1.2 Corpus linguistics in combination

In the research, we find plenty of examples of studies where corpus linguistics is combined with other types of language analysis, with a view to capitalising on the strengths of the approach(es) and mitigating some of the potential drawbacks. In what follows, I review some of the more common and effective combinations that have emerged in studies in applied linguistics.

1.2.1 Corpus-assisted discourse studies (CADS)

Discourse analysis is often cited as a broad term to capture the many different ways in which researchers explore 'language-in-use' (Blommaert, 2005: 2). Jucker et al. (2009a: 5) define 'discourse' as "the totality of linguistic practices that pertain to a particular domain or that create a particular object", emphasising the role of language (and other semiotic systems) in shaping our understanding of our everyday realities, objects, actions and processes. As such, there is a greater focus on meaning as it unfolds within the parameters of a (set of) text(s) or interaction(s). According to Jones et al. (2015: 4), discourse analysts tend to focus on four things: texts; contexts; actions and interactions; power and ideology. Consideration of these dimensions, with varying degrees of focus, enables researchers to examine the relationships between the 'micro' level and the 'macro' level of discourse to consider how language choices and the composition of texts contribute to certain social practices and orders.

There have been a number of book-long explorations and edited collections of how corpus-based methods can be used for discourse analysis, including: Baker (2006); Biber et al. (2007); Ädel and Reppen (2008); Partington et al. (2013); Baker and McEnery (2015); and Taylor and Marchi (2018), alongside the *Journal of Corpora and Discourse Studies* that was launched in 2017 and which publishes twice-per-year. Partington (2004) is attributed with having first proposed the term corpus-assisted discourse studies (CADS), which is defined as "that set of studies into the form and/or function of language as communicative discourse which incorporate the use of computerised corpora in their analyses" (Partington et al., 2013: 10). The aim, in involving corpus techniques alongside other conventional forms of discourse analysis, is to uncover 'non-obvious meaning', which to some extent offers a response to Cameron's (1998) concern that corpus linguistics is not suited to getting to the 'hidden story' of meaning. It is argued in CADS that this level of meaning can be elicited through the combination of identifying those regular patterns through procedures of corpus analysis alongside a close familiarity with the texts.

1.2.2 Corpus linguistics and critical discourse analysis

Arguably, what distinguishes CDA (or Critical Discourse Studies: CDS) from discourse analysis is that studies in CDA will assume a politicised stance, setting out to expose or understand some aspect of political, social or cultural power imbalance or ideology. As Van Dijk (2001: 96) puts it, CDA is "discourse analysis with an attitude". As such, linguistic analysis alone is not sufficient for CDA, which "requires the overlay of a social theoretic discourse for explaining and explicating the social contexts, concomitants, contingencies and consequences of any given text or discourse" (Luke, 2002: 102). Adopting an overtly politicised stance has raised questions of the objectivity of CDA (Widdowson, 1995), which has been criticised for foregrounding the negative aspects (Martin, 2004), or at least those that fit with the researcher's political objectives at the expense of other aspects of the data. A combined CDA and corpus linguistics approach has been cited as one of the ways in which researchers can attend to this issue (Hardt-Mautner, 1995). Adopting critical discourse analysis as a starting point, Hardt-Mautner (1995: 22) argues that "Drawing on corpus evidence fundamentally redefines the nature of interpretation, turning it from an introspective undertaking into an empirical one". Following this work, researchers have continued to explore this combination, with Baker et al. (2008) providing an effective demonstration in their study of the representations of refugees, asylum seekers, immigrants and migrants (RASIM) in the U.K. press.

1.2.3 Corpus pragmatics

Pragmatics is often defined in contrast to semantics, in the sense that if semantics is concerned with the more enduring and universal meaning of language (e.g. what we might include in a dictionary definition), then pragmatics is concerned with how meaning is informed by and changes with context. This distinction is perhaps best captured in the use of deictic terms, such as 'I', 'here' and 'now'. In terms of semantics, we can say that 'I' refers to an individual in the first person; in terms of pragmatics, we need to know something about the context in order to understand the referent, namely who is using 'I'. There are concerns that basic corpus queries will not capture all of the information, or perhaps the forms, that determine pragmatic meaning, since, as Rühlemann and Aijmer (2015: 10) observe, "for most pragmatic phenomena there is no one-to-one relationship between form and function". However, Adolphs (2008: 2) asserts that, assuming that form and function are integral to 'meaning', such meaning can be described on the basis of recurrent patterns and that we "should be able to extract functional information from such recurrent uses".

Speech act theory is one area of pragmatics in which researchers have demonstrated effective applications of corpus methods. Adolphs (2008) demonstrates that the different functions of 'why don't you' (operating as either a question or a suggestion) can be identified through analysis of the words that frequently occur with the phrase. 'Apologies' are a specific category of speech act that has been investigated through methods in corpus linguistics (e.g. Deutschmann, 2003; Harrison and Allton, 2013; and Page, 2014) and Lutzky and Kehoe (2017) demonstrate using the Birmingham Blog Corpus that an automated corpus analysis of the words that follow the terms 'sorry', 'apologise', 'afraid', 'excuse', 'apology', 'forgive', 'pardon' and 'regret' can help to distinguish occurrences that constitute an apology from other uses of the terms.

Corpora such as the Speech Act Annotated Corpus for Dialogue Systems (Leech and Weisser, 2003), the Corpus of Verbal Response Mode (VRM) (Stiles, 1992) and a subset of the Michigan Corpus of Academic Spoken English (MICASE) (Maynard and Leicher, 2007) have been tagged in order to capture some aspect of their pragmatic meaning, again, with a focus on speech acts. The tagging of this data means that corpus search queries can be carried out in relation to speech act functions, however as Rühlemann (2010) and Lutzky and Kehoe (2017) conclude, since these rely on manual microanalysis to generate and implement appropriate tags, there are limitations as to how much data can be analysed in this way.

There have been a handful of edited collections dedicated to studies combining corpus and pragmatics analysis (Romero-Trillo, 2008; Jucker et al., 2009b; Aijmer and Rühlemann, 2014; Weisser, 2018) and in 2017 the *International Journal of Corpus Linguistics and Pragmatics* ('Corpus Pragmatics') was launched, with the objective of "develop[ing] pragmatics with the aid of quantitative corpus methodology" (http://www.springer.com/education+%26+language/linguistics/journal/41701). In the Introduction to the first issue of *Corpus Pragmatics*, Romero-Trillo (2017: 1) writes: "the use of corpora of different sizes and varied topics is essential to understand human communication and […] corpus pragmatics provides an invaluable toolkit for linguistics due to its rigorous methodology and its multi-faceted methodological implications".

1.2.4 Corpus approaches to sociolinguistics

Sociolinguistics explores varieties of language, typically with respect to groups that share some form of social characteristic, such as region, ethnicity, age, gender etc. This approach helps us to understand how individual language choices are informed by broader social categories, along with situational factors such as who is being addressed, or the (in)formality of the encounter. As with corpus linguistics, in sociolinguistics there are degrees to which researchers focus on quantitative and/or qualitative data. 'Interactional sociolinguistics', for example, tends to rely on ethnographic approaches and looking in close detail at communicative behaviours in context (Gumperz and Hymes, 1972; Rampton, 2017). 'Variationist sociolinguistics', in its simplest form, examines linguistic variables in a quantitative and comparative way to say something meaningful about different social groups, or the same speaker(s) in different contexts (Labov, 1963; Tagliamonte, 2012).

We can see how corpus linguistics is closely aligned with, in particular, variationist sociolinguistics, which argues that language variation is 'systematic' and can be described using empirical, quantitative and frequency-based methods (Biber, 1988). As Andersen (2010: 548) observes, "Computerised corpora form a well-prepared basis for systematic, descriptive studies of instances of actual speech, for language variation and for how social context constrains communicative practices". However, writing in 2010, Baker (2010: 1) points out that despite a number of publications demonstrating the wide applications of corpus linguistics, there had yet to be a book-length treatment of corpus linguistics and sociolinguistics. In the same year, Murphy (2010) reported a study of variation across age groups using a corpus of spoken talk from 3 generations of female speakers in Ireland. She found that a corpus approach enabled her to illustrate "how age-related variation permeates all levels of language: discourse, grammar and lexis" and that "using a corpus-based methodology allowed for these subtleties to be explored in great detail" (Murphy, 2010: 205).

Corpora such as the Helsinki Corpus of British English Dialects (Ihalainen, 1990) show that there had been some recognition of the potential of corpus approaches to dialectology and the International Corpus of English (ICE) (Greenbaum and Nelson, 1996) facilitated explorations of global varieties of English. A number of corpora that capture broad representations of both U.S. English and British English over extensive periods of time (American National Corpus [ANC], Corpus of Contemporary American English [COCA], Corpus of Historical American English [COHA], BNC, the Brown Family) also supported comparisons of British and American English – a comparison that continues to be explored through corpus-based inquiry (Baker, 2017).

More recently, we find examples of 'sociolinguistic corpora' examining language variation in Toronto, Canada (Tagliamonte, 2006), and in London through the Linguistic Innovators Corpus (LIC) (Kerswill et al., 2008). The corpus of Global Web-based English (GloWbE) (Davies and Fuchs, 2015) allows us to continue to explore World Englishes as they manifest on the Web and Huang et al. (2015) use Twitter and geo-tagging to demonstrate that studies of regional variation can be carried out using corpora of social media data. Researchers have already begun to report sociolinguistic studies of the spoken component of the BNC (BNC2014) (Brezina et al., 2018) and Friginal (2018) has recently edited a collection of studies in corpus-based sociolinguistics that demonstrates how researchers have continued to examine questions of: language and dialects, including varieties of global Englishes; corpora and social demographics; and corpora and register characteristics.

1.2.5 Corpus stylistics

Despite the emphasis in definitions of corpus linguistics on 'natural' and authentic use of language, there is as much to be gained in the study of creative or 'literary language', whether it appears in fictional creative writing or in everyday speech. Corpus linguistics has supported explorations of metaphor (Semino, 2008; Krennmayr and Steen, 2017) and irony (Louw, 1993), for example. Mahlberg and McIntyre (2011: 205) demonstrate in a study of Ian Fleming's *Casino Royale* how "a corpus analysis can provide insights into characterization, the creation of particular stylistic effects and the construction of the fictional world of the text". Corpus approaches have been applied in explorations of 'literary style', across a range of literary periods and genres of fiction, for example (see: Scott and Tribble, 2006;

O'Halloran, 2007; Culpeper, 2009; Toolan, 2009; Bednarek, 2010; McIntyre, 2010; Lischinsky, 2018). As McIntyre and Walker (2010: 529) conclude, "for the stylistician, a corpus-methodology provides a way of achieving the more objective kind of analysis that is the hallmark of the stylistic approach to criticism".

The fruitful combination of corpus linguistics and stylistics has given rise to 'corpus stylistics', a discipline that gives particular emphasis to the relationship between linguistics description and literary appreciation (Mahlberg, 2013). As with other disciplinary combinations, "It is exactly the counting and comparing that contributes the additional systematicity to literary stylistics which seems to make corpus stylistics such an attractive undertaking" (Mahlberg, 2014: 380) and corpus approaches provide "a useful means of relatively objectively determining starting-points for a qualitative analysis" (Mahlberg and McIntyre, 2011: 224). This allows researchers to bring in more established approaches to literary linguistics and conduct close readings of the material, beginning with concordance lines (Mahlberg et al., 2016).

The CLiC Dickens project (Mahlberg et al., 2016) and associated Corpus Linguistics in Context (CLiC) tool (http://clic.bham.ac.uk/) is a demonstration of work in forms of literary linguistics that has fully embraced corpus linguistics and integrated corpus analysis tools into its approach. Mahlberg et al. (2016) demonstrate their iterative process for exploring the stylistic features of free indirect discourse and speech representation, concluding from their own work that in developing the concordance feature of their CLiC tool, "There is a payoff for cognitive poetics, narratology, corpus stylistics and literary criticism" (Mahlberg et al., 2016).

1.3 Types of corpora

It is useful for researchers, whatever their experience with corpus linguistics, to be aware of the vast number of publicly available corpora. A number of corpora are freely available to search through the BYU Web Interface (https://corpus.byu.edu/) created by Mark Davies at Brigham Young University, as shown in Figure 1.1. You can register a free profile with the site and this will extend the number of search queries you can run. As you can see, these examples represent largely (American and British) English language data, but from a range of time periods and of a range of text types. Corpora can typically be characterised through particular criteria, reflecting (in most cases) the research purposes for which they were designed and this is the focus of this section. A summary table of the corpora discussed here is provided as an Appendix.

1.3.1 General and specialised corpora

Many of the earliest corpora followed the model set by the Brown Corpus, in order to facilitate direct comparison. As such, the Brown Corpus (American English) was followed by LOB (British English), the Wellington Corpus of Written New Zealand English and by the 1980s, the Australian Corpus of English (ACE)

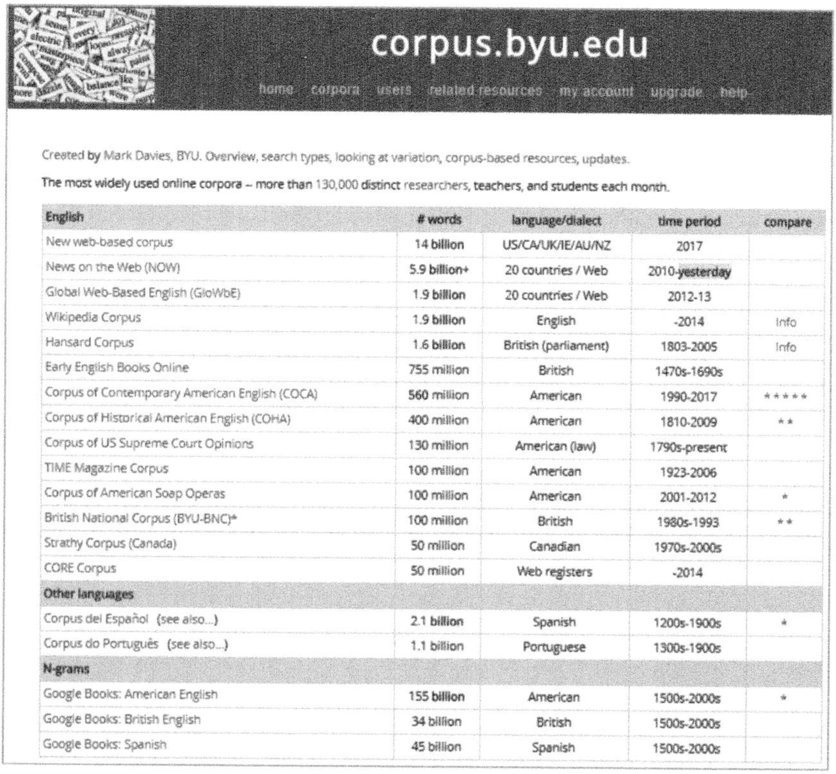

Figure 1.1 Corpora available at corpus.byu.edu.

corpus.byu.edu

home corpora users related resources my account upgrade help

Created by Mark Davies, BYU. Overview, search types, looking at variation, corpus-based resources, updates.

The most widely used online corpora – more than 130,000 distinct researchers, teachers, and students each month.

English	# words	language/dialect	time period	compare
New web-based corpus	14 billion	US/CA/UK/IE/AU/NZ	2017	
News on the Web (NOW)	5.9 billion+	20 countries / Web	2010-yesterday	
Global Web-Based English (GloWbE)	1.9 billion	20 countries / Web	2012-13	
Wikipedia Corpus	1.9 billion	English	-2014	Info
Hansard Corpus	1.6 billion	British (parliament)	1803-2005	Info
Early English Books Online	755 million	British	1470s-1690s	
Corpus of Contemporary American English (COCA)	560 million	American	1990-2017	*****
Corpus of Historical American English (COHA)	400 million	American	1810-2009	**
Corpus of US Supreme Court Opinions	130 million	American (law)	1790s-present	
TIME Magazine Corpus	100 million	American	1923-2006	
Corpus of American Soap Operas	100 million	American	2001-2012	*
British National Corpus (BYU-BNC)*	100 million	British	1980s-1993	**
Strathy Corpus (Canada)	50 million	Canadian	1970s-2000s	
CORE Corpus	50 million	Web registers	-2014	
Other languages				
Corpus del Español (see also...)	2.1 billion	Spanish	1200s-1900s	*
Corpus do Português (see also...)	1.1 billion	Portuguese	1300s-1900s	
N-grams				
Google Books: American English	155 billion	American	1500s-2000s	*
Google Books: British English	34 billion	British	1500s-2000s	
Google Books: Spanish	45 billion	Spanish	1500s-2000s	

Figure 1.1 Corpora available at corpus.byu.edu.

and the Kolhapur Corpus of Indian English. FROWN and FLOB followed in the early 1990s and the tradition continued into the twenty-first century with an addition to the Brown Family, BE06 (Baker, 2009). This patterning of the original Brown Corpus supports diachronic study (more on this below) but was also motivated by the desire to collect a broad representation of each respective regional variety of English. Each of these corpora can be described as a **general corpus**, designed to cover a range of genres and often to function as a reference point (hence their alternative appellation as **reference corpora**).

In contrast, **specialised corpora** are designed to capture a particular variety; subject matter; type of text (i.e. textbook, conversation); genre; particular communicative setting; or particular grammatical or lexical items (Flowerdew, 2004: 21). Most examples of corpora would be considered specialised, since so many are compiled as part of specific research projects. Notable examples include: the Michigan Corpus of Spoken English (MICASE), which contains 1.7 million words based on 200 hours of recordings of spoken data in academic settings at the University of Michigan (https://quod.lib.umich.edu/cgi/c/corpus/

corpus?c=micase;page=simple); the Air Traffic Control Corpus; and the ENRON Corpus, which contains 600,000 business emails that were made publicly available through an investigation following the company's bankruptcy (Klimt and Yang, 2004). Because general corpora typically incorporate samples across genres, it is often possible to use a sub-corpus of a reference corpus as a specialised corpus. With specialised corpora, there will likely be some degree of 'saturation': that is, the degree of variation will be finite and so researchers will endeavour to collect sufficient texts to a point that little or no more variation can be gathered through the inclusion of any more data.

Understandably, general corpora are typically much larger than specialised corpora. By the 1990s, the size and scope of corpora had greatly increased and rather than having distinct corpora for (national) varieties of English, examples such as the International Corpus of English (ICE) collected one million words of data from each of over 20 different varieties of English (13 are accessible as standalone corpora), including spoken data (Greenbaum and Nelson, 1996). It was around the same time that the Bank of English (Järvinen, 1994) and the British National Corpus (BNC) (Burnard, 1995) were created and with these, general corpora had surpassed the 100-million-word mark. The Bank of English has since reached 450 million words.

The BNC has proven to be the most widely cited reference corpus for British English and has inspired a number of other 'national' equivalents in various languages, including Polish (PELCRA), Czech (CNC), Chinese (Modern Chinese Language Corpus: MCLC), Korean (Sejong/Korean National Corpus: KNC) and the American National Corpus (ANC) (see Xiao, 2008). In 2017, the release of the spoken component of the British National Corpus 2014 was announced, as a corpus designed as a 'successor' to the original BNC, with the written component scheduled to be released in late 2019 (Love et al., 2017). This prompted a retrospective renaming of the original BNC as 'BNC1994', which will be adopted from this point on to distinguish it from BNC2014. Another announcement in 2017 saw the launch of the The CorCenCC project (Corpws Cenedlaethol Cymraeg Cyfoes – the National Corpus of Contemporary Welsh) (Knight et al., 2017) which aims to collect 10 million words of Welsh language data across spoken, written and e-language sources (http://www.corcencc.org/).

From this brief overview, it is clear that in many cases comparison between languages and, more specifically, varieties of English is made possible by the number of general corpora built to capture broad representations of those varieties. Researchers can – and have – also designed corpora to offer more direct comparisons between languages, as we will see in the next section.

1.3.2 Multilingual corpora

Researchers in translation studies may (build and) make use of **parallel corpora**, which offer exactly the same materials in 2 (or more languages). Often, they are linked so that users can select a specific example from the corpus and be shown the corresponding translation. Examples include the English-Norwegian Parallel Corpus (ENPC), the English-Swedish Parallel Corpus (ESPC) (which both come from the Oslo Multilingual Corpus) and InterCorp, which includes translations of (largely) fictional texts originally produced in Czech in 27 languages (Čermák and Rosen, 2012). Koehn (2005) presents EUROPAL, a corpus of parallel text from the proceedings of the European parliament in 11 different languages. The Canadian Hansard Corpus, which consists of debates from the Canadian Parliament, also constitutes a parallel corpus, since texts are published in the country's two official languages, English and French.

Comparable corpora are also multilingual corpora but are not based on the same text data. Instead, a comparable corpus will be designed to represent similar genres and types of text in multiple languages, as is the case with ICE. For more examples of parallel and comparable corpora, as well as a discussion of their applications, see Kenning (2010).

1.3.3 Diachronic corpora

Diachronic corpora capture representations of language over time and are key to studies of language change. In contrast, a **synchronic corpus** contains a range of texts from a singular point in time. Thus, while the Brown Family enables direct comparison between time periods (diachronic), each corpus is itself synchronic. Other examples include the Diachronic Corpus of Present-Day Spoken English (DCPSE), which takes 400,000 words from the London-Lund Corpus (1960s–1980s) along with 400,000 words from ICE-GB (1990s) (http://www.ucl.ac.uk/english-usage/projects/dcpse/); the TIME Magazine Corpus represents around 275,000 articles collected between 1923–2006 and allows researchers to observe language change from within 100 million words of data; the Corpus of Historical American English (COHA) comprises texts from 1800 onwards and at 400 million words is much larger than other historical corpora (Davies, 2012). This is one of the corpora that can be searched at https://corpus.byu.edu/.

Many diachronic corpora can also be referred to as **historical corpora**, particularly if they recall data from a period that would not be classified as (near-)contemporary. The Helsinki Corpus of English Texts, for example, contains texts from Old, Middle and Early Modern English (Rissanen, 1994). Biber et al. (1994) generated A Representative Corpus of Historical English Registers (ARCHER), collecting American and English texts across multiple genres in the period 1600–1999 and this work has continued among a consortium of colleagues from 14 different universities in seven different countries (López-Couso and Rodríguez-Puente, 2012). The International Computer Archive of Modern and Medieval English (ICAME) (http://clu.uni.no/icame/) has been pivotal to the creation and dissemination of historical corpora and maintains its commitments to promote all branches of corpus linguistics, to compile and share English text corpora, to include corpus-based studies of other languages for comparison and to provide a forum for research and discussion by way of its annual conference.

COHA can also be described as a **monitor corpus** (Davies, 2010): a dynamic corpus that is continually updated and thereby supports studies of incremental language change. Davies (2010) writes that although there were some 'near misses', there were no monitor corpora of general English prior to COHA. Other researchers have cited the Bank of English as a monitor corpus; however, Davies (2010) highlights that the sampling design did not remain consistent enough across genres to enable us to identify actual language change (as opposed to changes as an artefact of the changing sampling process). Monitor corpora are defined in contrast to **static corpora**, which have a set of texts and are not updated. The benefit of static corpora is that studies can be replicated on the same data and generate the same results. With a monitor corpus, the data changes but this in turn helps to generate the most up-to-date material.

1.3.4 Multimodal corpora

Communication often involves "making meaning in multiple articulations" (Kress and van Leeuwen, 2001: 4). For example, materials that we find online may have audio and visual elements that signify meaning and that in all likelihood were key considerations in the construction of the text. The various system logs (computational recordings of interactional activity, such as the timestamp for when an instant message was posted) can also be integrated as part of the communication to help us to understand language in context (Adolphs et al., 2015). Adolphs et al. (2015) provide an example of how audio/video-recorded conversational data was aligned with location tracking information and smartphone activity (such as sending text messages, taking photos and recording videos) to analyse communicative behaviours in relation to specific locations.

When we talk about spoken forms of communication, we use the term 'paralinguistics' to refer to features that operate 'alongside' the language context, for example audible aspects such as pitch, prosody, intonation as well as visual elements such as facial expressions and gesture. Increasingly in corpus design, we are seeing the alignment of, for example, audio and video files, as with TalkBank, the Scottish Corpus of Texts and Speech (SCOTS) and the Spoken Chinese Corpus of Situated Discourse (SCCSD). There are also examples of corpora that have prosodic features included in the transcript, such as the London-Lund Corpus of Spoken English (LLC) and the Intonational Variation in English (IViE) Corpus.

Zappavigna (2012: xi) argues that the analysis of such texts "demands not just a linguistics of words but a semiotics of multimodality, with all the implications for data gathering, analysis, interpretation and theorizing such entails". Similarly, Caple (2018: 86) argues that "one can only access the full meaning-potential of the text by engaging with the whole text in its multimodal richness", and "examining only one semiotic mode elides the complexity of construction of meaning across modes, and will at best give only a partial picture of what is actually going on in the modal ensemble" (103).

For the most part, paralinguistic data in corpora are a form of co-text to the transcribed data and it is only the orthographically transcribed component that can be analysed using corpus methods. On this basis, we might distinguish 'multimedia corpora' from 'multimodal corpora', with the latter supporting analyses of the interaction between modes. With SCCSD, video streams are segmented and annotated, and so users can search the video-text components through conventional corpus searches (Gu, 2006) and as such, this can be considered a **multimodal corpus**.

Knight et al. (2009) explore the Nottingham Multi-Modal Corpus (NMMC) for lexical and gestural features of spoken discourse during academic supervision meetings. Lin (2017) similarly examines co-gesture speech in a Multimodal Corpus of Intercultural Communication (MMCOIC) to determine preferences for gesture alongside particular semantic categories of information in speech. Such studies, however, tend to generate coding schemes that are specific to the dataset and which do not naturally translate to broader datasets. The degree of specificity also means that these works necessarily focus on comparatively small datasets in very specific contexts.

Task 1.2

Categorise each of the corpora available at https://corpus.byu.edu/ based on the descriptors above (e.g. synchronic vs. diachronic, general, spoken etc.) In order to help you, you can click on the title of each corpus to get more information about what it comprises.

1.4 Corpora of (digital and) online communication

Some corpora focus specifically on forms of digital and online communication, computer-mediated communication (CMC) and e-language (we will discuss these terms in Chapter 4). In most cases, these are specialised corpora that have been collected opportunistically, for a specific research purpose and so incorporate a particular type of digital communication. Corpora of SMS text messages have been reported by Tagg (2010), Chen and Kan (2011) and Tagg et al. (2012). The ENRON Corpus has produced a breadth of studies into professional relationships, network analyses, explorations of gender and of (in)formality, as well as opportunities for discussing the methods involved in working with such data (see Hardin and Sarkis (2015) for a summary). Orasan and Krishnamurthy (2002) also report a corpus of emails, focusing specifically on junk emails and have published the corpus along with some initial corpus analysis: http://rgcl.wlv.ac.uk/resources/junk-emails/index.php. A corpus of 33,000 emails sent and received by Hilary Clinton during her time as U.S. Secretary of State was released via the U.S. Government's Freedom of Information Act website and De Felice and Garretson (2018) have discussed how researchers can work with this data.

Chat rooms and discussion boards have also been the basis for corpus analysis; examples include the Dortmund Chat-Korpus (Beißwenger, 2007), the NPS Chat Corpus (Forsyth and Martell, 2007), the WestburyLab USENET Corpus (http://www.psych.ualberta.ca/~westburylab/downloads/usenetcorpus.download.html) and a corpus of Reddit comments (Baumgartner, 2015). Social media have provided the Edinburgh Twitter Corpus (Petrović et al., 2010) and HERMES (Zappavigna, 2012). Schler et al. (2006) examine a blog corpus (http://u.cs.biu.ac.il/~koppel/BlogCorpus.htm) to determine vocabulary features associated with age and gender, which even allows them to determine the age and gender of unknown authors. Kehoe and Gee (2012) introduce the Birmingham Blog Corpus: a 600-million-word collection of blog posts and reader comments and demonstrate that the reader comments can be examined to get a broader sense of what the content 'means'.

As a way of comparing genres of 'e-language', the Cambridge and Nottingham e-language Corpus (CANELC) includes data from Twitter, blogs, discussion boards, emails and SMS text messages (Knight et al., 2014). This also enables an exploration of how e-language more broadly is distinct from spoken and written forms. Tagliamonte (2016) has shown how data collected from individual speakers can be compared across registers in the Toronto Internet Corpus (TIC). Among the corpora available at https://corpus.byu.edu/, we find: the News on the Web (NOW) corpus, which is a live corpus of online news data from 2010 onwards; the corpus of Global Web-based English (GloWBE), which contains data collected from blogs and webpages in English from 20 different countries around the world; the Corpus of Online Registers of English (CORE), which contains more than 50 million words of online data, selected to represent a range of Web registers; and the iWeb corpus, which contains 14 billion words of data from across 22 million webpages. The TenTen Corpus Family (Jakubíček et al., 2013) is a collection of Web data in over 30 languages over a period of ten years, with a target size of 10+ billion words. This will enable researchers to carry out studies of multiple languages, of characteristics of particular varieties and language change over time, all with respect to online communication. The results of the work with such corpora, including the design and collection of data, analysis and key findings, will be discussed in more detail in the chapters that follow.

Summary

In this chapter, we have begun to look at some of the characteristic features of corpus analysis and how corpus linguistics has been combined effectively with other types of language analysis. In the second section of the book, which presents some applications of corpus approaches to online communication, we will also see how some of these other areas of linguistics can inform corpus analysis. This chapter has introduced some existing corpora and outlined some of the defining categories for the vast number of corpora that have been compiled, which also demonstrate some of the core functions of corpora for language studies (e.g. language change, language varieties). Finally, we have seen some of the existing corpora that focus specifically on forms of digital and online communication, demonstrating the growing interest in this area. Through the BYU Web Interface there are some corpora that can be freely accessed and searched; however, these types of tools do not allow users to upload and analyse their own corpora. In Chapter 3, we will discuss some publicly available corpus analysis software tools that allow users to upload data. In the next chapter, we will discuss what is involved in designing and building your own corpus.

References

Ädel, A. and Reppen, R. (eds) (2008). *Corpora and Discourse: The Challenges of Different Settings*. Amsterdam: John Benjamins.

Adolphs, A. (2008). *Corpus and Context: Investigating Pragmatic Functions in Spoken Discourse*. Amsterdam: John Benjamins.

Adolphs, S., Knight, D. and Carter, R. (2015). Beyond modal spoken corpora: A dynamic approach to tracking language in context, in P. Baker and T. McEnery (eds) *Corpora and Discourse Studies: Integrating Discourse and Corpora*. Hampshire: Palgrave Macmillan, 41–62.

Aijmer, K. and Rühleman, C. (eds) (2014). *Corpus Pragmatics: A Handbook*. Cambridge: Cambridge University Press.

Andersen, G. (2010). How to use corpus linguistics in sociolinguistics, in A. O'Keeffe and M. McCarthy (eds) *The Routledge Handbook of Corpus Linguistics*. London: Routledge, 547–562.

Baker, P. (2006). *Using Corpora in Discourse Analysis*. London: Continuum.

Baker, P. (2009). The BE06 corpus of British English and recent language change. *International Journal of Corpus Linguistics*, 14, 3, 312–337.

Baker, P. (2010). *Sociolinguistics and Corpus Linguistics*. Edinburgh: Edinburgh University Press.

Baker, P. (2017). *American and British English: Divided by a Common Language?* Cambridge: Cambridge University Press.

Baker, P. and McEnery, T. (2015). Introduction, in P. Baker and T. McEnery (eds) *Corpora and Discourse Studies: Integrating Discourse and Corpora*. Basingstoke: Palgrave Macmillan, 1–19.

Baker, P., Gabrielatos, C., Khosravinik, M., McEnery, T. and Wodak, R. (2008). A useful methodological synergy? Combining critical discourse analysis and corpus linguistics to examine discourses of refugees and asylum seekers in the UK press. *Discourse & Society*, 19, 3, 273–305.

Baumgartner, J. (2015). Complete Public Reddit Comments Corpus. Available at: https://archive.org/details/2015_reddit_comments_corpus, accessed 20 April 2018.

Bednarek, M. (2010). *The Language of Fictional Television: Drama and Identity*. London: Continuum.

Beißwenger, M. (2007). *Sprachhandlungskoordination in der ChatKommunikation (Linguistik – Impulse and Tendenzen 26)*. Berlin: de Gruyter.

Biber, D. (1988). *Variation Across Speech and Writing*. Cambridge: Cambridge University Press.

Biber, D., Finegan, E., Atkinson, D., Beck, A., Burges, D. and Burges, J. (1994). The design and analysis of the ARCHER Corpus: A progress report [A representative corpus of historical English registers], in M. Kytö, M. Rissanen and S. Wright (eds) *Corpora Across the Centuries: Proceedings of the First International Colloquium on English Diachronic Corpora*. Amsterdam: Rodopi, 3–6.

Biber, D., Connor, U. and Upton, T. A. (eds) (2007). *Discourse on the Move: Using Corpus Analysis to Describe Discourse Structure*. Amsterdam: John Benjamins.

Blommaert, J. (2005). *Discourse: A Critical Introduction*. Cambridge: Cambridge University Press.

Brezina, V., Love, R. and Aijmer, K. (eds) (2018). *Corpus Approaches to Contemporary British Speech: Sociolinguistic Studies of the Spoken BNC2014*. London: Routledge.

Burnard, L. (1995). The British National Corpus Users Reference Guide. Oxford University Computing Services. Available at: http://homepages.abdn.ac.uk/k.vdeemter/pages/teaching/NLP/practicals/bnc-doc.pdf, accessed 18 April 2018.

Cameron, D. (1998). Dreaming the dictionary: Keywords and corpus linguistics. *Keywords*, 1, 35–46.

Caple, H. (2018). Analysing the multimodal text, in C. Taylor and A. Marchi (eds) *Corpus Approaches to Discourse: A Critical Review*. London: Routledge, 85–109.

Čermák, F. and Rosen, A. (2012). The case of InterCorp, a multilingual parallel corpus. *International Journal of Corpus Linguistics*, 17, 3, 411–427.

Chen, T. and Kan, M.-Y. (2011). Creating a Live, Public Short Messaging Service Corpus: The NUS SMS Corpus. Technical Report. National University of Singapore. Available at: https://arxiv.org/pdf/1112.2468.pdf, accessed 20 April 2018.

Culpeper, J. (2009). Keyness: words, parts-of-speech and semantic categories in the character-talk of Shakespeare's *Romeo and Juliet*. *International Journal of Corpus Linguistics*, 14, 1, 29–59.

Davies, M. (2010). The Corpus of Contemporary American English as the first reliable monitor corpus of English. *Literary and Linguistic Computing*, 25, 4, 447–464.

Davies, M. (2012). Expanding horizons in historical linguistics with the 400-million-word corpus of Historical American English. *Corpora*, 7, 2, 121–157.

Davies, M. and Fuchs, R. (2015). Expanding horizons in the study of World Englishes with the 1.9-billion-word Global Web-based English Corpus (GloWbE). *English Worldwide*, 36, 1, 1–28.

De Felice, R. and Garretson, G. (2018). Politeness at work in the Clinton email corpus: A first look at the effects of status and gender. *Corpus Pragmatics*. Online first. Available at: https://link.springer.com/article/10.1007/s41701-018-0034-2, accessed 1 June 2018.

Deutschmann, M. (2003). *Apologising in British English*. Umeå: Umeå University.

Egbert, J. and Schnur, E. (2018). The role of the text in corpus and discourse analysis: Missing the trees for the forest in C. Taylor and A. Marchi (eds) *Corpus Approaches to Discourse: A Critical Review*. London: Routledge, 159–173.

Flowerdew, L. (2004). The argument for using English specialized corpora to understand academic and professional settings, in U. Connor and T. Upton (eds) *Discourse in the Professions: Perspectives from Corpus Linguistics*. Amsterdam : John Benjamins, 11–33.

Forsyth, E. and Martell, C. (2007). Lexical and discourse analysis of online chat dialog. *Proceedings of the 1st IEEE International Conference on Semantic Computing (ICSC 2007)*. 19–26 September 2007. Irvine, California, U.S.A.

Friginal, E. (ed.) (2018). *Studies in Corpus-based Sociolinguistics*. London: Routledge.

Greenbaum, S. and Nelson, G. (1996). The International Corpus of English (ICE) project. *World Englishes*, 15, 1, 3–15.

Gu, Y. (2006). Multimodal text analysis: A corpus linguistic approach to situated discourse. *Text & Talk*, 26, 2, 127–167.

Gumperz, J. and Hymes, D. (eds) (1972). *Directions in Sociolinguistics: The Ethnography of Communication*. Oxford: Blackwell.

Hardin, J. S. and Sarkis, G. (2015). Network analysis with the Enron email corpus. *Journal of Statistics Education*, 23, 2. Available at: http://ww2.amstat.org/publications/jse/v23n2/hardin.pdf, accessed 20 April 2018.

Hardt-Mautner, G. (1995). 'Only connect': Critical discourse analysis and corpus linguistics. *UCREL Technical Paper* 6. Lancaster: Lancaster University. Available at: http://ucrel.lancaster.ac.uk/papers/techpaper/vol6.pdf, accessed 14 April 2018.

Harrison, S. and Allton, D. (2013). Apologies in email discussions, in S. C. Herring, D. Stein and T. Virtanen (eds) *Pragmatics of Computer-mediated Communication*. Berlin: Walter de Gruyter, 315–337.

Huang, Y., Guo, D., Kasakoff, A. and Grieve, J. (2015). Understanding US regional linguistic variation with Twitter data analysis. *Computers, Environment and Urban Systems*, 59, 244–255.

Ihalainen, O. (1990). A source of data for the study of English dialectal syntax: The Helsinki Corpus, in J. Aarts and W. Meijs (eds) *Theory and Practice in Corpus Linguistics*. Amsterdam: Rodopi, 83–104.

Jakubíček, M., Kilgariff, Kovář, V., Rychlý, P. and Suchomel, V. (2013). The TenTen Corpus Family. *Proceedings of the International Corpus Linguistics Conference*. 23–26 July 2013. University of Lancaster, U.K. 125–127.

Järvinen, T. (1994). Annotating 200 million words: The Bank of English project. *Proceedings of the 15th International Conference on Computational Linguistics*. 5–9 August 1994. Kyoto, Japan. 565–568.

Jones, R. H., Chik, A. and Hafner, C. A. (2015). Introduction: Discourse analysis and digital practices, in R. H. Jones, A. Chik and C. A. Hafner (eds) *Discourse and Digital Practices: Doing Discourse Analysis in the Digital Age*. London: Routledge, 1–17.

Jucker, A., Schreier, D. and Hundt, M. (2009a). Corpus linguistics, pragmatics and discourse, in A. Jucker, D. Schreier and M. Hundt (eds) *Corpora: Pragmatics and Discourse*. Amsterdam: Rodopi, 3–9.

Jucker, A., Schreier, D. and Hundt, M. (eds) (2009b). *Corpora: Pragmatics and Discourse*. Amsterdam: Rodopi.

Kehoe, A. and Gee, M. (2012). Reader comments as an aboutness indicator in online texts: Introducing the Birmingham Blog Corpus, in S. Oksefjell, J. Ebeling and H. Hasselgård (eds) *Studies in Variation, Contacts and Change in English – Volume 12: Aspects of Corpus Linguistics: Compilation, Annotation, Analysis*. Available at: http://www.helsinki.fi/varieng/series/volumes/12/kehoe_gee/, accessed 20 April 2018.

Kenning, M.-M. (2010). What are parallel and comparable corpora and how can we use them?, in A. O'Keeffe and M. McCarthy (eds) *The Routledge Handbook of Corpus Linguistics*. London: Routledge, 487–500.

Kerswill, P., Cheshire, J., Fox, S. and Torgersen, E. N. (2008). *Linguistic Innovators: The English of Adolescents in London*. ESRC End of Award Report, RES-000-23-0680. Swindon: ESRC. Available at: http://doc.ukdataservice.ac.uk/doc/6127/mrdoc/pdf/6127uguide.pdf, accessed 13 April 2018.

Klimt, B. and Yang, Y. (2004). The Enron Corpus: A new dataset for email classification research. *European Conference on Machine Learning*, 3201, 217–226.

Knight, D., Evans, D., Carter, R. and Adolphs, S. (2009). HeadTalk, HandTalk and the corpus: towards a framework for multi-modal, multi-media corpus development. *Corpora*, 4, 1, 1–32.

Knight, D., Adolphs, S. and Carter, R. (2014). CANELC: constructing an e-language corpus. *Corpora*, 9, 1, 29–56.

Knight, D., Fitzpatrick, T. and Morris, S. (2017). CorCenCC (Corpws Cenedlaethol Cymraeg Cyfoes – The National Corpus of Contemporary Welsh): An overview. Paper presented at the *British Association for Applied Linguistics (BAAL) Conference*. 31 August–2 September 2017. University of Leeds, Leeds, U.K.

Koehn, P. (2005). Europarl: A parallel corpus for statistical machine translation. *Proceedings of the 10th Machine Translation Summit*. 13–15 September 2005. Phuket, Thailand. Available at: http://homepages.inf.ed.ac.uk/pkoehn/publications/europarl-mtsummit05.pdf, accessed 20 April 2018.

Krennmayr, T. and Steen, G. (2017). VU Amsterdam Metaphor Corpus, in N. Ide and J. Pustejovsky (eds) *Handbook of Linguistic Annotation*. Dordrecht: Springer, 1053–1071.

Kress, G. and van Leeuwen, T. (2001). *Multimodal Discourse: The Modes and Media of Contemporary Communication*. London: Arnold.

Labov, W. (1963). The social motivation of a sound change. *Word*, 19, 273–309.

Leech, G. and Weisser, M. (2003). Pragmatics in dialogue, in R. Mitkov (ed.) *The Oxford Handbook of Computational Linguistics*. Oxford: Oxford University Press, 135–156.

Lin, Y.-L. (2017). Co-occurrence of speech and gestures: A multimodal corpus linguistic approach to intercultural interaction. *Journal of Pragmatics*, 117, 155–167.

Lischinsky, A. (2018). Overlooked text types: from fictional texts to real-world discourses, in C. Taylor and A. Marchi (eds) *Corpus Approaches to Discourse: A Critical Review*. London: Routledge, 60–81.

López-Couso, M. J. and Rodríguez-Puente, P. (2012). Corpus compilation within the research unit variation, linguistic change and grammaticalization: COLMOBAENG, ARCHER, and CHELAR. Paper presented at *IV Congreso Internacional de Lingüística de Corpus*. 22–24 March 2012. Universidad de Jaén, Jaén, Spain.

Louw, W. E. (1993). Irony in the text or insincerity in the writer? The diagnostic potential of semantic prosodies, in M. Baker, G. Francis and E. Tognini Bonelli (eds) *Text and Technology: In Honour of John Sinclair*. Amsterdam: John Benjamins, 152–176.

Love, R., Dembry, C., Hardie, A., Brezina, V. and McEnery, T. (2017). The spoken BNC2014: Designing and building a spoken corpus of everyday conversations. *International Journal of Corpus Linguistics*, 22, 3, 319–344.

Luke, A. (2002). Beyond science and ideology critique: Developments in Critical Discourse Analysis. *Annual Review of Applied Linguistics*, 22, 1, 96–110.

Lutzky, U. and Kehoe, A. (2017). "I apologise for my poor blogging": Searching for apologies in the *Birmingham Blog Corpus. Corpus Pragmatics*, 1, 1, 37–56.

Mahlberg, M. (2013). *Corpus Stylistics and Dickens's Fiction*. London: Routledge.

Mahlberg, M. (2014). Corpus stylistics, in M. Burke (ed.) *The Routledge Handbook of Stylistics*. London: Routledge, 378–392.

Mahlberg, M. and McIntyre, D. (2011). A case for corpus stylistics: Ian Fleming's *Casino Royale*. *English Text Construction*, 4, 2, 204–227.

Mahlberg, M., Stockwell, P., de Joode, J., Smith, C. and O'Donnell, M. B. (2016). CLiC Dickens: novel uses of concordances for the integration of corpus stylistics and cognitive poetics. *Corpora*, 11, 3, 433–463.

Martin, J. R. (2004). Positive discourse analysis: solidarity and change. *Revista Canaria de Estudios Ingleses*, 49, 179–200.

Maynard, C. and Leicher, S. (2007). Pragmatic annotation of an academic spoken corpus for pedagogical purposes, in E. Fitzpatrick (ed.) *Corpus Linguistics Beyond the Word: Corpus Research From Phrase to Discourse*. Amsterdam: Rodopi, 107–115.

McEnery, T. and Hardie, A. (2012). *Corpus Linguistics: Method, Theory and Practice*. Cambridge: Cambridge University Press.

McIntyre, D. (2010). Dialogue and characterization in Quentin Tarantino's *Reservoir Dogs*: A corpus stylistic analysis, in D. McIntyre and B. Busse (eds) *Language and Style*. Basingstoke: Palgrave MacMillan, 162–182.

McIntyre, D. and Walker, B. (2010). How can corpora be used to explore the language of poetry and drama?, in A. O'Keeffe and M. McCarthy (eds) *The Routledge Handbook of Corpus Linguistics*. London: Routledge, 516–530.

Murphy, B. (2010). *Corpus and Sociolinguistics: Investigating Age and Gender in Female Talk*. Amsterdam : John Benjamins.

O'Halloran, K. (2007). The subconscious in James Joyce's *Eveline*: a corpus stylistic analysis that chews on the "Fish hook". *Language and Literature*, 16, 3, 227–244.

Orasan, C. and Krishnamurthy, R. (2002). A corpus-based investigation of junk emails. *Proceedings of Language Resources and Evaluation Conference (LREC-2002)*. 29–31 May 2002. Las Palmas, Canary Islands, Spain. Available at: http://publications.aston.ac.uk/5675/1/2002-LREC-113-junk-emails.pdf, accessed 20 April 2018.

Page, R. (2014). Saying 'sorry': Corporate apologies posted to Twitter. *Journal of Pragmatics*, 62, 30–45.

Partington, A. (2004). Corpora and discourse: A most congruous beast, in A. Partington, J. Morley and L. Haarman (eds) *Corpora and Discourse*. Bern: Peter Lang, 11–20.

Partington, A. (2008). The armchair and the machine: Corpus-assisted discourse research, in C. Taylor Torsello, K. Ackerley and E. Castello (eds) *Corpora for University Language Teachers*. Bern: Peter Lang, 95–118.

Partington, A., Duguid, A. and Taylor, C. (2013). *Patterns and Meanings in Discourse: Theory and Practice in Corpus-assisted Discourse Studies (CADS)*. Amsterdam : John Benjamins.

Petrović, S., Osborne, M. and Lavrenko, V. (2010). The Edinburgh Twitter Corpus. *Proceedings of the NAACL HLT 2010 Workshop on Computational Linguistics in a World of Social Media*. 6 June 2010. Los Angeles, California, U.S.A. Available at: http://www.aclweb.org/anthology/W/W10/W10-0513.pdf, accessed 20 April 2018.

Rampton, B. (2017). Interactional Sociolinguistics. *Tilburg Papers in Culture Studies*, 175. Available at: https://www.tilburguniversity.edu/upload/4e31ee44-c429-49c1-a51a-c2c6c219bf50_TPCS_175_Rampton.pdf, accessed 13 April 2018.

Rissanen, M. (1994). The Helsinki Corpus of English Texts, in M. Kytö, M. Rissanen and S. Wright (eds) *Corpora Across the Centuries: Proceedings of the First International Colloquium on English Diachronic Corpora*. Amsterdam: Rodopi, 73–80.

Romero-Trillo, J. (ed.) (2008). *Pragmatics and Corpus Linguistics: A Mutualistic Entente*. Berlin: Mouton de Gruyter.

Romero-Trillo, J. (2017). Corpus pragmatics. *Corpus Pragmatics*, 1, 1, 1–2.

Rühlemann, C. (2010). What can a corpus tell us about pragmatics?, in A. O'Keeffe and M. McCarthy (eds) *The Routledge Handbook of Corpus Linguistics*. London: Routledge, 288–301.

Rühlemann, C. and Aijmer, K. (2015). Introduction: corpus pragmatics – Laying the foundations, in K. Aijmer and C. Rühlemann (eds) *Corpus Pragmatics: A Handbook*. Cambridge: Cambridge University Press, 1–26.

Schler, J., Koppel, M., Argamon, S. and Pennebaker, J. (2006). Effects of age and gender on blogging. *Proceedings of 2006 AAAI Spring Symposium on Computation Approaches for Analyzing Weblogs.* 27–29 March 2006. Palo Alto, California, U.S.A. Available at: http://u.cs.biu.ac.il/~schlerj/schler_springsymp06.pdf, accessed 20 April 2018.

Scott, M. and Tribble, C. (2006). *Textual Patterns: Key Words and Corpus Analysis in Language Education.* Amsterdam: John Benjamins.

Semino, E. (2008). *Metaphor in Discourse.* Cambridge: Cambridge University Press.

Stiles, W. B. (1992). *Describing Talk: A Taxonomy of Verbal Response Modes.* Newbury Park: Sage.

Tagg, C. (2010). A Corpus Linguistics Study of SMS Text Messaging. PhD Thesis. The University of Birmingham. Available at: http://etheses.bham.ac.uk/253/1/Tagg09PhD.pdf, accessed 20 April 2018.

Tagg, C., Baron, A. and Rayson, P. (2012). "i didn't spel that wrong did i. Oops": Analysis and normalisation of SMS spelling variation, in L. A. Cougnon and C. Fairon (eds) *SMS Communication: A Linguistic Approach. Special Issue of Linguisticae Investigationes,* 35, 2, 367–388.

Tagliamonte, S. A. (2006). *Analysing Sociolinguistic Variation.* Cambridge: Cambridge University Press.

Tagliamonte, S. A. (2012). *Variationist Sociolinguistics.* Oxford: Wiley-Blackwell.

Tagliamonte, S. A. (2016). So sick or so cool? The language of youth on the internet. *Language in Society,* 45, 1, 1–32.

Taylor, C. and Marchi, A. (eds) (2018). *Corpus Approaches to Discourse: A Critical Review.* London: Routledge.

Tognini Bonelli, E. (2010). Theoretical overview of the evolution of corpus linguistics, in A. O'Keeffe and M. McCarthy (eds) *The Routledge Handbook of Corpus Linguistics.* London: Routledge, 14–27.

Toolan, M. (2009). *Narrative Progression in the Short Story: A Corpus Stylistic Approach.* Amsterdam: John Benjamins.

Van Dijk, T. A. (2001). Critical discourse analysis, in D. Schiffrin, D. Tannen and H. E. Hamilton (eds) *The Handbook of Discourse Analysis.* Oxford: Blackwell, 352–371.

Weisser, M. (2018). *How to do Corpus Pragmatics on Pragmatically Annotated Data: Speech Acts and Beyond.* Amsterdam: John Benjamins.

Widdowson, H. G. (1995). Discourse analysis: A critical review. *Language and Literature,* 4, 3, 157–172.

Xiao, R. (2008). Well-known and influential corpora, in A. Lüdeling and M. Kytö (eds) *Corpus Linguistics: An International Handbook.* Berlin: Walter de Gruyter, 383–457.

Zappavigna, M. (2012). *Discourse of Twitter and Social Media: How We Use Language to Create Affiliation on the Web.* London: Bloomsbury.

Chapter 2

Designing and building corpora

2.1 What makes a good corpus?

A **corpus** is a representative collection of language data, generated for the purposes of enabling researchers to make some kind of statement about authentic language use. Crawford and Csomay (2016: 79) assert that: "a well-designed corpus includes texts that address the research question(s) of the study, saves the texts into a file format that allows different software programs to analyse the texts and identifies the texts with relevant contextual material so that the different contexts are easily identifiable in the corpus". This concise summary foregrounds some of the key concerns of corpus design and of this chapter, relating to size, representativeness, formatting and metadata.

2.1.1 Size

Given the prominence of frequency in corpus analysis, it is reasonable to want to collect as much data as is possible and Sinclair (2004: 189) argues that in a large corpus, "underlying regularities have a better chance of showing through the superficial variations". If we are looking for patterns, they are more likely to be established and become discernible in larger datasets and this helps to identify aspects of the text that perhaps would not be recognised through a manual reading. As Sinclair (1991: 100) puts it, "language looks rather different when you look at a lot of it at once". If we look back at those corpora available at https://corpus.byu.edu/, they routinely comprise multiple millions, if not billions of words. Even the more specialised corpora, such as the TIME Magazine Corpus (though of course, not as specialised as some) include 100 million words of data – the same as the BNC.

Corpus builders recognise though, that it is not possible to capture every aspect of language and therefore, any corpus is a sample of sorts. This reiterates the significance of the sample design and this will inform the decision about how much data to include, along with the practical issues of collecting the data. Weber (2017: 129) writes that "although there is much to be said for the appeal of large datasets, there is often much to be gained from exploring the nuances of smaller datasets". Similarly, Koester (2010: 67) argues that smaller, more specialised corpora "allow a much closer link between the corpus and the contexts in which the texts in the corpus were produced". She points out that while larger corpora may be better suited to identifying **lexico-grammatical** patterns in the language as a whole, "smaller specialised corpora give insights into patterns of language use in particular settings" (Koester, 2010: 67). She refers to the findings of Handford (2007) as an example of where the limited size of a corpus – in this instance, the Cambridge and Nottingham Business English Corpus (CANBEC) – allowed the researcher to identify subtle differences in the use and meaning of 'issue' and 'problem' in a business context. Handford (2007) found that 'issue' was more frequent in human resources and marketing meetings, whereas 'problem' was more commonly found in procedural and technical meetings. Furthermore, 'issue' occurred more in interactions between managers and subordinates, while 'problem' occurred more in interactions between peers. The subsequent analysis of the terms in context allowed Handford (2007) to conclude that 'problem' indicated more of a concrete obstacle, whereas 'issue' referred to something more nebulous and was more euphemistic, which could appear as less confrontational and encourage further discussion of the 'issue'.

The size of a corpus must be appropriate to the research question, which may mean assessing at what point the corpus is likely to reach 'saturation': i.e. that there is sufficient material to reflect the range of linguistic variation in a population and that the addition of more texts is unlikely to contribute anything new. This is not only a question of the number of texts, but also of the type of texts included in the corpus, which brings us to the question of **representativeness**. As Lischinsky (2018: 60) reminds us, "however large it may be, a sample will remain partial and incomplete unless it adequately covers the range of genres and contexts in which a given discourse circulates".

2.1.2 Representativeness

Representativeness can be defined as "the extent to which a sample includes the full range of variability in a population" (Biber, 1993: 243). According to Biber (1993), there are two types of variability: situational and linguistic. In capturing the situational variability within a set of language, we need to draw from a range of registers and genres. Linguistic variability refers to the range of language characteristics within a population and often, this is what we are looking to identify through our analysis. As such, in ensuring situational variety, we can 'discover' the linguistic variety in the data through corpus analysis. When we refer to the design of general corpora such as the BNC or COCA, we can see that the selection criteria ensured that a range of text domains and media were included. The BNC, for example, includes in its written component texts from the domains of applied sciences, arts, commerce and finance, world affairs and literary and creative works (http://www.natcorp.ox.ac.uk/corpus/creating.xml), which are represented through data from textbooks, periodicals, advertising leaflets and personal letters. Aston and Burnard (1998: 28) recall:

> In selecting texts for inclusion in the [BNC], account was taken of both production, by sampling a wide variety of distinct types of material, and

reception, by selecting instances of those types which have a wide distribution. Thus, having chosen to sample such things as popular novels, or technical writing, best-seller lists and library circulation statistics were consulted to select particular examples of them.

Representativeness also refers to time i.e. that the corpus should reflect variability contemporaneous to the topic. In the case of historical corpora, this is more explicitly fundamental to the nature of the corpus. With the launch of the BNC2014, we are also reminded of the importance of using up-to-date materials. Love et al. (2017) show that in the BNC1994, references to public figures (e.g. John Major), technology (e.g. VHS tape cassettes) and television shows (e.g. *Noel's House Party*) serve as a stark reminder that the corpus was compiled in the early 1990s and that because of such references (and perhaps more significantly, what is not referenced), it could no longer be treated as representative of contemporary English use.

As has been discussed above, any corpus must really be thought of as a sample of any given population. In order to be representative, the sample must maintain the characteristics of the larger corpus, in terms of the distribution of the dimensions across which the population varies. A quality associated with representativeness is **balance**, which ensures that not only is the appropriate variety of texts included but they are also represented in the appropriate proportions. If we return to the design of the Brown Family, compilers have had to consider both the number of texts within a domain and the number of words for each text, settling on a very strict sampling method of using 2,000-word extracts. Specifying the number of words is one way of ensuring balance; however, this does raise questions about which features of a text are included within that, since, as Stubbs (1996: 23) points out, "few linguistic features of a text are distributed evenly throughout". While 2,000 words might be sufficient for collecting the entirety of, say a news report, it will only capture part of an academic journal or a literary work and this may favour particular language features (consider how the discussion of results and analysis in an academic journal in linguistics differs from its introduction). In the original Brown Corpus, the selection of samples of 2,000 words meant that extracts were likely to begin and end in the middle of sentences. For researchers compiling corpora, the issue of balance forces us to consider whether we want to retain texts in their entirety (which will mean that there is variability in the number of texts across domains) or whether samples are consistent for the number of texts and words (which will mean collecting extracts from larger texts).

Representativeness might not only refer to texts in a corpus, but also the participants. In certain communities, a sample can be matched to the wider population with respect to say, age, gender ethnicity etc. King (2009: 309) raises an interesting question with respect to online chat communities in that corpus builders "need to decide the extent to which their corpus accurately reflects the actual frequencies of types of people in a given population […] or tries to balance every single variable so that every *possible* type of person is represented in the data equally (even if this does not reflect the reality of usage patterns". In most cases, it is probable that the researchers will want to capture something of the reality of the community they are reporting, including its membership, and will also use this to inform their interpretation of the data. What this does remind us, however, is the context-dependent nature of any findings, as reflective of the population at the time that the data was collected.

Ultimately, a corpus needs to be fit for purpose and if you are designing and collecting your own corpus, the primary motive must be that it supports you in achieving your research aims. Love et al. (2017: 320) report that the design of the Spoken BNC2014 "necessarily represents a compromise between the ideally representative corpus and the constraints of what is realistically possible" and they describe their approach as 'opportunistic'. In practice, whatever our intentions for the design of our corpus, it is often practical considerations that prove most significant.

Task 2.1

Imagine you are conducting studies into the following areas. What data would you need in order to compile a representative corpus? How much data do you think you would need?

- How is climate change reported in the press?
- How do teenagers in Manchester use language in casual conversation?
- How do the participants of a forum for parents manage their identities through language?

2.2 Web as corpus (WaC)

At first glance, the Web seems to overcome many of the practical limitations associated with building offline corpora: it is freely available, encompasses a breadth of texts from around the world and is of unimaginable size. Texts are already in a computer-readable format, so researchers do not need (on the whole) to undergo tasks of digitisation (as with written texts) or transcribing spoken data. Bernardini et al. (2006: cf. 10–17) suggest four ways in which we can conceive of the Web as a corpus:

1. The Web as a corpus surrogate: the researcher carries out a linguistic query through a commercial search engine. This can provide results for ad hoc translation tasks, or, say, show frequencies for the use of particular terms over time (see Google Trends https://trends.google.com/trends/ and Google N-Gram Viewer https://books.google.com/ngrams).
2. The Web as a corpus shop: the researcher compiles a specialised corpus using a commercial search engine to locate the pertinent texts for download.

3 The Web as corpus proper: if the researcher is specifically interested in Web content and Web-based language, they might employ some form of Web sampling to collect webpages as a corpus.
4 The mega-corpus/mini-web: the researcher creates an extremely large corpus of texts derived from the Web that are annotated and support sophisticated corpus querying.

Kilgarriff et al. (2010) highlight the potential for corpus-building through 'piggybacking' on the work of commercial search engines, which complete some of the initial tasks as a matter of course and are what have facilitated Kilgarriff et al.'s (2010) 'corpus factory' that generates large general-language corpora. Renouf et al. (2007) distinguish between the Web as archive and the Web as a resource for studying contemporary texts designed specifically for the Web, consistent with the latter points outlined by Bernardini et al. (2006). However, Kehoe and Gee (2009) demonstrate how this distinction quickly becomes blurred by referring to online news articles, which can be thought of as distinct from the published hard copies of a newspaper in that they make use of features of online communication (hyperlinking, audio and video features, online comments etc.), but, on the other hand, will largely be a replication of the print version.

Lew (2009) offers a comparison of the Web as corpus with traditional corpora, in terms of: size (of the resources); linguistic representativeness; balancing and noisiness; functionality and access mechanism. He concludes that while the Web as corpus has advantages in terms of size and speed of retrieval, "the more sophisticated needs of the working linguist may be better fulfilled by means of traditional corpora or the WWW enhanced with a specialized access interface" (Lew, 2009: 298). He further cautions that "the more sophisticated the tool, the greater its complexity, and the skills required of the user" (Lew, 2009: 298). However, there have been significant advances in the software tools that facilitate corpus analysis, as we will see in the next chapter. When we look at the applications of such tools to online communication in the second part of this book, we will see that much can be achieved with a very basic familiarity with features of corpus analysis.

In addition to serving as an archive or as the source of the actual corpus material, the Web can also be a resource for recruiting the support in carrying out the collection – and even the analysis – of corpus data. Researchers are increasingly employing crowdsourcing methods to build and analyse corpora, recognising language users as authorities who can inform various stages of the research process. Callison-Burch and Dredze (2010) and Lane et al. (2010) both used crowdsourcing in the creation and collection of speech and language data; Novotney and Callison-Burch (2010) crowdsourced participants to transcribe their data and Callison-Burch (2009) recruited participants to evaluate the quality of their transcripts. Others have produced bespoke applications to facilitate crowdsourced contributions; McGraw et al. (2009) generated an online educational game to get their participants involved and Goldman et al. (2014) built the Dialäkt and Voice Äpp (see also Leemann et al., 2016) to elicit user evaluations of different Swiss German dialects in locations around Switzerland.

In 2017, Knight et al. (2017) announced the launch of the CorCenCC project, a key part of which was the development of the CorCenCC Crowdsourcing App (Neale et al., 2017). Part of the motivation for crowdsourcing contributions was to give Welsh speakers "the opportunity to directly involve themselves in the creation of the corpus", since "community pride is strong" and the 'proper' representation of contemporary Welsh speakers "is expected to have a wide-reaching impact on the way publishers, policy-makers, the education sector, academic researchers and many more work with Welsh going forward" (Neale et al., 2017). Users record their own conversations and edit the metadata through the app (including where the recording was made and who was involved), which allows the researchers to monitor contributions and manage the balance and representativeness of the corpus. This project demonstrates the ways in which the Web (and associated tools) can facilitate the inclusion of ordinary members of the public in research, who can also complete some of the work of corpus building and analysis.

2.3 Ethics

The expanding areas of research that involve participants, to a greater or lesser extent, in the study of online communication have foregrounded key ethical issues and challenges, which we can apply to studies in corpus linguistics. Such issues have been the focus of numerous publications (see for example McKee and Porter, 2009; Whiteman, 2012; Fossheim and Ingierd, 2015) and research guides, such as those published by the Association of Internet Researchers (http://aoir.org/ethics/) (Markham and Buchanan, 2012). Current research practices will need to be adapted to the E.U. General Data Protection Regulation (GDPR) (The European Parliament, 2016), which is applicable to all member states of the E.U. but is expected to be a model for global practices and which came into effect on 25 May 2018. Townsend and Wallace (2016) outline 4 key areas of concern within social media research: private versus public; informed consent; anonymity; and risk of harm. These are discussed below, with consideration of the relevant updates to the GDPR.

2.3.1 Public versus private

There are many areas of the Web that are openly accessible and this has raised significant questions about what can be considered 'public', with the implication that if something is public, it is 'fair game' for research. However, researchers have begun to question whether this distinction is sufficient. Koene and Adolphs (2015) highlight that while social media can be thought of as fundamentally public, users often use the platform to communicate with friends and suggest that this can be characterised more like a private conversation in a public space, rather than a radio broadcast. Similarly, books are accessible through public libraries but are still subject to copyright restrictions and so it is key that participants and researchers alike are aware of – and can clearly articulate – what is appropriate and ethical conduct.

As Mackenzie (2017) shows, researchers recognise the significance of participants' own perceptions and expectations about privacy and users are particularly apprehensive that the 'meaning' of the post will be lost when taken out of context (Golder et al., 2017). Orgad (2009) argues that researchers need to consider not only whether the user can be identified from their online posts, but also whether the users have invested in the material a private part of themselves, i.e. if the user treats a publicly-posted message as private, then the researcher should follow suit. This may be possible (though not guaranteed) to determine in ethnographic ('netnographic') approaches, where the researcher can familiarise themselves with the discourse norms of the virtual community; it is more difficult for corpus builders who are looking to collect a range of texts and for whom it is not feasible to ascertain the perceptions of all of the participants, across a range of platforms and contexts.

2.3.2 (Informed) consent

Participants need to be able to make informed decisions about their contribution to research, which relies on researchers being able to provide information prior to the study (or at least the data collection) about what participation involves (including the extent of any inconvenience, what will be documented, how it will be analysed, who will have access to it etc.). For corpus linguists, who are typically aiming to capture some degree of representativeness and generality by collecting data from large numbers of participants, there are particular challenges in the practicalities of contacting each potential participant and providing sufficient information, along with the opportunity to ask questions: consistent with the principle of 'informed' consent.

Koene and Adolphs (2015) recommend – as a minimum requirement – that following data collection from online contexts, researchers should post a message about the research on the platform and offer some form of 'data withdrawal' procedure. This emphasises the value of an 'opt-out' rather than an 'opt-in' process. King (2009), for example, contacted users of an online forum he had analysed as a corpus and made available (only to those who were originally involved) the conversations that were to be included, offering the opportunity for users to withdraw. King (2009: 309) took an approach of implied consent, in that the email invited users to comment on any amendments or removal of data, but also notified that "if they did not mind their data being used for research purposes, they could signal their consent by remaining silent". King (2009) chose this approach as a way to collect consent without compromising anonymity; however, he acknowledges that consent-by-silence is problematic (for example, some users may simply have not seen the email). Indeed, such processes would no longer be permissible according to the GDPR, which states that consent "should be given by a clear affirmative act establishing a freely given, specific, informed and unambiguous indication of the data subject's agreement to the processing of personal data relating to him or her, such as by a written statement, including by electronic means, or an oral statement" (The European Parliament, 2016: 6). As such, participation in research requires an 'opt-in' process and "Silence, pre-ticked boxes or inactivity should not therefore constitute consent" (The European Parliament, 2016: 6).

2.3.3 Anonymity

Research publication is, by definition, a process of 'making public' and for those who have participated in research (knowingly or otherwise), this means that there is information about them that is available to a greater number of people. In order to mitigate any risk to the individual following the disclosure of such data, Personally Identifiable Information (PII) is typically removed from corpus data; however, there are different definitions for PII (Buchanan and Zimmer, 2013). In the GDPR, 'personal data' means:

> any information relating to an identified or identifiable natural person; an identifiable natural person is one who can be identified, directly or indirectly, in particular by references to an identifier such as a name, an identification number, location data, an online identifier or to one or more factors specific to the physical, physiological, genetic, mental, economic, cultural or social identity of that natural person.
>
> (The European Parliament, 2016: Article 4)

Within this definition, there are orders of 'sensitive personal data'. The principles of data protection outlined in the GDPR do not apply to anonymised data, where the data subject is truly beyond identification (The European Parliament, 2016: 5). Researchers are also encouraged to take measures to reduce the possibility of re-identification by, for example, removing links to forums and avoiding extended verbatim quotes that can be retrieved through Internet searches.

In a systematic review of ethics research with respect to social media, Golder et al. (2017) ascertained that "Respondents were much more likely to support the use of numerical aggregate data (such as overall statistics) than qualitative research involving quotes or interpretation of quotes" (Golder et al., 2017:13). This might encourage the use of methods of corpus linguistics, in that corpus approaches are able to report aggregated patterns in language and often do not need to cite specific examples, but of course become more problematic when researchers want to look closer at, say, key words in context.

2.3.4 Risk of harm

Elgesem (2015: 18) argues:

> there is an ethically relevant distinction between situations in which participating in the research entails a risk of harm or discomfort and those in which there is no risk but the research nonetheless challenges the individual's interest in retaining control over information about [them].

She goes on to assert her belief that "in the first case, there must be a *requirement* to obtain consent, whereas information and consent in the other type of situation is an important *consideration*, which in some cases may be weighed against other considerations" (Elgesem, 2015: 18, italics in original). In practice, this relies on the researcher anticipating potential risks and assessing what constitutes 'harm'. This assessment might factor in the vulnerability of the people being studied; the sensitivity of the topic; searchability of the information being presented (and the possibility for re-identification); the degree of interactivity with those being studied; and the participants' understanding or perception of the visibility of the platform (Elgesem, 2015). The risks might manifest as embarrassment, reputational damage, prosecution, abuse or threatening behaviour. While it seems as though many of these risks can be mitigated by ensuring that participants cannot be identified through any quoted corpus material, researchers must remain conscientious of the impact of their work and this not only relates to the publication of results, but also to the processes involved in carrying out the research.

Golder et al. (2017: 13) conclude that "each research project requires individual consideration of ethics" and we should resist a 'one rule fits all' approach. Similarly, Markham and Buchanan (2012) advocate what they call a 'casuistic' approach. Their report offers a 'characteristic' range of questions for internet researchers to consider, rather than a prescriptive set of practices and they reiterate that researchers should draw on previous scholarship, but they should also continue to document their specific challenges and approaches for the benefit of everyone (Markham and Buchanan, 2009).

2.3.5 Censorship/moderation

The Web has made it possible for researchers to carry out studies with 'hard-to-reach' groups in a way that previously was not possible. However, there are still some ways in which the Web is 'closed off' and inaccessible. Perhaps the most explicit manifestation of this comes in the form of censorship and we can refer to countries where the government imposes strict censorship in online content (e.g. Iran, North Korea, Syria, China [Deibert et al., 2011]). In China, the government employs "sophisticated censorship technologies to monitor and intervene in the online public sphere" (Mou et al., 2016: 838), resulting in what has become known as the 'Great Firewall'. A very recent example of this type of initiative came via the microblogging site Weibo, who announced a 'clean-up campaign' to remove 'illegal' content, referring to manga and videos with pornographic implications, promoting violence or (related to) homosexuality (https://news.sky.com/story/iamgay-trends-in-china-as-weibo-targets-homosexual-content-in-clean-up-11330334). Reactions to this included a surge in the use of the hashtag #IAmGay, adopted by 170,000 users, as well as other protests.

This demonstrates the role of censorship in modifying online behaviours, which may not only be to inhibit them but to encourage creativity and adaptation. Mou et al. (2016) review some of the circumvention tools that have been developed in response to censorship, believed to be used by 2–3% of the population, but there are also examples of language innovation, which will be of interest to corpus linguists. Weibo was the site of another censorship controversy when it closed the Feminist Voices group, citing 'inappropriate content' that 'violated regulations' as the reason (https://www.wired.com/story/china-feminism-emoji-censorship/). At around the same time, it blocked the hashtag #MeToo, which was being used internationally as part of a movement against sexual harassment and assault: the hashtag an expression by the victims of sexual assault to show how pervasive it has been. Participants using the hashtag on Weibo debated (in)appropriate sexual conduct; however, the Feminist views expressed in such a discussion were perceived to be a threat to Communist rule, hence the closing down of the group. In response, Chinese Feminists adopted the #RiceBunny hashtag, which was typically accompanied by the emoji 🍚🐰. The Chinese articulation of this is 'mi tu', constituting a homophone that calls to mind the wider global discussion and demonstrated a creative social media response to censorship and the technical restrictions of the platform.

Researchers need to be aware of censorship issues when considering the representativeness and balance of their corpus data, as well as when considering what are suitable resources from which they can collect data. It is also useful to be aware of censorship issues when analysing data and making sense of innovations such as #RiceBunny.

Task 2.2

Imagine you are going to carry out a corpus linguistic study of the following research topics. What ethical considerations would be involved in carrying out this research?

- Personal profiles posted on an online dating website
- The social media pages of an extremist political group
- An online forum oriented around discussions of mental health issues.

2.4 Extracting your corpus from the Web

Once you have decided to build your own corpus and considered your sampling design, you can set about collecting the data. In this section, we will look at some of the key considerations and processes involved in building corpora of Web-derived data.

Web crawling is a process by which a researcher provides a software tool with a sample of URLs associated with their research topic, from which the software collects ('scrapes') the Web content and then 'follows' any hyperlinked data within that content to locate additional webpages. This process continues until the researcher terminates the crawl, or when certain parameters have been met (e.g. sufficient data has been collected). The user can also manage the search parameters for which hyperlinked pages are downloaded. For example, sticking to a particular domain (i.e. .com/.co.uk) can be a proxy for language; or only collecting data from pages with HTML can help to avoid types of content that are less suitable for language study (e.g. predominantly image content).

Researchers have found that this approach can return materials of variable quality and relevance and in corpus building, having to remove Web content that is limited in what it can offer for the study of language. Subsequently, a number of tools have been developed to support a more discerning crawling process. Suchomel and Pomikálek (2012), for example, developed SpiderLing (http://corpus.tools/wiki/SpiderLing), with the aim of excluding from the original crawl texts that are likely to be manually removed at a later stage and thereby, make the process more efficient. On the simple basis that it favours texts containing (largely) full sentences, they argue that it returns content that offers more language material and thereby is of more value to researchers interested in studying (written) language (Suchomel and Pomikálek, 2012).

2.5 Preparing your corpus

Corpus analysis relies upon a standard form of regular text; however, webpages are not just made of language content, but also navigation bars, panels and frames, page headers and footers, advertisements etc. Once you have collected your data from the Web you need to ensure that it is 'machine-readable' and this may require some editing and formatting to convert your Web material into a working corpus.

Task 2.3

Open a webpage in your Web browser. For the purposes of this task, the 'simpler' the webpage, the better. Press Ctrl+U (Option+Command+U for Mac) to view the source code. Can you identify the components of the webpage within the source code? Some elements, such as hyperlinks and images, will be relatively easy to spot. Can you identify where any text on the webpage appears within the source code?

2.5.1 Cleaning your corpus

Boilerplate removal

'Boilerplate' refers to features of a webpage that are external to its unique content, such as headers, footers, copyright notices and navigation links. These tend to be part of the wider website design and carry over from page to page, so do not tell us much about the specific content of a webpage. In fact, they are likely to over-represent terms such as 'Home', 'About', 'Links' etc. Figure 2.1 offers an example of the parts of a webpage that might be determined as 'boilerplate' and removed in order to separate out the main content of the webpage.

Web crawlers do not simply 'ignore' this material though and can use it not only to determine the main 'body' of a text, but also to identify the page links (such as 'Next' or 'More') in order to piece together sections of a text that run over a series of pages. Removal tools analyse HTML to determine the 'segments' of a webpage and then algorithms are applied to each segment to determine textual properties, such as: number of words or characters, number of links, average sentence length, number of function words, proportion of punctuation marks, etc. It is on this basis that the segments that are likely to represent the linguistic content that the researcher is most interested in are identified. Boilerplate content can be any content that the researcher considers 'noise' in their corpus, as any material that is not the primary content they determine to be part of the text. But this is not always straightforward to determine based on the organisation of the page alone. For example, a webpage that hosts news articles or academic journals is likely to offer suggestions of associated articles, based on content and these often appear 'within' the organisation of the text. Furthermore, many Web crawlers are programmed to favour text in full sentences, since this is thought to be more 'valuable' to language studies; this does mean that lists and tables tend to be excluded and it is with respect to this type of material that there will be differing opinions on whether this is a core part of the text.

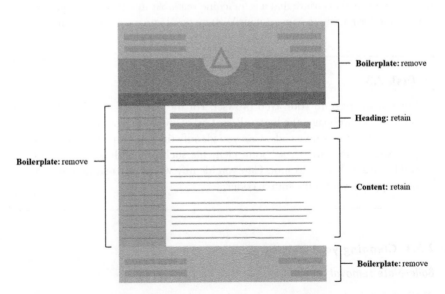

Figure 2.1 Features of a webpage for boilerplate removal (Author's own).

De-duplication

A subsequent process to 'boilerplate removal' is to remove duplications of texts in your corpus. There are many ways in which texts are duplicated on the Web and in most instances, this type of repetition is not helpful to the examination of variation in language. There may be research questions where repetition is significant; for example, if the researcher is exploring a question of exposure to a particular language feature, it may be pertinent that the user comes across particular texts and the features within it in multiple ways. Nevertheless, the duplication of texts will inevitably affect the outputs of an analytical process predicated on frequency and so it is often desirable to limit this type of repetition. Pomikálek (2011) distinguishes between 'natural' repetition, where phrasal constructs are repeated and which is of interest to language studies; and 'artificial' repetition that is simply a 'copy and paste' of a text and therefore does not constitute an independent and natural use of language. Pomikálek (2011) offers a review of the processes through which duplication and near-duplication have been identified – including for the purposes of plagiarism detection – before introducing the algorithm which became the basis for the Onion (ONe Instance ONly) tool (http://corpus.tools/wiki/Onion). This tool has subsequently been applied by Benko (2013) to a collection of Slovak corpora and shown to be an effective tool for de-duplication at the text and paragraph level and can be combined effectively with other methods to ensure comprehensive de-duplication at the sentence level.

Non-standard orthography

In their study of Internet Relay Chat and Yahoo Messenger chat sessions, Al-sa'di and Hamdan (2005: 409) found that "economy is a salient attribute of e-English" and this manifests in characteristically short and simple sentences, truncated and distorted words, abbreviations and acronyms, and taboo words. As such, we can expect a prevalence of non-standard orthography in online communications, which is of course significant for corpus analysis queries that rely on patterns of consistent word forms, but also for automated tagging processes that rely on recognising the grammatical form and/or semantic meaning of a word (more on this in the next chapter). Some studies may be interested in, for example, varieties of English as manifest in spelling differences, such as 'organisation' (favoured in British English) and 'organization' (favoured in U.S. English). But if we are not interested in looking specifically at dialect variation, it is likely that we would want the corpus analysis tool to collate these forms when determining frequency.

Given the immediacy of Internet chat interactions and the efforts to perhaps compensate for paralinguistic features that would be apparent in spoken interaction (facial expressions, pitch, prosody, gesture), it is reasonable to think that non-standard orthography is the result of hurried typing and it has often been characterised as an error. Ringlstetter et al. (2006: 297) identify 4 classes of error found in large English and German corpora from the Web:

- Typing errors
- Spelling errors (presumed to be a result of insufficient language competence)
- Errors resulting from inadequate character encoding
- Optical Character Recognition (OCR) errors.

These categories capture different aspects of the communicative act, which is reliant upon the user's competence, articulation (typing), the technological realisation of this (encoding) and the reproduction/retrieval of this for analysis (OCR). Ringlstetter et al. (2006: 336–7) report that Web corpora "typically contain a non-negligible number of pages with an unacceptable number of orthographic errors" and that "typing errors represent the most important subclass". They also demonstrate some approaches to building error dictionaries, which can aid the researcher in filtering out webpages that are high in error content and subsequently, improve the automated collection of translation correspondences.

Smith et al. (2014) discuss spelling errors in a corpus of 'agony aunt' style health queries submitted online as part of the 'Teenage Health Freak' project. They found use of abbreviations and acronyms (e.g. u > you; 4 > for; cuz > because) as well as typographical errors (iam > I am; alchohl > alcohol) and phonetic errors (probarbly > probably; egsisting > existing) – some of which were likely to be an attempt to recover some sense of audible emphasis (soooooo > so). A large proportion of their token corrections (39.6%) simply reinserted a missing apostrophe, suggesting that these were errors of convenience. Nevertheless, even simple frequency counts are compromised, as demonstrated in the variant spellings of 'embarrassed': 'embarrased', 'embarassed', 'embaressed', 'embarresed', 'embrassed', 'embarrassed', 'embarased', 'embarrsed', 'embaresed', 'embarrised', 'embarested', 'embarised', 'embarresd', 'embarsed', 'imbarrased' (Smith et al., 2014: 147). However, Smith et al. (2014) maintain that while spelling correction affects the number of words (types) in a corpus, analytical processes will still identify which terms are the most prominent in a dataset (which they confirm through comparison with a normalised version of the dataset). In this instance, the corpus comprised quite a specific lexicon, where references to, for example, 'tonsillitis' or 'tetanus' are likely to be reported as characteristic words whether they are spelt correctly or not. The authors therefore recommend that similar procedures be carried out on more general computer-mediated communication in order to assess whether corpus analysis can 'cope' with such spelling errors (Smith et al., 2014).

Researchers have explored ways in which to deal with variant forms of words, with a view to mitigating the impact of typographical errors. One approach can be found in the Variant Detection (VARD) tool (Rayson et al., 2007), which was initially developed to process spelling variations in historical English, but has since been developed to deal with any kind of variation (including on the basis of error) and is customisable to any dictionary (including languages other than English) (Baron and Rayson, 2009). It has subsequently been applied to studies of Early Modern English (Baron et al., 2009; Lehto et al., 2010); learner corpora (Rayson and Baron, 2011); and studies of SMS and Twitter data (Baron et al., 2011; Tagg et al., 2012). Laurence Anthony (2017) has developed a tool called VariAnt that finds variants of a search word within a corpus http://www.laurenceanthony.net/software/variant/. This can be used by the user to identify legitimate variants that can then be entered into tools like VARD and ensure that multiple iterations of what is perceived by the researcher to be a single term can be collated in corpus analyses.

There are circumstances and research purposes for which it may be useful for the researcher to retain non-standard orthography. The use of non-standard orthography is not exclusively a case of limited language competence, or the product of hurried typing. Non-standard forms serve a range of functions (as we will see in Chapter 4) and can therefore be the basis for a range of sociolinguistic questions regarding language in an online context. There may be some non-standard forms that are not only considered 'acceptable' but preferred, in which case it seems more 'authentic' to maintain a distinction from standardised forms. This is often the case in spoken data. For example, in the BNC1994, 'isn't' is orthographically realised as 'isn't', 'ain't', 'isnae' (Scottish dialect form), 'in't' and 'in' (from 'innit'), based on its vocal realisation. Most of us would recognise (and probably use) a number of these forms and recognise that saying 'ain't' is not the same as saying 'isn't'. The same must be said for the use of non-standard forms in online communication.

Lin (2016) examines the use of vocal spelling, focusing on emulated prosody and lexical surrogates. These categories cover attempts to replicate stretched out syllables or prosodic changes in spoken conversation (e.g. helloooo), as well as the lexicalisation of vocal sounds such as laughter (e.g. hehe). Lin (2016) found that non-standard capitalisation was used to emulate prosody and was most commonly used with degree adverbs (e.g. REALLY), demonstrating its being used for emphasis. Vocal spelling was also used for degree adverbs, but also for interjections (e.g. yeahhh) and discourse markers (e.g. ooooh), which we might consider to be characteristic of spoken discourse. For the purposes of corpus analysis, the researcher must decide if they want to retain these non-standard forms or normalise them so that all forms of 'yeah' (whether 'yeahh' or 'yeahhhh') for instance, are counted together. One possibility for reaching a compromise is to normalise the variants but to provide some form of annotation to indicate that an edit had been made and perhaps record the original form; it is annotation to which we now turn our focus.

2.5.2 Corpus annotation

Alongside textual data, we can document different types of information about that language data in our corpus, which can be categorised as either **metadata**, **textual markup** or **linguistic annotation**.

Metadata

Metadata refers to information about the primary language data. Typically, this recalls something of the context from which the data was taken, or the form it takes. There are different types of metadata that can be applied to the same data, as Page et al. (2014: 157) demonstrate with the example of a digital image, which might be described in terms of its technical specifications; by the tags that have been ascribed by the individual who posted it (or other users); and/or with respect to licensing information. With most types of user content online, there is a record of the date and time at which we have posted materials and if it is a platform that enables user profiles, some components of these (e.g. usernames, avatars) will appear alongside posts.

One of the criticisms of the BNC1994, particularly in relation to the spoken component, is the limited and inconsistent availability of metadata, which is acknowledged by Burnard (2001) in his reflections on the design. The principle metadata categories used for the BNC2014 with respect to the speakers included: age, gender, accent/dialect and occupation, though the compilers also collected information on nationality, birthplace, current location, duration of stay in current location, mother tongue, most influential country on language, additional languages, educational level (Love et al., 2017). Some of these, such as 'Accent/dialect' relied on self-report and the researchers outline the benefits of having such data for the purposes of perceptual dialectology alongside the audio recordings, which in any case can be classified according to more objective linguistic criteria. Metadata relating to the recordings was also captured, pertaining to: the number of speakers, recording location, the range of conversation topics and the main conversation topic.

Barbaresi (2016) describes a tool for automatically extracting metadata from WordPress to compile a corpus of blogs that also has data on: the title of the post, title of the blog, date of publication, canonical URL, author, categories and tags, as well the functionality for extracting comments. Barbaresi (2016) shows that with better metadata, a more refined analysis of the blog genre can be carried out to understand more about the 'hybridity' of blogs.

Ultimately, metadata can help us to understand more of the circumstances in which our language data were generated and make informed assessments about the 'meaning' of the data with details about the context in which it was originally disseminated and received. This is shown in Deutschmann's (2003) analysis of 'apologies' in British English, which is based on data from the spoken component of the BNC1994 and which enables an examination of speech behaviour with respect to gender, age and social class of speakers, as well as aspects of the conversational setting (e.g. group size, genre, formality). It is the inclusion of this metadata that enables Deutschmann (2003) to consider the use of apologies for the purposes of self-representation.

Textual markup

Markup refers to information about the physical appearance and formatting of a document, e.g. headings, paragraph breaks, sections. We can use markup information in our searches, for example looking only for instances of a word in a newspaper headline (perhaps as a way of increasing the likelihood that the article is about that topic). eXtensible Markup Language (XML) is routinely used for the textual markup of corpus files and the Text Encoding Initiative (TEI) (Sperberg-McQueen and Burnard, 1994) provides guidelines for applying tags in XML. Another notable set of conventions is outlined in the Corpus Encoding Standard (CES) (https://www.cs.vassar.edu/CES/) (Ide, 1998). For an introduction to the basics of XML markup, Rühlemann and Gee (2017) describe its principal features and functions, as well as arguing for the value of producing transcripts in XML for 'big data' conversation analysis and introducing tools for converting transcripts to XML format and running queries. Hardie (2014) proposes a 'modest' set of XML features for enabling corpus linguists to apply markup without necessarily having a developed understanding of the more substantive standards, such as the TEI.

Markup is thought to refer to more objective phenomena, in contrast to annotation, which is seen as more evaluative; however, this distinction is not always clear-cut. For example, Smith et al. (2014: 144) provide the following demonstration of their use of the TEI tags (<choice>, <sic> and <corr>) to indicate where an instance of non-standard orthography ('plz') had been corrected (to 'please'):

```
<choice>
        <sic>plz</sic>
        <corr>please</corr>
</choice>
```

Though we can refer to standardised spelling and would probably recognise a fairly routine variant of the word 'please', this has involved some degree of interpretation of the form and an assessment of the intended meaning. Even basic elements, such as sentence boundaries, may require some interpretation, so the distinction between markup and annotation is not absolute.

Linguistic annotation

Leech (1997: 2) defines annotation as "the practice of adding interpretative, linguistic information to an electronic corpus". You can find out more about the annotation of the BNC1994 here: http://www.natcorp.ox.ac.uk/corpus/creating.xml?ID=annotation. Interpretation and evaluation can be applied at various levels, including: syntactic analysis, semantic analysis, error tagging, discourse and pragmatic analysis. The University Centre for Computer Corpus Research on Language (UCREL) at Lancaster University has developed a number of annotation tools that correspond to these different levels of interpretation (http://ucrel.lancs.ac.uk/annotation.html). We will look at some of these in the next chapter when we explore features of corpus analysis. Some of these tools are fully automated, some require manual input; each has been developed to support corpus analysis and been applied to various corpus data.

Leech (1993) proposed 7 maxims of annotation as a guide for good practice:

1 **It should be possible to remove the annotation from an annotated corpus in order to revert to the raw corpus.** Typically, tags do not interrupt the unit (e.g. 'shoes_NN2', <word pos="N">dog</word>).
2 **It should be possible to extract the annotations by themselves from the text.** The text and its annotations are often stored as one XML file; however, it is also common to keep them as separate files.
3 **The annotation scheme should be based on guidelines which are available to the end user.** Most annotation schemes come with a freely available user guide.
4 **It should be made clear how and by whom the annotation was carried out.**
5 **The end user should be made aware that the corpus annotation is not infallible, but simply a potentially useful tool.** Annotation provides interpretative information, so it is always possible that the user's reading may differ from that of the annotator.
6 **Annotation schemes should be based as far as possible on widely agreed and theory-neutral principles.**
7 **No annotation scheme has the a priori right to be considered as a standard.** The value of an annotation scheme is in its applicability.

Annotation procedures offer another opportunity for us to make use of computational processes, but these must be informed by linguistic theory and what researchers have determined from various areas of language analysis. They have also been developed in response to the questions that we have about language use and in the next chapter, we will look at the different units of analysis involved in corpus linguistics and how we can use annotation schemes to identify and measure them.

Summary

In this chapter, I have outlined some of the key considerations behind designing and building a corpus, including how we determine what to include and some of the processes for extracting data for our corpus from the Web. We have discussed the different ways we can utilise the Web as a corpus and as a resource for carrying out some of the tasks involved in corpus-building, alongside some of the ethical considerations relating to research on the Web. On the basis of what has been covered in this chapter, you should be well-prepared to construct your own corpus and begin to consider what exactly we look for in corpus analysis, which is the focus of the next chapter.

References

Al-sa'di, R. A. and Hamdan, J. M. (2005). "Synchronous online chat" English: Computer-mediated communication. *World Englishes*, 24, 4, 409–424.

Anthony, L. (2017). *VariAnt* (Version 1.1.0) [Computer Software]. Tokyo, Japan: Waseda University. Available from http://www.laurenceanthony.net/software, accessed 21 April 2018.

Aston, G. and Burnard, L. (1998). *The BNC Handbook: Exploring the British National Corpus with SARA*. Edinburgh: Edinburgh University Press.

Barbaresi, A. (2016). Efficient construction of metadata-enhanced web corpora. *Proceedings of the 10th Web as Corpus Workshop (WAC-X) and the EmpiriST Shared Task*. 7–12 August 2016. Berlin, Germany, 7–16.

Baron, A. and Rayson, P. (2009). Automatic standardization of texts containing spelling variation, how much training data do you need? *Proceedings of the Corpus Linguistics Conference, CL2009*. 20–23 July 2009. University of Liverpool, U.K. Available at: http://ucrel.lancs.ac.uk/publications/cl2009/314_FullPaper.pdf, accessed 17 April 2018.

Baron, A., Rayson, P. and Archer, D. (2009). Word frequency and key word statistics in historical corpus linguistics, in R. Ahrens and H. Antor (eds) *Anglistik: International Journal of English Studies*, 20, 1, 41–67.

Baron, A., Tagg, C., Rayson, P., Greenwood, P., Walkerdine, J. and Rashid, A. (2011). Using verifiable author data: Gender and spelling differences in Twitter and SMS. Presented at *ICAME 32*. 1–5 June 2011. Oslo, Norway.

Benko, V. (2013). Data deduplication in Slovak corpora, in K. Gajdošová and A. Žáková (eds) Slovko 2013: Natural Language Processing, Corpus Linguistics, E-learning. Lüdenscheid: RAM-Verlag, 27–39.

Bernardini, S. Baroni, M. and Evert, S. (2006). A WaCky introduction, in M. Baroni and S. Bernardini (eds) *WaCky! Working Papers in the Web as Corpus*. Bologna: GEDIT Edizioni, 9–40.

Biber, D. (1993). Representativeness in corpus design. *Literary and Linguistic Computing*, 8, 4, 243–257

Buchanan, E. A. and Zimmer, M. (2013). Internet research ethics, in E. N. Zalta (ed.) *The Stanford Encyclopedia of Philosophy*. Fall 2013 Edition. Available at: https://plato.stanford.edu/archives/fall2013/entries/ethics-internet-research/, accessed 22 April 2018.

Burnard, L. (2001). Where did we go wrong? A retrospective look at the design of the BNC, in B. Ketterman and G. Markus (eds) *Teaching and Learning by Doing Corpus Analysis*. Amsterdam: Rodopi, 51–71.

Callison-Burch, C. (2009). Fast, cheap and creative: Evaluating translation quality using Amazon's Mechanical Turk. *Proceedings of Empirical Methods in Natural Language Processing (EMNLP)*. 6–7 August 2009. Singapore, 286–295.

Callison-Burch, C. and Dredze, M. (2010). Creating speech and language data with Amazon's Mechanical Turk. *NAACL HLT 2010 Workshop on Creating Speech and Language Data with Amazon's Mechanical Turk*. 6 June 2010. Los Angeles, California, U.S.A., 1–12.

Crawford, W. J. and Csomay, E. (2016). *Doing Corpus Linguistics*. New York.: Routledge.

Deibert, R., Palfrey, J., Rohozinski, R. and Zittrain, J. (eds) (2011). *Access Contested: Security, Identity, and Resistance in Asian Cyberspace*. Cambridge: The MIT Press.

Deutschmann, M. (2003). Apologising in British English. PhD Dissertation. Umeå University: Umeå, Sweden.

Elgesem, D. (2015). Consent and information – ethical considerations when conducting research on social media, in H. Fossheim and H. Ingierd (eds) *Internet Research Ethics*. Oslo: Cappelen Damm Akademisk, 14–34.

The European Parliament and the Council of the European Union (2016). Regulation (E.U.) 2016/679 of the European Parliament and of the Council of 27 April 2016 on the protection of natural persons with regard to the processing of personal data and on the free movement of such data, and repealing Directive 95/46/EC (General Data Protection Regulation). *Official Journal of the European Union*. Available at: https://eur-lex.europa.eu/legal-content/EN/TXT/PDF/?uri=CELEX:32016R0679&from=EN, accessed 1 June 2018.

Fossheim, H. and Ingierd, H. (eds) (2015). *Internet Research Ethics*. Oslo: Cappelen Damm Akademisk.

Golder, S., Ahmed, S., Norman, G. and Booth, A. (2017). Attitudes toward the ethics of using social media: A systematic review. *Journal of Medical Internet Research*, 19, 6, e195.

Goldman, J. P., Leemann, A., Kolly, M.-J., Hove, I., Almajai, I., Dellwo, V. and Moran, S. (2014). A crowdsourcing smartphone application for Swiss German: putting language documentation in the hands of the users. *Proceedings of Language Resources and Evaluation Conference (LREC) 2014*. 26–31 May 2014. Reykjavík, Iceland, 3444–3447.

Handford, M. (2007). The Genre of the Business Meeting: A Corpus-based Study. PhD Thesis. The University of Nottingham. Available at: http://eprints.nottingham.ac.uk/11893/1/438546.pdf, accessed 20 April 2018.

Hardie, A. (2014). Modest XML for corpora: not a standard, but a suggestion. *ICAME Journal*, 38, 1, 73–103.

Ide, N. (1998). Corpus Encoding Standard: SGML guidelines for encoding linguistic corpora. *Proceedings of the 1st International Language Resources and Evaluation Conference (LREC)*. 28–30 May 1998. Granada, Spain. Available at: https://www.cs.vassar.edu/~ide/papers/CES.granada.pdf, accessed 23 March 2018.

Kehoe, A. and Gee, M. (2009). Weaving web data into a diachronic corpus patchwork, in A. Renouf and A. Kehoe (eds) *Corpus Linguistics: Refinements and Reassessments*. Amsterdam: Rodopi, 255–279.

Kilgarriff, A., Reddy, S., Pomikálek, J. and PVS, A. (2010). A corpus factory for many languages. *Proceedings of the 7th International Conference on Language Resources and Evaluation (LREC)*. 17–23 May 2010. Valletta, Malta. Available at: http://kilgarriff.co.uk/Publications/2010_KilgReddyPomikalekAvinesh_LREC_CorpFactory.pdf?format=raw, accessed 20 April 2018.

King, B. (2009). Building and analysing corpora of computer mediated communication, in P. Baker (ed.) *Contemporary Corpus Linguistics*. London: Continuum, 301–320.

Knight, D., Fitzpatrick, T. and Morris, S. (2017). CorCenCC (Corpws Cenedlaethol Cymraeg Cyfoes – The National Corpus of Contemporary Welsh): An overview. Paper presented at the *British Association for Applied Linguistics (BAAL) Conference*. 31 August–2 September 2017. University of Leeds, Leeds, U.K.

Koene, A. and Adolphs, S. (2015). Ethics considerations for corpus linguistic studies using internet resources. HORIZON: University of Nottingham. Available at: https://casma.wp.horizon.ac.uk/wp-content/uploads/2015/04/CL2015-CorpusLinguisticsEthics_KoeneAdolphs.pdf, accessed 22 April 2018.

Koester, A. (2010). Building small specialised corpora, in A. O'Keeffe and M. McCarthy (eds) *The Routledge Handbook of Corpus Linguistics*. London: Routledge, 66–79.

Lane, I. Eck, M., Rottmann, K. and Waibel, A. (2010). Tools for collecting speech corpora via Mechanical-Turk. *Proceedings of the North American Chapter of the Association of Computational Linguistics (AACL) Human Language Technologies Workshop 2010*. 1–6 June 2010. Los Angeles, California, U.S.A., 184–187.

Leech, G. (1993). Corpus annotation schemes. *Literary and Linguistic Computing*, 8, 4, 275–281.

Leech, G. (1997). Introducing corpus annotation, in R. Garside, G. Leech and T. McEnery (eds) *Corpus Annotation*. London: Longman, 1–18.

Leemann, A., Kolly, M. J., Purves, R., Britain, D. and Glaser, E. (2016). Crowdsourcing language change with smartphone applications. *PLoS ONE*, 11, 1, e0143060.

Lehto, A., Baron, A., Ratia, M. and Rayson, P. (2010). Improving the precision of corpus methods: The standardized version of Early Modern English medical texts, in I. Taavitsainen and P. Pahta (eds) *Early Modern English Medical Texts: Corpus description and studies*. Amsterdam: John Benjamins, 279–290.

Lew, R. (2009). The web as corpus versus traditional corpora: their relative utility for linguists and language, in P. Baker (ed.) *Contemporary Studies in Linguistics: Contemporary Corpus Linguistics*. London: Continuum, 289–300.

Lin, Y.-L. (2016). Non-standard capitalisation and vocal spelling in intercultural computer-mediated communication. *Corpus*, 11, 1, 63–82.

Lischinsky, A. (2018). Overlooked text types: From fictional texts to real-world discourses, in C. Taylor and A. Marchi (eds) *Corpus Approaches to Discourse: A Critical Review*. London: Routledge, 60–81.

Love, R., Dembry, C., Hardie, A., Brezina, V. and McEnery, T. (2017). The Spoken BNC2014: Designing and building a spoken corpus of everyday conversations. *International Journal of Corpus Linguistics*, 22, 3, 319–344.

Mackenzie, J. (2017). Identifying informational norms in Mumsnet Talk: A reflexive-linguistic approach to internet research ethics. *Applied Linguistics Review*, 8, 2–3, 293–314.

Markham, A. and Buchanan, E. (2012). *Ethical Decision-making and Internet research: Recommendations from the AoIR Ethics Working Committee*. Version 2.0. Available at: http://aoir.org/reports/ethics2.pdf, accessed 22 April 2018.

McGraw, A., Gruenstein, A. and Sutherland, A. (2009). A self-labeling speech corpus: Collecting spoken words with an online educational game. *Proceedings of Interspeech 2009*. 6–10 September 2009. Brighton, U.K., 3031–3034.

McKee, H. A. and Porter, J. (2009). *The Ethics of Internet Research: A Rhetorical, Case-based Process*. Oxford: Peter Lang.

Mou, Y., Wu, K. and Atkin, D. (2016). Understanding the use of circumvention tools to bypass online censorship. *New Media & Society*, 18, 5, 837–856.

Neale, S., Spasić, I., Needs, J., Watkins, G., Morris, S., Fitzpatrick, T., Marshall, L. and Knight, D. (2017). The CorCenCC Crowdsourcing App: A bespoke tool for the user-driven creation of the National Corpus of Contemporary Welsh. Paper Presented at the *Corpus Linguistics Conference 2017*. 24–28 July 2017. University of Birmingham, Birmingham, U.K. Available at: https://www.birmingham.ac.uk/Documents/college-artslaw/corpus/conference-archives/2017/general/paper273.pdf, accessed 18 April 2018.

Novotney, S. and Callison-Burch, C. (2010). Cheap, fast and good enough: automatic speech recognition with non-expert transcription. *Human Language Technologies: The 2010 Annual Conference of the North American Chapter of the Association for Computational Linguistics, HLT '10*. 1–6 June 2010. Los Angeles, California, U.S.A., 207–215.

Orgad, S. (2009). Question two: How can researchers make sense of the issues involved in collecting and interpreting online and offline data?, in A. N. Markham and N. K. Baym (eds) *In Internet Inquiry: Conversations About Method*. Los Angeles : Sage, 33–53.

Page, R., Barton, D., Unger, J. W. and Zappavigna, M. (2014). *Researching Language and Social Media: A Student Guide*. London: Routledge.

Pomikálek, J. (2011). Removing Boilerplate and Duplicate Content from Web Corpora. PhD Thesis. Masaryk University Faculty of Informatics, Brno, Czech Republic.

Rayson, P. and Baron, A. (2011). Automatic error tagging of spelling mistakes in learner corpora, in F. Meunier, S. De Cock, G. Gilquin and M. Paquot (eds) *A Taste for Corpora: In Honour of Syviane Granger*. Amsterdam : John Benjamins, 109–126.

Rayson, P., Archer, D., Baron, A., Culpeper, J. and Smith, N. (2007). Tagging the bard: Evaluating the accuracy of a modern PoS tagger in Early Modern English corpora. *Proceedings of the Corpus Linguistics Conference: CL2007*. 27–30 July 2007. University of Birmingham, U.K. Available at: https://www.birmingham.ac.uk/documents/college-artslaw/corpus/conference-archives/2007/192Paper.pdf, accessed 17 April 2018.

Renouf, A., Kehoe, A. and Banerjee, J. (2007). WebCorp: an integrated system for web text search, in C. Nesselhauf, M. Hundt and C. Biewer (eds) *Corpus Linguistics and the Web*. Amsterdam: Rodopi, 47–67.

Ringlstetter, C., Schulz, K. U. and Mihov, S. (2006). Orthographic errors in web pages: Toward cleaner web corpora. *Computational Linguistics*, 32, 3, 295–340.

Rühlemann, C. and Gee, M. (2017). Conversation analysis and the XML method. *Gesprächsforschung*, 18, 274–296.

Sinclair, J. (1991). *Corpus, Concordance, Collocation*. Oxford: Oxford University Press.

Sinclair, J. (2004). *Trust the Text: Language, Corpus and Discourse*. London: Routledge.

Smith, C., Adolphs, S., Harvey, K. and Mullany, L. (2014). Spelling errors in born-digital data: a case study using the Teenage Health Freak Corpus. *Corpora*, 9, 2, 137–154.

Sperberg-McQueen, C. M. and Burnard, L. (1994). *Guidelines for Electronic Text Encoding and Interchange*. Oxford: Text Encoding Initiative.

Stubbs, M. (1996). *Text and Corpus Analysis*. Oxford: Blackwell.

Suchomel, V. and Pomikálek, J. (2012). Efficient web crawling for large text corpora. *Proceedings of the 7th Web as Corpus Workshop (WAC7)*. 17 April 2012. Lyon, France, 39–43.

Tagg, C., Baron, A. and Rayson, P. (2012). "i didn't spel that wrong did i. Oops": Analysis and normalisation of SMS spelling variation, in L. A. Cougnon and C. Fairon (eds) *SMS Communication: A Linguistic Approach*. Special Issue of *Linguisticae Investigationes*, 35, 2, 367–388.

Townsend, L. and Wallace, C. (2016). Social Media Research: A Guide to Ethics. The University of Aberdeen. Available at: http://www.dotrural.ac.uk/socialmediaresearchethics.pdf, accessed 22 April 2018.

Weber, M. S. (2017). The challenge of 25 years of data: An agenda for web-based research, in N. Brügger (ed.) *Web 25: Histories from the First 25 Years of the World Wide Web*. New York: Peter Lang, 125–137.

Whiteman, N. (2012). *Undoing Ethics: Rethinking Practice in Online Research*. London: Springer.

Chapter 3

Analysing corpora

In this chapter we will be looking at some of the fundamentals of corpus analysis, as well as introducing some of the publicly available software tools through which researchers can upload and explore their own corpora and compare them with some of the pre-existing corpora we have seen in previous chapters. Many of the examples provided here and throughout the rest of the book will make use of #LancsBox: a 'toolbox' of corpus analysis software programs developed at Lancaster University (Brezina et al., 2015).

> **Task 3.1**
>
> Go to http://corpora.lancs.ac.uk/lancsbox/download.php and follow the instructions to download #LancsBox to your computer. The site also hosts a comprehensive user guide (http://corpora.lancs.ac.uk/lancsbox/help.php), including video demonstrations and exercises to help you familiarise yourself with the interface and functionality. It is recommended that you engage with that material alongside reading this chapter, which will outline some of the key terms and processes that #LancsBox supports.

3.1 What can we analyse in a corpus?

So far in this book I have discussed how corpus linguistics allows us to search for particular terms and language features, without going into too much detail. In this section we will look at precisely what can be queried through corpus analysis, how this is made possible by corpus analysis tools and what users need to do carry out those queries. As we consider the different ways we can organise language, I will demonstrate how these can be queried simply by using the search bar in a corpus analysis tool. To do this, I will be referring to https://corpus.byu.edu/ to demonstrate how to navigate retrieval tools and #LancsBox in order to support readers in working with a tool that allows them to work with their own data. Many of the freely available corpus analysis tools use the same notation for search queries or will make available user guides for how to navigate corpus data through their search interfaces.

3.1.1 Tokenisation

One of the simplest ways to query a corpus is to look for particular words. In Chapter 1, we saw a series of concordance lines for the term 'viral', through a process of what is referred to as concordancing. In this format, the analyst can sort the lines to manually look for patterns or to look for other words that appear in the surrounding co-text; the user guide for the KWIC tool in #LancBox outlines some of the sort and filter functions (http://corpora.lancs.ac.uk/lancsbox/docs/pdf/LancsBox_3.0_KWIC.pdf). Often, the identification of a search term or node word comes from the researchers' own interests or prior knowledge of the topic, though any word items identified through preliminary corpus analysis (such as keywords, which will be discussed below) can also be viewed as concordance lines. Even this requires that we program corpus analysis tools to recognise what a 'word' is. In the first instance, corpus tools need to ascertain where a unit begins and ends, which to some extent, can be determined by spaces. However, what happens when we include punctuation? What happens when punctuation appears between letters, such as 'I'm' or 'can't'? In these instances, a manual reader would recognise the pronoun and the verb ('I' and 'am') and the verb with negation ('can' and 'not'), so we must train our computer tools to do the same. There are also some units that operate as multiple words, for example 'Great Britain', or 'drum 'n' bass'.

Task 3.2

How many words would you say there are in each of the following extracts? What features do you need to consider in order to decide?

Extract A

How he had managed to climb through the portrait hole was anyone's guess, because his legs had been stuck together with what they recognized at once as the Leg-Locker Curse.

(Rowling, 1998)

Extract B

There's just one point I'd make on erm, the first one, regarding the, th-, Wiltshire and Thamesdown Racial Equality Council.

(BNC1994)

> **Extract C**
>
> An exclusive look at my new @kkwbeauty collab with #GlamMasters'
> Argenis! Watch now: http://bit.ly/2qMNmYJ
> (Kim Kardashian, Twitter, 12:56 PM 19 April 2018)
>
> You will find a commentary on this task at the end of the book.

The process for segmenting a text into words is called **tokenisation**. It is an important process in that many subsequent forms of analysis rely on accurate identification of tokens in the first instance. While there are some words that appear as one unit but require segmentation, such as 'I'll', 'c'mon' and 'gonna', there are also some cases where it seems more logical to treat a series of words as one unit – for example, 'in front of', 'of course' and 'up to date'. These are what we refer to as **multi-word units** and we can program tagging software tools to recognise these and treat them as single units. However, it is often the case that a multi-word unit comprises words that can also be understood individually; for example, we might recognise 'spot on' as an adjective to mean 'accurate', but this would not be the case in 'there's a spot on the mirror'. In this instance, because 'spot' is preceded by the indefinite article ('a'), 'spot' is likely to be used as a noun and therefore, not part of the multi-word unit 'spot on'. Tokenisation relies on not only recognising the arrangement of letters within the boundaries of white spaces or punctuation, but will also use the surrounding co-text (e.g. the presence of a determiner) to discern, for example, what is a multi-word unit and what is a series of individual tokens.

In practice, any basic corpus analysis software program will carry out tokenisation for you. Nevertheless, it will be useful to understand the process for conducting subsequent manual analysis and understanding a frequency list that has, for example, 'n't' and ''m' in it. You can see what contracted forms (http://ucrel.lancs.ac.uk/bnc2/fused.htm) and multi-word units (http://ucrel.lancs.ac.uk/bnc2/multiwd.htm) have been tagged in the BNC1994 to get a sense of how this is carried out by automatic computational tools that provide annotation – known as **taggers** – most typically in terms of its grammatical or semantic function, as is discussed below.

Forms of online communication introduce new challenges for these automatic tagging processes in the use of contracted forms, non-standard orthography, hyperlinks, emoticons etc. Hallsmar and Palm (2016: 10) detail some of the measures they carried out to simplify the tokenisation process, including:

- Converting all characters to lowercase
- Replacing all hyperlinked usernames (mentions) with '@USER'

- Replacing all URLs (strings beginning with http[s], ftp[s] and www) with 'URL'
- Reducing occurences characters appearing more than twice in succession down to two characters. For example, reducing 'Helloooooooo' to 'Helloo'. This allowed the researchers to capture instances of elongation (whether by two, three characters etc.) as distinct from standard orthography ('Hello').

Hallsmar and Palm (2016) also used TweetTokenizer, a tool designed specifically to deal with hashtags and emojis to determine tokens. The development of such tools attests to the recognition that in order to carry out studies of online communication, we need to program our tools to recognise, for example, emoticons as combined punctuation :). It is often the case in social media platforms (and word processors) that these are automatically converted into emoji ☺ (expressible in Unicode (U+1F60A)), which in turn, might make tokenisation more straightforward.

Tokenisation allows researchers to make an assessment of the lexical variation within a text, by way of the **type-token ratio (TTR)**. The number of **tokens** is determined by the words (word units) within a text and the number of **types** is determined by the number of unique words forms. Repetitions of word units increase the number of tokens, but not the number of types. The TTR is calculated by dividing the number of types by the number of tokens, which will generate a number between 0 and 1 (which can be multiplied by 100 to be expressed as a percentage). For the purposes of comparison, we must remember that larger texts are likely to have greater repetition of tokens (i.e. relatively fewer types) and so this tends to be standardised for comparison between texts of different sizes. Type-token ratio can be a useful measure when investigating language learning and language teaching (Jiménez et al., 2006) as one indicator of fluency.

3.1.2 N-grams and lexical bundles

It may be that we are interested in identifying patterns of series of words that appear in our corpus. Phraseological units are common in English and along with the multi-word units described above, there may be other sequences of words that are particular to our dataset but nonetheless appear with regularity. In corpus linguistics, the term **n-gram** is used to refer to a combination of two or more words that "repeatedly occur consecutively in a corpus" (Cheng, 2012: 72). The label 'n-grams' allows for an unspecified number of words, where we might use bi-grams, tri-grams etc. to be more specific about the number. Biber et al. (1999) refer to the outputs of their n-gram method as **lexical bundles**, and they have alternatively been named 'recurrent combinations' (Altenberg, 1998) and 'clusters' (Scott, 1999). A 'cluster analysis' will automatically return sequences of two, three, four or more words that appear multiple times in the corpus, allowing us to consider whether there is any particular meaning behind this sequencing. The identification of lexical bundles is based on the most frequent sequences within a register as a means of register analysis (Biber et al., 1999), relying on pre-selected lengths (typically four, such as 'as a result of') and frequency rates.

3.1.3 Lemmatisation

Tokenisation allows us to distinguish individual word units, but it is often useful to be able to collate and count the inflected forms of a word. For example, if we are querying the discussion of 'playing' we might want to include all forms of the word 'play', i.e. plays, playing, played. This is achieved through a process called **lemmatisation**. Corpus analysis tools are programmed to identify the root word, called a **lemma** (i.e. 'play'), along with the different realisations of the lemma, which are called **lexemes** (including 'play', but also 'playing', 'plays', 'played'). For regular patterns, having associated lexemes with -s, -ing and -ed endings is a good way to identify a verb. However, there are numerous irregular forms, such as 'is' (am, are, be, was etc.), that need to be programmed into a lemmatiser.

Task 3.3

When conducting a search through https://corpus.byu.edu/bnc/ you can search by lemma by putting the term in square brackets. For example, searching for [talk] returns 'talk', 'talking', 'talks', 'talked' as well as the contracted form 'talkin' and the punctuated form 'talk.'.

Before you run the corpus query below, write down all the different forms of the verb 'to be' you can think of. So, for example, 'be' is the infinitive, 'is' is the present tense singular form and 'were' is the past tense plural form. Then search for [be] in the BNC.

- How many different forms of [be] are there? How does this compare with your list?
- Are all of the forms listed actually to do with the verb? Which ones would you discount?
- What does this tell you about the different ways in which we use the word?
- What does this show you about how the program carries out lemmatisation?

Recognising what is a stem and what is an affix is fundamental to lemmatisation. Often, we will want to explore a category of words as characterised by the presence of a prefix such as 'anti-' or a suffix such as '-itis' as a way of exploring types of inflammatory disease. Of course, not all health complaints end in '-itis' and equally, not all words ending in '-itis' are illnesses (e.g. 'zitis' are a type of pasta). Nevertheless, this may be a way for us to observe the frequency of words constructed on this premise and understand its creative extrapolation, as in the case of "WhatsAppitis": a repetitive strain injury associated with overuse of the messaging system (Fernandez-Guerrero, 2014). We also have to be aware of words that look similar but are unrelated; for example, the more common use of the noun 'butter' has nothing to do with the verb 'to butt'. To distinguish these types of words requires identifying whether they are a noun or a verb, which is achieved through PoS-tagging.

3.1.4 Part-of-speech (PoS) tagging

Corpus analysis tools also carry out grammatical tagging known as **part-of-speech (PoS)** tagging, allocating each token to a grammatical word class (noun, adjective, verb, etc.). This is an important process not only for supporting queries of grammatical word classes, but also for disambiguation, as with homographs. If we were interested in 'play' as a verbal process then we might want the corpus analysis tool to discount instances of 'play' as a noun (a piece of drama performed in a theatre) and through PoS-tagging, this is made possible.

In the PoS-tagging annotation process, tags indicative of major word classes are assigned to each word and also provide further morpho-syntactic information. For example, in the Constituent Likelihood Automatic Word-tagging System (CLAWS) (http://ucrel.lancs.ac.uk/claws7tags.html), major word classes are indicated by letters i.e. conjunctions are indicated by tags beginning with 'C', nouns indicated with 'N', verbs indicated by 'V' etc. This follows the categorisation scheme established in the Penn Treebank PoS tagset (Marcus et al., 1993), which was a simplification of the original tagset used to annotate the Brown Corpus. Subsequently, the tendency is to increase specificity within updated tagsets. Within the word class categories there are further specifications; for example, there are 19 categories for pronouns, delineating case, number and whether the pronoun is personal or indefinite (see Table 3.1).

Task 3.4

Familiarise yourself with the CLAWS tagset at http://ucrel.lancs.ac.uk/claws7tags.html. Use the tagset to manually PoS-tag the opening line from George Orwell's (1949) Nineteen Eighty-Four:

It was a bright cold day in April, and the clocks were striking thirteen.

Check your results against the automated tagger by entering the text here: http://ucrel.lancs.ac.uk/claws/trial.html. Make sure you select the C7 tagset.

How do your results compare? Was the annotation scheme straightforward to understand? How would you explain any discrepancies between your manual tagging and the automated tagging?

Table 3.1 Categories of pronouns in CLAWS

PN	indefinite pronoun, neutral for number (none)
PN1	indefinite pronoun, singular (e.g. anyone, everything, nobody, one)
PNQO	objective wh-pronoun (whom)
PNQS	subjective wh-pronoun (who)
PNQV	wh-ever pronoun (whoever)
PNX1	reflexive indefinite pronoun (oneself)
PPGE	nominal possessive personal pronoun (e.g. mine, yours)
PPH1	3rd person sing. neuter personal pronoun (it)
PPHO1	3rd person sing. objective personal pronoun (him, her)
PPHO2	3rd person plural objective personal pronoun (them)
PPHS1	3rd person sing. subjective personal pronoun (he, she)
PPHS2	3rd person plural subjective personal pronoun (they)
PPIO1	1st person sing. objective personal pronoun (me)
PPIO2	1st person plural objective personal pronoun (us)
PPIS1	1st person sing. subjective personal pronoun (I)
PPIS2	1st person plural subjective personal pronoun (we)
PPX1	singular reflexive personal pronoun (e.g. yourself, itself)
PPX2	plural reflexive personal pronoun (e.g. yourselves, themselves)
PPY	2nd person personal pronoun (you)

The CLAWS was used to tag the BNC1994 and has a reported 96–97% accuracy (Fligelstone et al., 1996), with a slightly lesser degree of accuracy on spoken texts (Leech and Smith, 2000). You can access an online version of the tagger at http://ucrel.lancs.ac.uk/claws/trial.html and PoS-tag up to 100,000 words.

Giesbrecht and Evert (2009) report that PoS-tagging accuracy drops to just below 93% when applied to a corpus of German Web texts. There are additional challenges with, for example, PoS-tagging Twitter data, where character restrictions and conventions of the genre mean that users often do not use fully lexicalised word forms or complete sentences (Derczynski et al., 2013). Other features that compromise the performance of automatic taggers included: absence of capitalisation on proper nouns (e.g. birmingham); non-standard spelling and orthography (e.g. LUVZ, 2night, suprising); omission of spaces between words (e.g. eventhough); and genre-specific vocabulary (e.g. unfollowing). Derczynski et al. (2013: 200) found that while standard taggers performed at an accuracy of 83.14% on known words, accuracy for unknown words was 38.56% and so they identify the handling of unknown words as a priority for improving tagging performance, which can be informed by increased sample-gathering.

3.1.5 Collocation

Collocation refers to the co-occurrence of words, which allows us to see how their occurring together informs their meaning. The probability of this co-occurrence can be statistically validated, as we will see below. Collocation refers to word pairings but we can also examine the co-occurrence of words with word class categories to examine the syntactic relationship between language features. For example, Sinclair (1998) shows that the word 'budge' is frequently preceded by a modal auxiliary verb (e.g. will, won't) and the phrase 'naked eye' is often preceded by a preposition and a definite article (e.g. to the, for the). The co-occurrence of a word with a grammatical category is referred to as **colligation**. Collocation can tell us about the patterning around our search term, but it can also offer insights by way of comparison with what are considered to be equivalent or synonymous words. Crawford and Csomay (2016) offer an effective demonstration of this by comparing the use of 'equal' and 'identical' among the 450 million words of the Corpus of Contemporary American English (COCA). These two words, in some instances, can be said to have the same meaning, as in "These two students are equal/identical in their performance on the exam". However, Crawford and Csomay (2016: 6) show us that 'equal' occurs more frequently in the corpus (22,480 times) than 'identical' (8,080 times) and is associated with the terms 'equal rights', 'equal opportunity' and 'equal protection'. In these instances, it would be unusual to substitute in 'identical'. Conversely, 'identical' collocates with 'twins' and 'copies', where to substitute this with 'equal' would seem odd. Similarly, Biber et al. (1998) show through colligation analysis that although 'little' and 'small' are similar in meaning, 'little' is considerably less likely to be used in the subject complement position.

Brezina et al. (2015) review the range of criteria pertaining to the identification of collocations, starting with the more established dimensions of:

1 Distance
2 Frequency
3 Exclusivity

In order to retrieve collocations in a corpus analysis tool, we need to set a **span** in relation to our node word that instructs the program as to how far from the node word we want it to look. In most corpus analysis tools, this will be set at a default (often 5) which means that the tool will consider that number of tokens prior to and following the node word. This is what is meant by distance. It is assumed that the closer a word to our search term, the more pertinent it is; however, there are some constraints on the basis of syntax that may mean, for example, that an adjective does not immediately precede a noun but appears earlier in the clause.

Frequency must also be considered, but again, may be more of a relative measure. On the basis of the size of the corpus, it may be that we want words to occur a minimum number of times in order to be considered as important. Frequency must be considered in relation to other measures, which may point to the importance of a **collocate** (a word that collocates with our search term) but if the pairing does not appear 'often enough', the researcher might overlook it.

Frequency can be evaluated with respect to exclusivity; this aspect considers whether a collocate occurs frequently with specific relation to our node word, as opposed to simply being frequent (i.e. also appearing alongside other words). Prepositions, for example, will be common in most datasets and their frequent co-occurrence with our node word may not be exclusive.

In addition to these more long-standing criteria, Gries (2013) proposed the next three measures:

4 Directionality
5 Dispersion
6 Type-token distribution

Though collocation identifies a recurrence of paired items, Gries (2013) points out that it is not often the case that the patterning of this co-occurrence is symmetrical, and directionality is a dimension that focuses on whether our node word has a stronger attraction to a collocate or vice versa. Brezina et al. (2015) use the example of 'love' and 'affair' to demonstrate that 'affair' is strongly associated with 'love', but because 'love' frequently occurs with a number of other words, its relationship to 'affair' is not as strong. It is also of interest to researchers to consider whether a feature appears across a range of texts in the corpus, or whether its strength as a collocate is on the basis of a limited number of texts. Dispersion is the term used to capture a sense of this distribution and we make a stronger case for the importance of collocate if it is shown to feature across a wider range of texts. We might also consider the level of 'competition' for the positions around our node word; it is useful to know how many alternatives there are that could occupy the same position as a reported collocate in order to assess its strength

7 Connectivity

In addition to these six criteria, Brezina et al. (2015) propose an additional dimension, 'connectivity' and they support the investigation of this aspect through the introduction of the GraphColl (graphical collocations) tool. Connectivity attends to the fact that collocates exist within a complex network of semantic relationships and as readers, we draw upon this network to determine meaning. Brezina et al. (2015) continue with the example of 'love' and 'affair' to demonstrate that while 'affair' does not collocate with 'unrequited' ('undying', 'madly' etc.), it is connected to these words through its association with 'love'. The GraphColl tool visualises this network and allows users to explore this network by following the collocates. Figure 3.1 demonstrates a very simple network, beginning with the node word 'table' and extending to the collocate 'tennis'. GraphColl is one of the tools within the #LancsBox toolkit and you will find more information on its

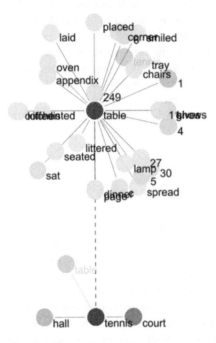

Figure 3.1 The collocation network for 'table' and 'tennis' displayed in GraphColl.

functionality in the user guide materials (http://corpora.lancs.ac.uk/lancsbox/docs/pdf/LancsBox_3.0_GraphColl.pdf) as well as in the paper introducing the tool (Brezina et al., 2015).

Semantic prosody

Related to the study of collocation is the concept of **semantic prosody**, which is defined as "a form of meaning which is established through the proximity of a consistent series of collocates" (Louw, 2000: 57). Semantic prosody is said to capture some of the implicit attitude or evaluation of the speaker/writer and it is argued that when a word collocates with another word that expresses positive or negative evaluation, this positivity/negativity is transferred to the node word. For example, Louw (1993) has shown that the word 'utterly' has a negative semantic prosody in that it tends to collocate with negative words. If we look at 'utterly' in the BNC1994, we see among the top 10 collocates words such as 'failed', 'ridiculous', 'impossible' and 'miserable'. Determining the semantic prosody of a word is based not simply on frequency, but the probability of its occurrence with particular words.

Such meanings are said to be "at least as inaccessible to a speaker's conscious introspection as collocation is" (Xiao, 2015: 112), i.e. speakers may contribute to a larger pattern of collocation through their language use without a real awareness that that is what they are doing. Researchers (Louw, 1993; Bublitz, 1996; Adolphs and Carter, 2002; Hunston, 2002) have therefore argued that the relationships that determine semantic prosody can only be revealed computationally, by looking at large corpora. However, there is still a degree of subjective interpretation in identifying notable collocates from a list that is returned by a corpus analysis tool, deciding which collocates are evaluative. Semantic prosody is apparent enough that speakers can appropriate a long-standing negative association for the purposes of irony; for example, given the strong collocation between 'break out' and war (or infection, say), we can read an implied negative evaluation in the statement 'when peace breaks out', despite 'peace' itself seemingly to be fundamentally positive (Stewart, 2010). Other examples of strong negative semantic prosody reported in the literature include: 'set in' (Louw, 1993); 'cause' (Stubbs, 1995); 'undergo' (Stubbs, 2001); 'occur', 'come about', 'take place' (Partington, 2004); and 'persistent' (Hunston, 2007). Stubbs (1995) reports that 'provide', in contrast, has a positive semantic prosody.

Along with semantic prosody, we can also refer to **semantic preference**, which refers to the pattern of collocates of a node word in terms of lexical sets. For example, Stubbs (2001) observes that 'large' typically collocates with words indicating quantities and sizes (e.g. 'number(s)', 'scale', 'quantities', 'amounts'). It is the patterning of the collocates belonging to particular lexical sets that distinguishes semantic preference from semantic prosody. Semantic prosody is said to be more concerned with attitudes and evaluations (Partington, 2004) and to tell us more about the node word (with semantic preference revealing more about the collocates), though of course, one contributes to the other. The overall effect is that language users are 'primed' to use terms in the context of regularised collocates or patterns of evaluation.

3.1.6 Semantic categorisation

UCREL semantic analysis system (USAS)

UCREL have developed an automated software tool for the semantic field annotation of corpora known as the UCREL Semantic Analysis System (USAS) (Rayson et al., 2004; Rayson, 2008). This is a unique annotation scheme that operates in a similar way to the PoS-tagging scheme: it has a multi-tier structure that begins with 21 major discourse fields at the top level, as follows:

A: General and abstract terms
B: The body and the individual
C: Arts and crafts

E: Emotion
F: Food and farming
G: Government and public
H: Architecture, housing and the home
I: Money and commerce in industry
K: Entertainment, sports and games
L: Life and living things
M: Movement, location, travel and transport
N: Numbers and measurement
O: Substances, materials, objects and equipment
P: Education
Q: Language and communication
S: Social actions, states and processes
T: Time
W: World and environment
X: Psychological actions, states and processes
Y: Science and technology
Z: Names and grammar.

Within the major discourse fields, there are subdivisions that offer more specificity on the basis of hyponymy. For example, in the category 'L: Living things', there is a subcategory of 'L3 Plants', within which we would find the terms, 'azaleas', 'rhubarb', 'evergreen' etc. The annotation scheme is also founded on a principle of synonymy and antonymy, so that polar realisations of the same concept are collected with one semantic category. For example, the word 'excited' is allocated to the category 'X5.2+ Interested/excited/energetic' and the word 'bored' is allocated to the category 'X5.2- Uninterested/bored/unenergetic', with the +/- indicating their related but oppositional meaning. USAS is also able to process multi-word units, on the basis that meaning is derived from the combination (as opposed to the individual word units), as shown by the example 'jump_on_the_bandwagon', which is allocated to the category 'S1.1.3+ Participating' (Piao et al., 2005). The full tagset can be found here: http://ucrel.lancs.ac.uk/usas/semtags_subcategories.txt. Rayson et al. (2004) report a 91% accuracy for the USAS when applied to a corpus of informal conversations.

USAS has been developed to work with historical Englishes (Archer et al., 2003) as well as Chinese, Dutch, Italian, Portuguese, Spanish and Malay (Piao et al., 2015), with the view to extending this to 12 languages overall (Piao et al., 2016). USAS is currently available through the WMatrix corpus analysis tool, which requires registration and payment of a license fee. Researchers can upload up to 100,000 words of text to the online tagger (http://ucrel.lancs.ac.uk/usas/tagger.html), though this does not allow for subsequent analysis, such as frequency lists for tokens, PoS-tags and USAS tags; collocation; and keyness (see below), as is possible through the full WMatrix tool.

> **Task 3.5**
>
> Having already carried out PoS-tagging on the opening line from George Orwell's (1949) Nineteen Eighty-Four, now familiarise yourself with the USAS tagset and repeat the process, this time assigning semantic tags to the text.
>
> It was a bright cold day in April, and the clocks were striking thirteen.
>
> You can check your results against the automated tagger by entering the text here: http://ucrel.lancs.ac.uk/usas/tagger.html.

Linguistic inquiry word count (LIWC)

Pennebaker et al. (2007) developed the Linguistic Inquiry and Word Count (LIWC) text analysis application, designed to automatically assess emotional, cognitive and structural components according to a psychometrically validated internal dictionary. For example, the word 'cried' is part of five word categories: sadness, negative emotion, overall affect, verb and past tense verb (Pennebaker et al., 2007). Tumasjan et al. (2010) showed how the LIWC application can be applied to Twitter messages by analysing over 100,000 tweets in the lead up to the 2009 German federal election. They found that sentiment profiles of politician and parties "plausibly reflect[ed] many nuances of the election campaign" (Tumasjan et al., 2010: 183) and ultimately conclude that the content of Twitter is a valid indicator of political sentiment.

3.1.7 Images

Computational analyses of images have largely relied upon developing manual coding processes that support quantification and querying, showing more of the potential for the application of corpus methods, rather than a demonstration. For example, Selfiecity.net (http://selfiecity.net/#selfiexploratory) is a project that involves the computational analysis of 16 million Instagram photos shared from locations around the world (Manovich, 2017). Researchers have combined automatic image analysis and human judgement, articulated through a coding scheme and assessment of age and gender, to generate an annotation scheme for 120,000 photos. This can then facilitate systematic searches of particular image components (and combinations thereof).

Caple (2018) applied a Corpus-Assisted Multimodal Discourse Analysis (CAMDA) approach (Bednarek and Caple, 2014) to Instagram posts made in relation to the Australian federal election in July 2016. The images were assessed for "(dis)affiliative strategies realised visually", with affiliative strategies capturing aspects such as: positive gestures along with signage, items of clothing, colour filters, posters and linguistic content added to the image (Caple, 2018: 101). Distancing strategies included: obscene gestures, negative verbal text on the image and on posters, as well as photos of the ballot card indicating that a party was the posters least-favoured choice. These codes were entered into a relational database and assessed alongside frequency and cluster analyses of the captions. Caple (2018) shows what can be gained from querying and annotating the data at a multimodal level and while the specificity of the coding scheme is its strength, it is also its limitation in terms of its transferability to other corpus-assisted studies. Corpus analyses of photographic (and other non-linguistic) modes would benefit from annotation schemes that extend beyond individual projects, though we must be wary of losing any meaningful specificity.

3.1.8 Register

Researchers have set out to determine the range and characteristics of Web registers through corpora of Web data. 'Register' refers to a kind of language associated with a particular situation of use and "the underlying assumption of the register perspective is that core linguistic features like pronouns and verbs are functional, and, as a result, particular features are commonly used in association with the communicative purposes and situational contexts of texts" (Biber and Conrad, 2009: 2). Biber and Conrad (2009: 2) use the term 'register' as distinct from 'genre', which focuses on "the conventional structures used to construct a complete text within the variety, for example, the conventional way in which a letter begins and ends".

A common method for characterising registers – both online and offline – is Multi-Dimensional (MD) analysis (Biber, 2014), which is characterised by its capacity to empirically identify sets of linguistic features that tend to co-occur in texts. MD analysis is supported by the Biber grammatical tagger (Biber, 1988), which identifies a range of grammatical features including word classes (e.g. nouns, verbs, adjectives); syntactic constructions (such as conditional adverbial clauses); semantic classes (e.g. activity verbs); and lexical–grammatical classes. It is on the basis of these grammatical features, and the particular co-occurrence of the types within them, that a dimension is scored and the description of a register is determined by these dimension scores. For example, Biber et al. (2015: 16) analysed URLs collected from the 'General' component of the GloWBE Corpus and found that Narrative, Informational Description/Explanation and Opinion registers account for well over 80% of the documents on the Web (and that blogs featured in all of these categories). However, they do acknowledge that their method of data collection excluded primarily visual/limited text registers such as advertising. They also highlight the prominence of 'hybrid registers': "registers that combine the communicative purposes and other situational characteristics of two or more general registers" (Biber et al., 2015: 33). The most frequent combinations further confirmed the prevalence of the Narrative, Informational Description/Explanation and Opinion registers (which was the case for two-part and three-part combinations).

3.2 What measures are used in corpus analysis?

3.2.1 Frequency

Wordlists are one of the basic outputs of corpus analysis and present the frequencies of items in a corpus, which can be sorted alphabetically or by frequency to show the most common words/lemmas/parts-of-speech etc. Simple frequency analysis has been useful in demonstrating some of the fundamental differences between varieties and registers of language. For example, Carter and McCarthy (2017) report that spoken communication contains a higher number of personal pronouns (e.g. 'you' and 'I'), response tokens (e.g. 'right') and organisational discourse markers (e.g. 'now' used at the beginning of sentences). These features help to structure spoken conversation and attest to its more personal nature. Frequency has also been particularly useful for studies of vocabulary, from which researchers have been able to determine that a basic spoken vocabulary of English must contain around 1,800 words (McCarthy and Carter, 2013).

Task 3.6

Put the list of words below in the order of which you think is most frequently used in English.

> time, okay, however, party, song

These are all terms we can expect to find in written, spoken and online forms of communication. Would the order of which was most frequently used be the same for each format? Go to https://corpus.byu.edu/bnc/ and from the help box, click on the link for 'comparison between genres'. Run search queries for the words above separately for the SPOKEN genre and one of the written genres (e.g. MAGAZINE). Make a note of the frequencies. Then go to https://corpus.byu.edu/core/ to search the Corpus of Online Registers of English and run the queries here too.

You now have frequency values for each of the terms for spoken and written and online data.

- What differences do you notice in the order of most frequent across each format?
- Is there anything about these words that explain those frequencies?
- What is the overall order for the most frequent? How does this compare with your original list?
- Does the order of frequency suggest anything in terms of whether online communication is more like spoken or written language?

You will find a commentary for this task at the end of the book.

In order to make comparisons of frequencies between corpora of different sizes, the data must be 'normalised'. This helps us to make sense of the significance of the numbers. For example, CORE comprises 50 million words and a search for 'social media' tells us it appears 3,331 times. In NOW, which contains more than 5.9 billion words, 'social media' appears 630,000 times. These raw frequencies indicate that we can find 190x as many examples of 'social media' in the NOW Corpus, but in terms of their normalised (or 'relative') frequency, this difference is much smaller. Using a measure of 'words-per-million' (**wpm**), we see that the value for 'social media' in CORE is 66.62, compared with 106.93 for NOW, indicating that the difference in frequency between the two corpora is more like twice-as-often in NOW. You will find in the literature that normalised frequency can be reported in terms of words-per-(ten) thousand, or as a decimal, depending on the researcher's preference and the size of the corpora being analysed.

3.2.2 Keyness

One of the defining measures of corpus linguistics is **keyness**. Though any unit of analysis can be measured for keyness (key collocates, key PoS-tags, key semantic tags), it is most often discussed with respect to **keywords**, which Scott (1997: 236) defines as "a word which occurs with unusual frequency in a given text". In order to understand what is an 'unusual' frequency, we first have to determine what is 'usual' and for this, we refer to a reference corpus. The reference corpus, as a representation of 'general' language use, establishes a baseline norm for how frequently we might expect a language feature to appear. Our data, referred to as the target corpus, is then processed to determine if the relative frequency of the language feature is much higher or much lower than what we would expect (based on frequency in the reference corpus). The difference in frequency – whether high or low – must be statistically significant and the measures for determining this are discussed below. A word that appears with unusually high frequency in our target corpus (compared with the baseline norm) is referred to as a **positive keyword**, whereas a word that appears with unusually low frequency is called a **negative keyword.**

The value of keyness as a measure is very quickly demonstrated when we compare it with what is generated through a simple frequency analysis. Table 3.2 provides lists of the most frequently occurring words from the BNC1994, LOB, Brown and *Harry Potter and the Sorcerer's Stone* (Rowling, 1998). You will see that many of these words are the same and they tend to be functional words, i.e. prepositions, articles, conjunctions, pronouns etc. What this indicates is that in English, some words are simply more frequent than others, across domains and registers. This, therefore, does not tell us much about the individual corpus or text (although, the centrality of 'Harry' in the novel is indicated).

When we look at keywords, we begin to get more of a representation of what is particular to our data. Scott (1999) makes the observation that typically, three types of keywords are found: keywords that give indications of the 'aboutness' of a particular

Table 3.2 Most frequent words across texts

	BNC1994	LOB	Brown	Harry Potter
1	the	the	the	the
2	of	of	of	and
3	and	and	and	he
4	a	to	to	a
5	in	a	a	to
6	to	in	in	Harry
7	it	that	that	was
8	is	is	is	it
9	was	was	was	of
10	i	it	he	's

Table 3.3 Keywords in *Harry Potter* when compared with BNC1994

	Harry Potter
1	Harry
2	Ron
3	he
4	Hagrid
5	Hermione
6	n't
7	Professor
8	Snape
9	said
10	Dumbledore
11	him
12	Professor
13	Dudley
14	you
15	his
16	yeh
17	Malfoy
18	'd
19	Neville
20	Quirrell

text (i.e. in terms of theme or topic); high frequency words that may be indicators of style (e.g. first-person narratives indicated by pronoun usage: 'I', 'me', 'my'); and proper nouns (which tend to relate to the specific individuals and locations mentioned in the text). Table 3.3 shows the top 20 (positive) keywords for *Harry Potter and the Sorcerer's Stone* when compared with the BNC1994 as a baseline. This offers more of an insight into what this text is 'about', with a number of character names and the keywords 'said', along with the speech-like 'yeh' might indicate a high use of direct speech. The main difference between these two measures is that while the pronoun 'he' appears in Table 3.2 (telling us that it is used frequently), its appearance in Table 3.3 indicates that it is used even more frequently than we would expect, based on ordinary language use. Indeed, the keyword list shows that male characters are prominent, both in character names and pronouns ('Hermione' is the only listed character who is not male), which offers a reasonable basis on which to explore representations of gender in the texts (as many have, such as Eberhardt (2017), who looks at gender representations through speech in the 'Harry Potter' series).

We can use keyness approaches to make direct comparisons between texts (as Rayson demonstrates in his tutorial for WMatrix, comparing the 2005 manifestoes of the Labour Party and the Liberal Democrats: http://ucrel.lancs.ac.uk/wmatrix/tutorial/), which would indicate what appears frequently in one text and infrequently in the other. In this sense, a positive keyword list for one text is effectively a negative keyword list for the other. This approach is fundamentally contrastive as it is predicated on difference. In addition to what words characterise each text, we might also be interested in what aspects they share and we can do this by having a common reference point for both texts. Conducting independent keyword analyses with a common reference corpus (e.g. BNC1994) allows for similarities, as well as differences, to emerge. This approach to keywords can be replicated for collocations, PoS-tags and semantic tags (as well as any other feature that is tagged in a reference corpus) and can provide useful 'entry points' to the data, identifying which features we might look at in context and in closer detail. When we look at statistical measures below, we will consider how to navigate the outputs of keyness analysis and determine which items on the list should be explored in closer detail.

3.2.3 Dispersion

One of the questions that we might be interested in answering is how evenly a term appears across the texts that make up our corpus. For example, if we wanted to say something about the significance of a term as characteristic of the corpus, this would be more convincing if we could say that the term was reasonably well distributed across the corpus in multiple texts. Gries (2008) discusses a number of the measures pertaining to dispersion, with a particular focus on deviation of proportions (DP). DP_{norm} (for normalised deviation of proportions) generates a measure between 0 and 1, where the higher the number, the better the distribution across texts. Another popular statistical measure for dispersion is coefficient of variation (CV), which is the ratio of standard deviation and shows the extent of variability in relation to the mean of the population. With this statistic, a low value indicates some degree of consistency across the data. In the next section, we will look at some of the other common statistical measures used in corpus linguistics and what they offer.

3.2.4 Statistical measures

Crawford and Csomay (2016) provide a thorough discussion across two chapters of the fundamental statistical measures and tests that characterise many of the functions of corpus analysis tools, demonstrating how these could be carried out manually. In practice, most corpus analysis software will automatically calculate statistical measures and provide optionality for which measures to apply. Here, I will offer a very brief introduction to the more conventional statistical measures reported in the literature, including those that will be cited throughout this book. Readers interested in learning more about these calculations can refer to the aforementioned chapters in Crawford and Csomay (2016), as well as Dunning (1993) and Rayson (2008) for mathematical explanations of log-likelihood.

T-score and mutual information (MI)

Two commonly cited statistical measures for collocation are **T-score** and **mutual information** (MI). T-score is a measure of the certainty of collocation, whereas MI measures strength of collocation and the choice of statistical measure is often informed by the collocation criteria discussed above, since no measure captures all of these aspects. T-score indicates what are high-frequency collocates, which may be more useful for the lexicographer or grammarian, since these will tend to be grammatical words. MI highlights lexical items that may appear with relatively low frequency, but occur more often than not with the node word. One way to ensure that our subsequent investigations are based on following the strongest patterns is to cross-reference frequency, T-score and MI score and include only those terms that score highly in each aspect (as Mautner (2007) does in her investigation of 'elderly'). The thresholds for what is considered 'high' are typically an MI score above 3 and a T-score higher than 2 (Hunston, 2002).

Chi-squared and log-likelihood (LL)

Keyness is determined by chi-squared (χ^2) or **log-likelihood** (LL) tests. Log-likelihood is typically favoured over chi-squared for the purposes of linguistic analysis, since chi-squared is best suited to datasets where there is a normal distribution and this cannot be said for language (Dunning, 1993). Both are null-hypothesis significance test statistics that have associated probability values (p-values). The p-value tells us the probability of observing our results due to chance; a very low p-value indicates that the results are unlikely to be the result of chance and more likely the effect of some other impetus (such as authorial intention or the established conventions for a language type) (Baker, 2006), which is what we as researchers are looking to argue. Across disciplines, it is generally accepted that a p-value of 0.05 is an acceptable threshold for claiming statistical significance. A p-value of 0.05 equates with an LL value of 3.84, though corpus linguists often find that their keyword lists return LL values much higher than this. An LL value of 15.13 equates with a p-value of 0.0001, but even this is likely to prove to be a modest value in keyword lists. Ultimately, LL values at this level and above allow us to say with confidence that our observed results are not the result of chance.

You can discover how LL is calculated, as well as inputting values for LL calculation here: http://ucrel.lancs.ac.uk/llwizard.html.

Effect size

Gabrielatos and Marchi (2012) have argued that effect size statistics (such as frequency difference: %DIFF) should be used instead of probability statistics for keyness analysis. Gabrielatos (2018: 238) explains that "The effect size score will enable the items returned from an automated frequency comparison to be ranked according to the size of the frequency difference". There is a tendency in the literature for researchers to begin at the top of a keyword list ordered by LL and work downwards with a view that the words at the top are the most 'key'. However, as Mujis (2010: 70) explains, "A very significant result may just mean that you have a large sample"; relying on LL alone might mean that some query results we are highly confident in do not actually reflect a notable difference in frequency. Effect size measures will indicate whether the difference between our data and the reference data is strong or weak. If a query returns a high LL value but a low %DIFF value, then we can be highly confident that there is a very small frequency difference. If a query returns a high %DIFF value and a low LL value, then there is a greater difference in the frequencies but we cannot be as confident that this is not the result of chance. Gabrielatos (2018) recommends that all corpus tools allow for the combination of effect-size and statistical significance metrics in order to support researchers in establishing difference as well as confidence.

3.3 What corpus analysis tools are available?

3.3.1 #LancsBox

You will already have encountered the #LancsBox corpus toolbox (Brezina et al., 2015) and located the extensive user guides available at the host website (http://corpora.lancs.ac.uk/lancsbox/help.php). Nevertheless, it is worth briefly summarising the tools within the collection and what type of corpus analysis they support. KWIC offers the standard Key Word in Context presentation format as well as enabling users to see annotation in the concordance lines and the larger text file simply by clicking on the concordance. Whelk provides information about relative frequencies and distribution (dispersion) across the corpus. The Words tool enables keyness analysis alongside analysis of types, lemmas and PoS categories. GraphColl finds collocations and colligations and displays them in list, table and network formats. Users can quickly return to the full-text file and explore the wider co-text by clicking on the Text tool. #LancsBox also comes with the LOB and Brown corpora available for download.

3.3.2 AntConc

AntConc is a "freely-available corpus software that was developed by Laurence Anthony as a lightweight, simple and easy-to-use corpus analysis toolkit" (Anthony, 2004: 12). Anthony (2004) intended to make available the key functions of corpus analysis without potentially overwhelming non-expert users with optionality for, say, statistical measures, as were available in other tools such as WordSmith (Scott, 1999). Nevertheless, the original toolkit included a concordancer, word and keyword frequency generator, tools for cluster and lexical bundle analysis and a word distribution plot (Anthony, 2004). Laurence Anthony has continued in his commitment to making user-friendly tools and provided ample instruction by way of user guides (http://www.laurenceanthony.net/software/antconc/resources/help_AntConc321_english.pdf) and instructional videos as to how to make the most of the tools that he has developed.

In addition to the AntConc toolkit, Anthony has developed tools to support researchers in a number of corpus-building processes, including file conversion (AntFileConverter), PoS-tagging (TagAnt), a tool for dealing with spelling variations (VariAnt); a social media and data analysis toolkit (FireAnt) and a parallel corpus analysis toolkit (AntPConc). The full range of tools is accessible at (and downloadable from) http://www.laurenceanthony.net/software.html.

3.3.3 WMatrix

WMatrix operates as an online interface for corpus analysis and comparison. In order to use the tool, researchers need to register an account and pay a (modest) license fee, though a free one-month trial is available. What distinguishes WMatrix best from other corpus analysis tools is that it has the USAS built into it and can automatically tag researchers' own corpus data semantically. It also supports keyness analysis at word, PoS-tag and semantic tag levels in comparison to various sub-corpora of the BNC, as well as BE06 and AmE06 from the Brown Family.

3.3.4 Programming languages

Many researchers are now using programming languages to carry out their data analysis. Popular examples include Perl, Python and R. These offer the researcher the flexibility to program their own commands and perform functions beyond those offered by the available software. The tools mentioned above provide all of the functionality required for the case studies reported here and so programming languages will not be discussed in detail, but you can find useful guides for Python (Downey, 2012), and Perl (Foy, 2007). Russell (2014) has produced an instructive text and practical workbook for working with APIs and Python script to collect data from various social media, including Twitter, Facebook, LinkedIn and Google+ and for carrying out some initial analysis.

Summary

In this chapter I have outlined what is involved in corpus analysis, including what can be considered a unit of analysis and how we measure it. We have discussed the processes involved in enabling corpus analysis and this will help us to assess the outputs of automated corpus analysis processes through an understanding of how they are generated. We have looked at a range of statistical measures that are used in corpus analysis, which constitute some of the parameters that can be managed by researchers in their corpus analysis, according to their research aims. Finally, we have briefly considered some tools that are available to use in our own corpus studies. In the next chapter, we will review some key studies of online communication with a focus on what has been found through corpus linguistics approaches.

References

Adolphs, S. and Carter, R. (2002). Corpus stylistics: point of view and semantic prosodies in Virginia Woolf's *To the Lighthouse*. *Poetica*, 58, 7–20.

Altenberg, B. (1998). On the phraseology of spoken English: The evidence of recurrent word-combinations, in A. P. Cowie (ed.) *Phraseology. Theory, Analysis, and Applications*. Oxford: Oxford University Press, 101–122.

Anthony, L. (2004). AntConc: A learner and classroom friendly, multi-platform corpus analysis toolkit. *Proceedings of the IWLeL 2004: An Interactive Workshop on Language and e-Learning*. 10 December 2004. Waseda University, Tokyo, Japan, 7–13.

Archer, D., McEnery, T., Rayson, P. and Hardie, A. (2003). Developing an automated semantic analysis system for Early Modern English. *Proceedings of the Corpus Linguistics 2003 Conference*. Available at: http://ucrel.lancs.ac.uk/people/paul/publications/cl2003_archerEtAl.pdf, accessed 20th December 2018.

Baker, P. (2006). *Using Corpora in Discourse Analysis*. London: Continuum.

Bednarek, M. and Caple, H. (2014). Why do news values matter? Towards a new methodological framework for analyzing news discourse in critical discourse analysis and beyond. *Discourse & Society*, 25, 2, 135–158.

Biber, D. (1988). *Variation Across Speech and Writing*. Cambridge: Cambridge University Press.

Biber, D. (2014). Multi-dimensional analysis: A personal history, in T. B. Sardinha and M. V. Pinto (eds) *Multi-Dimensional Analysis, 25 Years On: A Tribute to Douglas Biber*. Amsterdam: John Benjamins, xxix–xxxviii.

Biber, D. and Conrad, S. (2009). *Register, Genre, and Style*. Cambridge: Cambridge University Press.

Biber, D., Conrad, S. and Reppen, R. (1998). *Corpus Linguistics: Investigating Structure and Use*. Cambridge: Cambridge University Press.

Biber, D., Johansson, S., Leech, G., Conrad, S. and Finegan, E. (1999). *Longman Grammar of Spoken and Written English*. London: Longman.

Biber, D., Egbert, J. and Davies, M. (2015). Exploring the composition of the searchable web: a corpus-based taxonomy of web registers. *Corpora*, 10, 1, 11–45.

Brezina, V., McEnery, T. and Wattam, S. (2015). Collocations in context: A new perspective on collocation networks. *International Journal of Corpus Linguistics*, 20, 2, 139–173.

Bublitz, W. (1996). Semantic prosody and cohesive company. *Leuvense Bijdragen*, 85, 1–2, 1–32.

Caple, H. (2018). Analysing the multimodal text, in C. Taylor and A. Marchi (eds) *Corpus Approaches to Discourse: A Critical Review*. London: Routledge, 85–109.
Carter, R. and McCarthy, M. (2017). Spoken grammar: Where are we and where are we going? *Applied Linguistics*, 38, 1, 1–20.
Cheng, W. (2012). *Exploring Corpus Linguistics: Language in Action*. London: Routledge.
Crawford, W. J. and Csomay, E. (2016). *Doing Corpus Linguistics*. New York: Routledge.
Derczynski, L., Ritter, A., Clark, S. and Bontcheva, K. (2013). Twitter Part-of-Speech tagging for all: Overcoming sparse and noisy data. *Proceedings of Recent Advances in Natural Language Processing*. 7–13 September 2013. Hissar, Bulgaria, 198–206.
Downey, A. (2012). *Think Python: How to Think Like a Computer Scientist*. Needham: Green Tea Press.
Dunning, T. (1993). Accurate methods for the statistics of surprise and coincidence. *Computational Linguistics*, 19, 1, 61–74.
Eberhardt, M. (2017). Gendered representations through speech: The case of the *Harry Potter* series. *Language and Literature*, 26, 3, 227–246.
Fernandez-Guerrero, I. M. (2014). "WhatsAppitis". *The Lancet*, 383, 1040.
Fligelstone, S., Rayson, P. and Smith, N. (1996). Template analysis: bridging the gap between grammar and the lexicon, in J. Thomas and M. Short (eds) *Using Corpora for Language Research*. London: Longman, 181–207.
Foy, B. (2007). *Mastering Perl*. Sebastopol: O'Reilly Media.
Gabrielatos, C. (2018). Keyness analysis: Nature, metrics and techniques, in C. Taylor and A. Marchi (eds) *Corpus Approaches to Discourse: A Critical Review*. London: Routledge, 225–258.
Gabrielatos, C. and Marchi, A. (2012). Keyness: Appropriate metrics and practical issues. Available at: http://repository.edgehill.ac.uk/4196/1/Gabrielatos%26Marchi-KeynessCADS2012.pdf, accessed 20th December 2018.
Giesbrecht, E. and Evert, S. (2009). Is Part-of-Speech tagging a solved task? An evaluation of PoS taggers for the German Web as corpus. *Proceedings of the 5th Web as Corpus Workshop (WAC5)*. 7 September 2009. Donostia-San Sebastián, Basque Country, Spain, 27–35.
Gries, S. Th. (2008). Dispersions and adjusted frequencies in corpora. *International Journal of Corpus Linguistics*, 13, 4, 403–437.
Gries, S. Th. (2013). 50-something years of work on collocations: What is or should be next.... *International Journal of Corpus Linguistics*, 18, 1, 137–166.
Hallsmar, F. and Palm, J. (2016). Multi-class sentiment classification on twitter using an emoji training heuristic. Technical Report: KTH/Skolan for datavetenskap och kommunikation (CSC). Available at: https://kth.diva-portal.org/smash/get/diva2:927073/FULLTEXT01.pdf, accessed 21st April 2018.
Hunston, S. (2002). *Corpora and Applied Linguistics*. Cambridge: Cambridge University Press.
Hunston, S. (2007). Semantic prosody revisited. *International Journal of Corpus Linguistics*, 12, 2, 249–68.
Jiménez Catalán, R. M., Ruiz de Zarobe, Y. and Cenoz Iragui, J. (2006). Vocabulary profiles of English foreign language learners in English as a subject and as a vehicular language. *Vienna English Working Papers (VIEWS)*, 15, 3, 23–27.
Leech, G. and Smith, N. (2000). Manual to accompany The British National Corpus (Version 2) with improved word-class tagging. Available at: http://www.natcorp.ox.ac.uk/docs/URG/posguide.html, accessed 2 June 2018.

Louw, W. E. (1993). Irony in the text or insincerity in the writer? The diagnostic potential of semantic prosodies, in M. Baker, G. Francis and E. Tognini-Bonelli (eds) *Text and Technology: In Honour of John Sinclair*. Amsterdam: John Benjamins, 157–176.

Louw, W. E. (2000). Contextual prosodic theory: Bring semantic prosodies to life, in C. Heffer, H. Sauntson and G. Fox (eds) *Words in Context: A Tribute to John Sinclair on His Retirement*. Birmingham: University of Birmingham, 48–94.

Manovich, L. (2017). *Instagram and Contemporary Image*. Available at: http://manovich.net/content/04-projects/147-instagram-and-contemporary-image/instagram_book_manovich.pdf, accessed 20th December 2018.

Marcus, M. P., Santorini, B. and Marcinkiewicz, M. A. (1993). Building a large annotated corpus of English: The Penn treebank. *Computational Linguistics*, 19, 2, 313–330.

Mautner, G. (2007). Mining large corpora for social information: The case of *elderly*. *Language in Society*, 36, 1, 51–72.

McCarthy, M. J. and Carter, R. A. (2013).What constitutes a basic spoken vocabulary?*Cambridge ESOL Research Notes*, 13,5–7.

Mujis, D. (2010). *Doing Quantitative Research in Education with SPSS*. London: Sage.

Orwell, G. (1949). *Nineteen Eighty-Four*. London: Secker and Walburg.

Partington, A. (2004). "Utterly content in each other's company": semantic prosody and semantic preference. *International Journal of Corpus Linguistics*, 9, 1, 131–156.

Piao, S., Rayson, P., Archer, D., McEnery, T. (2005). Comparing and combining a semantic tagger and a statistical tool for MWE extraction. *Computer Speech and Language*, 19, 4, 378–397.

Piao, S. Bianchi, F., Dayrell, C., D'Egidio, A. and Rayson, P. (2015). Development of the multilingual semantic annotation system. *Proceedings of the 2015 Conference of the North American Chapter for the Association of Computational Linguistics – Human Language Technologies (NAACL HLT 2015)*. 31 May–5 June. Denver, Colorado, U.S.A., 1268–1274.

Piao, S., Rayson, P., Archer, D., Bianchi, F., Dayrell, C., El-Haj, M., Jiménez, R.-M., Knight, D., Kren, M., Löfberg, L., Muhammad Adeel Nawab, R., Shafi, J., Lee Teh, P. and Mudraya, O. (2016). Lexical coverage evaluation of large-scale multilingual semantic lexicons for twelve languages. *Proceedings of the 10th Edition of the Language Resources and Evaluation Conference (LREC 2016)*. 23–28 May. Portorož, Slovenia, 2614–2619.

Pennebaker J. W., Chung, C. K., Ireland, M., Gonzales, A. and Booth, R. J. (2007). The development and psychometric properties of LIWC2007. Austin, Texas, U.S.A. Available at: http://citeseerx.ist.psu.edu/viewdoc/download?doi=10.1.1.600.7227&rep=rep1&type=pdf, accessed 21st April 2018.

Rayson, P. (2008). From key words to key semantic domains. *International Journal of Corpus Linguistics*, 13, 4, 519–49.

Rayson, P., Archer, D., Piao, S. and McEnery, T. (2004). The UCREL semantic analysis system. *Proceedings of the Workshop on Beyond Named Entity Recognition: Semantic Labelling for NLP Tasks in Association with the 4th International Conference on Language Resources and Evaluation (LREC 2004)*. 25 May 2004. Lisbon, Portugal, 7–12.

Rowling, J. K. (1998). *Harry Potter and the Sorcerer's Stone*. New York: Scholastic Corporation.

Russell, M. A. (2014). *Mining the Social Web*. Second Edition. Sebastopol: O'Reilly Media.

Scott, M. (1997). PC Analysis of key words – and key key words. *System*, 25, 2, 233–245.

Scott, M. (1999). *Wordsmith Tools* [Computer Software]. Oxford: Oxford University Press.

Sinclair, J. (1998). The lexical item, in E. Weigand (ed.) *Contrastive Lexical Semantics*. Amsterdam: John Benjamins, 1–24.

Stewart, D. (2010). *Semantic Prosody: A Critical Evaluation*. London: Routledge.

Stubbs, M. (1995). Collocations and semantic profiles: on the cause of the trouble with quantitative studies. *Functions of Language*, 2, 1, 23–55.

Stubbs, M. (2001). *Words and Phrases: Corpus Studies of Lexical Semantics.* Oxford: Blackwell.

Tumasjan, A., Sprenger, T. O., Sandner, P. G. and Welpe, I. M. (2010). Predicting elections with Twitter: What 140 characters reveal about political sentiment. *Proceedings of the 4th International AAAI Conference on Weblogs and Social Media.* 23–26 May 2010. Washington, D.C., U.S.A., 178–185.

Xiao, R. (2015). Collocation, in D. Biber and R. Reppen (eds) *The Cambridge Handbook of English Corpus Linguistics.* Cambridge: Cambridge University Press, 106–124.

Chapter 4

Online communication
Corpus approaches

This chapter will focus on the features and subsequent corpus approaches to analysing forms of online communication that are distinct from, or have built on, approaches developed with respect to other (offline) modes of communication. Drawing on a concept originally developed in the context of ecological psychology, the online communicative environment presents a number of 'affordances' (Gibson, 1986) for language users. In this context, the format and the digital tools offer users means of expressing themselves and communicating with other users in ways that approximate offline forms of communication (e.g. emoticons that offer a typographic representation of a facial expression: ;)), but also in wholly innovative ways (e.g. emojis as pictorial representations of faces, symbols, objects etc.: 🤳 [selfie]).

Users also have a role to play in shaping the practices of online communication, finding new ways to utilise the tools of online communication and new forms of expression through those modes. Online communication is not simply the product of a 'technological determinism', whereby users have to adapt their expression in response to the limits of the communicative mode. Users are also driving the developments of what is made possible online and so we can consider the 'complementarity' of users and, in this instance, the online environment (Gibson, 1986).

As such, there are two questions that are the focus of this chapter and which are of broader concern to applications of corpus linguistics in an online context: the first has been articulated by Jones et al. (2015: 10), who ask "how [do] these new 'technologies of entextualisation' and the kinds of texts they result in allow people to do different things, or to do old things in different ways?". For example, how do users communicate irony, when they cannot rely on prosody? Second, this chapter will focus on the question of what corpus linguistics can tell us about the ways that people are (re)purposing features of online communication to say something and do things as part of an online community. For example, how might an emoji constitute an interactional turn? Knight (2015: 20) argues that "Corpus linguists are ideally situated to contribute to the investigation of digital discourse as they have the appropriate expertise to construct, analyse, and characterise patterns of language use in large-scale bodies of such digital discourse".

Task 4.1

In what ways has the Web changed the way we communicate in other modes? Do you find yourself 'carrying over' aspects of, say, social media communication to speech, for example? Can you think of particular vocabulary that has become part of 'ordinary speech', such as 'Friending'?

Conversely, what are the challenges in online forms of communication in communicating meaning as you might in other contexts? For example, how do you show someone that you are paying attention? What strategies do you use to compensate for the loss of certain communicative cues?

Studies of online forms of communication reside within a broader exploration of Computer-Mediated Communication (CMC), which "is a research field that explores the social, communicative and linguistic impact of communication technologies, which have continually evolved in connection with the use of computer networks (esp. the Internet)" (Beiβwenger and Storrer, 2008: 292). Given the prevalence of the Web and the Web-functionality of most digital tools, explorations of CMC have, largely, involved the Internet. However, we can also consider various forms of Human-computer Interaction (HCI) (such as self-service checkouts) and means of telephonic communication such as through SMS. Herring and Androutsopoulos (2015: 127) define Computer-Mediated Discourse (CMD) as "the communication produced when human beings interact with one another by transmitting messages via networked or mobile computers, where 'computers' are defined broadly to include any digital communication device".

With respect to language and the Internet, Herring (2014) has identified five key research areas:

1. Classification research: concerned with modes or genres, or in terms of features, such as whether it is asynchronous or synchronous.
2. Research on structural features: for example, typography, orthography and new word formations that manifest in abbreviations (smth for 'something'), acronyms (SMH for 'shaking my head'), number homophones (gr8 for 'great') and emoticons (:p).
3. Research on discourse patterns: concerned with interactional patterns such as turn-taking; register phenomena such as dialect; and pragmatic functions such as politeness.
4. Internet behaviour as a more general reflection of human interaction, dealing with issues such as identity, community and power, for example.
5. Language ecologies: examining the spread of English, for example, throughout the world.

This categorisation broadly guides the rest of this chapter, as I review corpus studies of online communication considering online registers, structural features and interactional elements of online communication.

4.1 Netspeak and registers of online communication

Crystal (2006: 20) uses the term 'Netspeak' to refer to forms of communication "displaying features that are unique to the Internet", which is positioned in relation to spoken and written forms of communication. Spoken communication is typically "time-bound, spontaneous, face-to-face, socially interactive, loosely-structured, immediately revisable, and prosodically rich". In contrast, writing is typically "space-bound, contrived, visually decontextualized, factually communicative, elaborately structured, repeatedly revisable, and graphically rich" (Crystal, 2006: 31). With online communication, Knight (2015: 20) argues that "there is a blurring of boundaries between what we traditionally understand as being characteristic of spoken and written discourse through the reduction of the temporal and social distance between the sender and the receiver".

However, while our understanding of online communication has often been facilitated by a comparison with spoken and/or written forms of communication, Crystal (2006: 51) argues that "Netspeak is more than an aggregate of spoken and written features", rather "it does things that neither of these mediums do, and must accordingly be seen as a new species of communication". He characterises Netspeak as "speech + writing + electronically mediated properties" (Crystal, 2006: 20). In a study of Internet Relay Chat interactions, Al-sa'di and Hamdan (2005: 422) examined sentence structure (length and complexity) and lexical analysis (word truncation, orthography, word formation, taboo words) and conclude that "e-chat English would be better viewed as a newly emerging, hybrid form with its own characteristics and uses". Similarly, Sindoni's (2013: 154) analysis of keywords in the blog corpus in comparison to those in ICE-GB shows that the blog corpus lies "somewhat in-between the spoken and written genre" and includes highly hybridised and polymorphic texts.

Nevertheless, in identifying what makes online communication distinct from written and spoken forms, we have also begun to outline the features that help us to distinguish types of online communication. In his exploration of *Language and the Internet*, Crystal (2001; 2006) offers separate chapters exploring e-mail, chatgroups and virtual worlds, with another chapter dedicated to language on the Web. Recognising the value in examining different types of online communication, the one-million-word Cambridge and Nottingham e-Language Corpus (CANELC) was compiled in order to provide "the facilities for exploring patterns of lexical, grammatical and semantic properties of language use within and across different communicative modes" (Knight et al., 2014: 32) and includes data from discussion boards, Twitter, blogs, emails and SMS messages.

The differences between written and spoken communication, and the subsequent evaluation of forms of online communication as more like one or the other, has often been spoken about as coming down to two aspects: (a)synchronicity and (in)formality (Ling, 2003; Shortis, 2007; Crystal, 2008; Tagg, 2009). Asynchronous modes such as email are closer to the written end of the written–spoken continuum; synchronous modes such as chat tend to exhibit more 'oral' features (Herring and Androutsopoulos, 2015). With respect to formality, we might consider whether the platform typically involves one-to-one communication (such as email) or one-to-many (such as Twitter), since there may be lower expectations for formality and markers of intersubjectivity when the user is not posting with a particular recipient in mind. Similarly, Tagg (2009: 17) argues that the "informal and intimate nature of texting encourages the use of speech-like language" in SMS messages. Of course, most platforms allow some flexibility with the nature of broadcast versus direct address: for example, we can communicate via mailing lists in emails and direct messages on Twitter.

(A)synchronicity is one of the features of the 'medium' that Herring (2007) refers to in her classification scheme for variability in forms of CMD, alongside one-way versus two-way message transmission and message format, for example. Alongside 'medium', Herring (2007) identifies 'situation' as another pertinent set of characteristics, taking into account the group size, participant characteristics, purpose of communication topic or themes, code or language used and the norms of social appropriateness. This reiterates the significance of understanding the 'affordances' of the platform in combination with the agency of the participants.

Task 4.2

Based on your own awareness and experience of the following forms of online communication, how would you describe the mode along the following criteria?

	Email	SMS/ Text-messaging	Blogs	Facebook Posts	Twitter
Asynchronous v.s. synchronous					
One-to-one v.s. one-to-many					
Can recipients respond?					
Can you determine group size?					
Is the message predominantly text-based?					
Is the communication professional/social?					

Does this help you to evaluate and demonstrate what is the appropriate degree of formality used in each communicative mode?

What contextual factors might determine how you use each mode (e.g. who is the addressee)?

Multi-dimensional (MD) analysis is a specialised research approach developed for analysing the linguistic characteristics of Internet registers, identifying how core grammatical features such as pronouns, nouns and verb tenses are used online (Biber et al., 2007; Grieve et al., 2010; Hardy and Friginal, 2012; Biber et al., 2018). Titak and Roberson (2013) used this approach to analyse an exploratory corpus of over 16 million words of online data and identified four primary functional dimensions of Web registers:

1   Personal narrative focus versus Descriptive, informational production
2   Involved, interactive discourse
3   Complex statement of opinion
4   Past versus present orientation.

Through this type of analysis, researchers have been able to describe key differences between Internet registers. For instance, Friginal et al. (2018: 358) report that, in comparison to Twitter texts, Facebook texts are "more personal, narrative, involved and interactive, complex and past oriented". Twitter texts are reported as exhibiting "a predominantly nominal and informational production focus" (Friginal et al., 2018: 358). It is not only the platform or the code that determines the level of formality evidenced in the way that interactants use language, but also the topic of conversation. Montero-Fleta et al. (2009) report that while "online asynchronous computer mediated communication in English displayed markedly more oral elements than in Catalan and Spanish, both in fora devoted to a serious topic and in fora devoted to sport […] the Catalan and Spanish showed more informal, conversational elements than the corresponding fora about politics" (Montero-Fleta et al., 2009: 770). Understanding the different functions and conventions of Internet registers informs our understanding of the use of different structural features, which is the focus of the next section.

4.2 Structural features of online communication

A thorough application of corpus methods (with other forms of discourse analysis) is demonstrated in Zappavigna's (2012) *Discourses of Twitter and Social Media*. A simple wordlist of the most frequent n-grams in a 100-million-word Twitter Corpus (labelled HERMES) allows Zappavigna (2012) to highlight some of the features of microblogging talk that are distinct from traditional, non-CMC corpora, including:

- @word – the 'at' character, typically used to address another user (where the username occupies the 'word' position)
- http – the acronym (for Hyper Text Transfer Protocol) that typically appears at the beginning of weblinks and which might be followed by a punctuation mark (such as a colon) that is read by corpus analysis tools as indicating a word break

- \# - the hashtag has become an iconic feature of Twitter discourse (and carried over to other social media, even to speech to replicate its function on social media) that signals the topic of a tweet, aligns the post with a wider discussion topic, or even functions as a contextualisation cue (Zappavigna, 2018)
- RT – these two letters indicate a 'retweet', the republishing of another tweet that also gives the user the opportunity to caption or comment on the original post.

Task 4.3

Conduct an informal search via Twitter by entering a search term here: https://twitter.com/search-home?lang=en. (Alternatively, if you have an account with Twitter you could simply scroll down your own feed). Go through the first 100 tweets and tally how many feature the following and how many times:

- @ tag
- Hyperlink (which may or may not include 'http'
- Hashtag(s) (#)
- A retweet (i.e. have another tweet embedded within it).

What other features are regularly used? Would you associate these with Twitter or do they also appear in other forms of online communication?

Zappavigna (2012) demonstrates that each of the features identified above (often) functions as a way of bringing in other voices to the tweet and in that sense is highly reflective of the 'heteroglossic' (Bakhtin, 1981) nature of social media. We can also see this as a result of the asynchronous nature of Twitter, in that responses may not immediately follow the original post and so users may need to indicate which tweet or tweeter they are responding to through the @username function (or by retweeting the post). Hashtags can be searched using corpus analytical techniques to aggregate tweets based on a mutual experience, but also to capture a sense of the metacommentary function, whereby users offer some form of evaluation and in that sense, hashtags contribute to interpersonal meaning in social media (Zappavigna, 2015).

Since online communication has historically been discussed in relation to forms of spoken and written communication, these offline forms have provided the standards against which 'Netspeak' has been evaluated. In comparison with spoken interactions, Crystal (2006: 44) asserts that "Addressing someone on the Internet is a bit like having a telephone conversation in which a listener is giving you no reactions at all: it is an uncomfortable and unnatural situation, and in the absence of such feedback one's own language becomes more awkward than it might otherwise be". Similarly, Frehner (2008: 76) has claimed that "computer-mediated communication can be considered incomplete for its lack of paralinguistic cues". The paralinguistic cues available in spoken interaction are based on audible aspects of our speech, such as intonation, prosody, pitch, volume, alongside gesture and facial expressions. Online, users may look to compensate for a lack of paralinguistic cues or find alternative ways to convey their message. Through an analysis of five online corpora, Riordan and Kreuz (2010) identified nine types of non-verbal cues commonly used in CMC: capitalised words, vocal spelling, repeated punctuation, emoticons, angled brackets, underscores, tildes and curly brackets. As with spoken communication, such cues serve a range of functions, including to disambiguate a message, to regulate the interaction, to express affect and to strengthen the message content. What online users have at their disposal is a range of visual elements for conveying meaning, which we might broadly label 'graphicons'.

4.2.1 'Graphicons'

Herring and Dainas (2017) use the term 'graphicons' to refer to the types of graphical devices most commonly seen in online contexts, which include emoji as well as stickers, Graphics Interchange Format files (GIFs), images and videos. Graphicons can – and often do – function as conversational turns in themselves i.e. with no text, as is the case with facial expressions and gesture (Herring and Dainas, 2017: 2190).

On microblogging sites such as Tumblr, animated GIFs typically function as reactions to previous posts and are shown to express "more emotion, more intense emotion and are more positive in valence than posts containing only text" (Bourlai and Herring, 2014: 171). As such, the functions of graphicons as features of online communication are complex and multifaceted.

Emoticons/emoji have long been recognised as a feature of CMC and they also function in multiple ways. 'Emoticons' are referred to as 'emotion icons'; they are constructed through ASCII characters, most notably, punctuation marks: :) and have long been associated with the expression of emotion in the absence of facial expressions (Walther and D'Addario, 2001). 'Emoji' are picture characters that were originally developed in Japan in the 1990s for display on mobile phones but have since become popularised around the world through their use in social media and on smartphones. Emoji are represented in Unicode characters and extend beyond representations of facial expressions to include objects, symbols, activities, animals etc. 🛐 (U+1F6C0).

Dresner and Herring (2010: 253) argue that "emoticons do not comprise new lexical or morphosyntactic constituents of English. Thus, what is required is a theoretical framework that situates emoticons (or rather, some of their uses) between the extremes of nonlanguage and language". The debate around the status of emoji and the potential for analysing emoji as a language system was in part sparked by the *Oxford English Dictionary's* announcement that their Word of the Year 2015 was the 'face with tears of joy' emoji: 😂 (U+1F602). The announcement did come with the qualification that the emoji is not 'a traditional word', but Casper Grathwohl, President of Oxford Dictionaries, said:

> You can see how traditional alphabet scripts have been struggling to meet the rapid-fire, visually focused demands of 21st Century communication. It's not surprising that a pictographic script like emoji has stepped in to fill those gaps—it's flexible, immediate, and infuses tone beautifully. As a result emoji are becoming an increasingly rich form of communication, one that transcends linguistic borders.
> (https://www.oxforddictionaries.com/press/news/2016/9/2/WOTY)

In this summary, we find a number of interesting aspects that challenge our traditional understanding of a 'word', in that the emoji is not composed of the traditional alphabet and, possibly because of that, it transcends linguistic borders, suggesting it is (or can be) a feature of language that can be understood within different linguistic codes. Nevertheless, we are reminded that there are cultural norms for the use of emoticons and emoji; Dresner and Herring (2010) remind us that sideways emoticons originated in Western culture and that there are also kaomoji that are specific to Japan and favour a 'right way up' orientation [^.^]. Finally, Miller et al. (2016) have found that people disagree on the sentiment and meaning of emoji, suggesting that emoji do not have the same restricted sense meaning of traditional words. In the way that facial expressions (such as a wink) and gestures (such as pointing) are paralinguistic features whose meaning can be modified by the preceding or accompanying verbal content, emoji are flexible in their meaning. There may be some regularity in their use, though Provine et al. (2007) refer to the 'punctuation effect', in that emoji/emoticons typically appear at the end of sentences or utterances in the same way that laughter and other non-verbal vocalisations tend to occur in predictable locations.

Task 4.4

- Do you use emoji? Are there particular platforms on which you would use emoji and how are they structured to support you in your use of emoji?
- Do you tend to favour particular emoji? Does your use of emoji fall under one of the functional categories described above?
- Find some examples of emoji use in your own interactions (i.e. either by you or by someone you have interacted with). If you removed the emoji, would this change the meaning of the utterance?

There are indications that since emoji can be encoded in a standardised form, they can be the subject of corpus query. Davis and Edberg (2017) provide the following example of how Unicode emoji function in Web searches:

> Searching includes both searching for emoji characters in queries, and finding emoji characters in the target. These are most useful when they include the annotations as synonyms or hints. For example, when someone searches for ⛽ on yelp.com, they see matches for "gas station". Conversely, searching for "gas pump" in a search engine could find pages containing ⛽. Similarly, searching for "gas pump" in an email program can bring up all the emails containing ⛽.

Allowing for variation at the same level of regional spellings, it is clear that the standardised Unicode characters could potentially be used to collate instances of the same emoji. Furthermore, these can be tagged and annotated in the same way as other features of language, so while current corpus tools do not support the entry of emoji as search terms, with the right encoding, this could be made possible.

Many forms of online communication are image-based, particularly on social media and Zappavigna (2016: 272) has discussed what she terms the 'social photograph'. She studied the construction of 'motherhood' through a collection of images posted to Instagram, analysing the images with respect to focalisation' and 'subjectification' (Zappavigna, 2016). 'Focalisation' can be discussed through the technical codes that have been established through other approaches to visual imagery (Kress, 2001). 'Subjectification' refers to the significance of the photographer–viewer relationship, the intersubjective functionality of social media and how this is achieved through compositional choices. Zappavigna (2016) developed a manual coding scheme that became searchable through an image annotation software tool. It is this type of approach that supports computational querying of image corpora, but does rely on implementing a manual coding scheme in the first instance.

Another (primarily visual) type of graphicon, made possible by the potential for immediate distribution on the Web and, in particular, social media, is the meme. A meme does not necessarily have to be a visual; as Knobel and Lankshear (2007: 202) explain, an Internet meme is "a particular idea presented as a written text, image, language 'move', or some other unit of cultural 'stuff' that is taken up and spreads rapidly". However, historically, Internet memes have been image templates, GIFs, or some reformulated phrase with a visual accompaniment. Milner (2013) describes memes as small still-pictures and animated GIF files predominantly used for satirical humour and for public commentary. Shifman (2013: 367) calls them "units of popular culture that are circulated, imitated, and transformed by internet users, creating a shared cultural experience".

Zappavigna (2012: 105) identifies some of the recurring features of social media memes, including:

- Phrasal templates – phrases with 'slots' available to be modified
- Catchphrases
- Image macros
- Initialisms.

Figure 4.1 shows a representation of one of the Internet's most popular memes and an example of the 'image macro' type: the 'distracted boyfriend' meme. Reformulation and spread of this 'object labelling' type meme is achieved through assigning different labels to the subjects in the image. The original image was published to iStock on 2 November 2015 by Antonio Guillem and entitled 'Disloyal man with his girlfriend looking at another girl' (https://www.istock-photo.com/gb/photo/disloyal-man-with-his-girlfriend-looking-at-another-girl-gm493656728-77018851). In meme culture, there is little regard – or indeed little reproach – with the unlicensed appropriation of visual content. On 21 August 2017, the image was posted to Reddit with labels that referred to the 'solar eclipse' (Slot A), 'me' (Slot B) and 'scientific evidence supporting the dangers of staring at the sun' (Slot C) (see Figure 4.2).

The 'solar eclipse' example captures what was the underlying sentiment expressed in reformulations of the meme, that the subject (typically the poster who would assume the role of 'B') was distracted or tempted away from a stable or sensible state of affairs to something unhelpful or non-sensical. Another example

Figure 4.1 A rendering of the 'distracted boyfriend' meme.

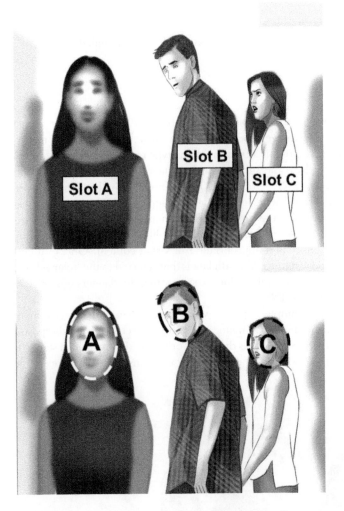

Figure 4.2 Labelling strategies of the 'distracted boyfriend' meme.

posited 'work' in Slot C alongside 'me' in Slot B, with 'anything else' in Slot A. Alternative labelling styles would involve photoshopping recognisable faces (or icons) over those in the image, rather than having written labels (Figure 4.2).

The concept of the 'meme' was established by Richard Dawkins (2006), likening culture and the spread of cultural units to evolutionary theory. He proposed that in order for a meme to survive and proliferate, it must have high longevity, high fecundity and high copying fidelity (Dawkins, 2006: 35). Zappavigna (2012: 101) observes that "Internet memes are deployed for social bonding rather than for sharing information" and that "humour is a very common strategy supporting this bonding". She goes on to explain that "within internet culture high status is given to being privy to an inside joke before it becomes well-known" (Zappavigna, 2012: 101). As Lankshear and Knobel (2006: 242) explain, "Online, contributing directly to spreading a new, mutating meme is considered cool, and generating an entirely new meme is even cooler. Being among the first to spot a potential online mutating meme is perhaps coolest of all". Zappavigna (2012: 102) makes the further point that "applying a meme beyond its semiotic used-by date is undesirable, lowering status". Even at the time of writing, the 'distracted boyfriend' meme has been 'played out'. This reiterates that the value of and participation in the spreading of a meme is short-lived and the 'death' of one meme is often at the emergence of another.

Because of the phrasal patterning of memes, this could be an aspect of online communication that benefits from corpus analysis. The lifespan of a meme is contingent upon the reformulations of a set template, so corpus analysis seems well-suited to examining the range of acceptable variation on the underlying template and approaching memes as "phrase long collocations" (Smadja, 1993: 149). However, this is difficult if the articulation of the phrasal template is embodied in or overlays the image and may only be possible when the memetic phrasal component is provided as a caption, in text.

4.3 Interpersonal features of online communication

Graphicons are a key structural component of online communication and in discussing their form, we have begun to consider their interpersonal and interactional function. Miltner and Highfield (2017: 9) argue that the

> diverse applications of the GIF underscore how the format's polysemy and affective capacity afford users with the opportunity to provide heightened and layered communication, demonstrate cultural knowledge, and occasionally engage in displays of resistance to certain ideologies and actors. This places the GIF at the root of digital cultures, as these features are also key to much of the practice and communities that thrive online.

Graphicons are rich with meaning and perhaps because of the capacity for broader interpretation (in comparison to, say, the written word) perform a range of functions, often simultaneously. Herring and Dainas (2017: 2185) show that emoticons are multifunctional and that they have "at least four uses in CMC that potentially overlap", including:

1   Expressions of emotion
2   Nonverbal signalling
3   Tone management or indication of illocutionary force
4   As punctuation or structural markers.

In a study of emoticons in 1,606 business emails gathered from three different countries and originally written in either Norwegian, Danish, Swedish or Finnish, Skovholt et al. (2014) show that emoticons function as contextualisation cues, performing important interpersonal functions in workplace discourse. They categorise these functions into three categories:

1   When following signatures, emoticons function as markers of a positive attitude.
2   When following utterances that are intended to be interpreted as humourous, they are joke/irony markers.
3   They are hedges; when following expressive speech acts (thanks, greetings etc.) they are strengtheners; when following directives (requests, corrections etc.) they function as softeners.

Through a free production task that asked participants to use emoticons to clarify the intent of a pre-written message, Thompson and Filik (2016) found consistency in the preferred selection and use of particular emoticons, most notably that the 'tongue face' (:p) and 'wink face' emoticons (;)) were most consistently used to signal sarcasm.

Returning to the work of Zappavigna (2012) and the HERMES Corpus, a cluster analysis identified patterns for how the interpersonal functions of social media manifest in particular phrasal constructs. The most frequent tri-gram was 'Thanks for the', which was also frequently accompanied by the @ character, indicating interpersonal reciprocity (Zappavigna, 2012: 47). 'Thanks for the' was also frequently used in reference to retweeting ('RT'), which highlights the value in rebroadcasting and the implicit endorsement (or explicit positive captioning) of such a practice, demonstrating the work of building interpersonal relationships within a social network.

More broadly, Zappavigna (2012) reflects on computational (linguistic) approaches to online social networks which have worked towards modelling social network structures (Puniyani et al., 2010) and 'influence', with respect to information diffusion (Weng et al., 2010). This exploration of 'influence' has enabled researchers to account for the growth of the 'micro-celebrity' in social media (Marwick, 2010). Zappavigna (2012) then turns her attention to how interpersonal meaning within these networks is communicated, drawing on social semiotics and systemic functional linguistics (SFL). Framing this through the concept of 'coupling' (Martin, 2000), which is concerned with the temporal relation of how semiotic elements occur 'with' others, Zappavigna (2012) combines a corpus analysis based on collocation and clustering with discourse analysis informed by SFL to explore 'affiliation'.

As discussed in Chapter 1, corpus linguistics can be combined effectively with other forms of applied linguistics to explore the interaction between structural components of online communication (such as the use of emoji) and their interpersonal function (e.g. as a politeness marker). Seedhouse (2005) has questioned how far Conversation Analysis (CA) principles could be applied to online interaction and Benson (2015: 83) has examined user behaviour on the video-platform YouTube to consider to what extent we can use spoken interaction analysis to account for YouTube pages as "products of multiple authorship". Benson (2015: 85) positions the uploading of a video as an "interactional turn which begins a process of multimodal social interaction" to show how existing methods in applied linguistics can be adapted to support us in analysing forms of online communication. However, the asynchronous nature of many forms of online communication means that we cannot conceive of 'turns' and 'turn-taking' in quite the same way. As Crystal (2006: 34) observes: "The time-delay (usually referred to as lag) is a central factor in many situations: there is an inherent uncertainty in knowing the length of the gap between the moment of posting a message and the moment of receiving a reaction". This inevitably has an effect on how participants in the interaction construct their utterances, when they may have to position their contribution in the sequence not through the sending of their post (if this is not immediately following the turn to which they are responding) but in their content, through '@ mentions' of the other participant, for example. Nevertheless, as has been shown by Zappavigna (2012), corpus analysis through keywords, collocations and cluster analysis, for example, can identify the prominent features of online forms of communication and facilitate an exploration of how these are functioning at the interpersonal level, in this context.

4.4 Identity, community and power in online communication

The high degree of interpersonal elements in online communication reminds us that the Web is a social space like any other, where relationships are managed and negotiated and where our (projected) identities can determine a great deal of how we harness language. Zappavigna (2012) examines a set of terms that could be considered 'internet slang' and shows that corpus analysis can help us to understand how the use of particular terms contributes both to online identities and membership to social networks. Using the examples, of 'geek', 'n00b', 'pwned' and 'fail', Zappavigna (2012) shows how the analysis of how such terms are used can give us an insight into how online communities admonish individuals who are not demonstrating familiarity or competence associated with that group, or how individuals can use the terms in a self-deprecatory way to show their (limited) awareness for such forms, as a way of ingratiating themselves to the online community.

Corpus analysis of Web-based communication can also support us in sociolinguistic inquiry, with respect to age and gender for example. Ooi et al. (2007) use the USAS built into WMatrix (see Chapter 3) to analyse a corpus of 100,000 words from personal blogs written in Singaporean English. This semantic category analysis provided evidence of the creativity associated with the language used by the younger age categories in these blogs and highlighted some of the contrastive language styles used across age groups. The authors are optimistic with regard to the robustness of the automatic tagging tool; however, Ooi (2009) highlights some of the features of Web-based communication that reflect the innovation and non-standard language used in that context and which demonstrate the need to continually update such automatic taggers.

4.4.1 Online disinhibition

One of the purported characteristics of the Web is that users have a tendency to express themselves more freely than they would in offline interactions and this can provide us with insights into the power dynamics of close-knit and, conversely, confrontational online communities. Suler (2004) outlines 6 factors relating to online platforms that contribute to what he terms the 'online disinhibition effect', which proposes that people self-disclose or act out more frequently or intensely online than they would in person. The first of these, 'dissociative anonymity', refers to the capacity for users to hide some or all aspects of their identity and thereby separate their actions online from their offline lifestyle and identity. This limits the sense of responsibility and potential for recriminations they may experience outside of a restricted online context. 'Invisibility' online means that users can visit spaces and observe online behaviours without making their presence known and thereby can be less concerned with how they are perceived – or would be perceived – for engaging with particular spaces or topics. Suler (2004: 322) further makes the point that users are not subject to the scrutiny of other's (potentially disapproving) gaze, which can enable disinhibition. The 'asynchronicity' of many forms of online communication means that users do not necessarily have to (immediately) confront the consequences of their actions, or that they can create some distance between themselves and their original post and the replies it may elicit.

Suler (2004) refers to the 'solipsistic introspection' of the Web experience, in that users can internalise the other users they encounter as 'characters' within their own experience – as with an author typing out a novel. This 'safer' mental space encourages users to play out fantasy sequences but also to project aspects of their own voice onto these representations of the other users, where talking 'to oneself' leads to disinhibition. This leads to 'Dissociative imagination', whereby users may perceive the online world to be one distinct from 'reality', one more like a game with different rules and norms from everyday life. Finally, Suler (2004) points out that signifiers of status and authority (such as uniforms) that are visible in the offline world are often not perceptible online. The Internet can be seen as a leveller of status and authority to some extent, where participants in online discussion are equal.

The degree of 'disinhibition' shown online poses a challenge for legal and administrative bodies who are responsible for addressing forms of abuse, as shown by Hardaker and McGlashan (2016), who explore manifestations of misogyny and rape threats directed at Caroline Criado-Perez, following her involvement in a petition to the Bank of England to (continue to) have a woman represented on the U.K.'s £5 note. Possibly for the reasons outlined above, online communication offers a unique perspective on what we might consider varying degrees of 'impoliteness'. (Im)politeness is a key area of pragmatics, in which researchers have long recognised the significance of context-dependent and participant-informed evaluations of what is considered '(im)polite', for example with 'mock politeness' (Leech, 1983). Given the potential for 'disinhibited' communication online, forms of anti-social talk such as 'flaming' and 'trolling' are of interest to researchers across linguistic disciplines, alongside other types of negatively marked behaviours such as spamming, cyberstalking and cyberbullying (Hardaker, 2010).

'Flaming' refers to hostile emotional expressions, characterised by the use of profanity, insults and offensive language, typically related to a specific topic and directed at a specific individual (Alonzo and Aiken, 2004; Crystal, 2006). Crystal (2006: 56) defines 'trolling' as the sending of a message specifically intended to cause irritation to others, such as the members of a chatgroup. Hardaker (2010: 237) defines a 'troll' as: "a CMC user who constructs the identity of sincerely wishing to be a part of the group in question, including professing, or conveying pseudo-sincere intentions, but whose real intention(s) is/are to cause disruption and/or to trigger or exacerbate conflict for the purposes of their own amusement". This definition was developed through the exploration of a corpus derived from a Usenet newsgroup, determining that online participants oriented their discussions around the key themes of deception, aggression, disruption and success. Hardaker (2013) has subsequently delineated forms of trolling, examined responses to trolling (Hardaker, 2015) and provided an updated definition for trolling, as "the deliberate (perceived) use of impoliteness/aggression, deception and/or manipulation in CMC to create a context conducive to triggering or antagonising conflict, typically for amusement's sake" (Hardaker, 2013: 79).

However, it is also important to note that not all 'disinhibited' exchanges online need be aggressive or confrontational. Suler (2004: 321) distinguishes between 'benign disinhibition' and 'toxic disinhibition', with the former referring to where users share very personal things about themselves, show kindness and generosity – perhaps more openly than they would offline. This has helped to cultivate important areas of the Web where users can seek support and forge significant relationships with other users because of this level of disclosure, for example, with respect to health issues and other highly personal aspects of their lives. Researchers recognise the value of these spaces in affording insights into aspects of users' experiences that are difficult to access (Loiacono, 2014; Hunt and Harvey, 2015; Kramer et al., 2015; Xu et al., 2015) and to encourage further engagement (Saxton et al., 2014). However, by the same token, the extent of the disclosures offered in such spaces prompts important ethical considerations, as discussed in the previous chapter (Taddicken, 2014).

> **Task 4.5**
> - How would you go about carrying out a corpus study of trolling online? What corpus would you use? Would you collect your own?
> - What practical challenges would there be for collecting examples of trolling? How, for example, would you locate instances of trolling? Would this be based on particular vocabulary?
> - What ethical challenges would there be for investigating trolling practices online?

The use of corpora and corpus analysis in studies of (im)politeness provides a basis on which we can develop our approach to flaming, trolling, etc. which seem to have emerged most prevalently in online contexts. There are particular challenges with understanding these kinds of social dynamics online, where the nature of the relationship is only really actualised as users interact. As such, in spaces where scant user information is available, we are left with the problem of making claims about the person based on their language use versus making observations of the use of language on the basis of the author. As best as we can, we must bring forward the knowledge we have of ideological discourse and power in offline forms of communication, under the presumption that users are communicating meaning at least to some degree along the same principles of spoken and written forms of communication. As Jones et al. (2015: 1) argue, "analytical tools designed to examine the ideological dimensions of discourse need to be adapted to contend with discursive environments in which the loci of power are much more diffuse and the instruments of ideological control and discipline are much more subtle and complex". In testing existing approaches in an online context, we can – and have already begun to – learn something about what precisely is different about online forms of communication, compared with offline forms, but also in what ways our approaches need to be adapted in order to remain effective.

Summary

In this chapter, I have outlined some of the features of online communication as they have been identified and examined through corpus analysis. Studies of CMC and, in particular, the Web have considered to what extent we can carry forward the insights generated from other applications of corpus linguistics to the online domain, positioning 'netspeak' in relation to written and spoken forms of communication, for example. Online communication, in part, demonstrates ways of replicating features of other modes of communication, though it is also clear the Web has enabled emergent forms of expression, that are complex, have multiple functions and are used to varying degrees across registers of online communication.

So far in this book, we have established some of the core principles of corpus linguistics, with a view to how they can be applied to online communication. We have seen what is involved in the design, collection and construction of corpora from the Web and what types of studies Web-derived corpora facilitate. What follows is four case study chapters, each introducing and analysing a specially collected corpus of Web-based communication. Through these case studies, we will see how what we have discussed so far works in practice.

References

Alonzo, M. and Aiken, M. (2004). Flaming in electronic communication. *Decision Support Systems*, 36, 3, 205–213.

Al-sa'di, R. A. and Hamdan, J. M. (2005). "Synchronous online chat" English: Computer-mediated communication. *World Englishes*, 24, 4, 409–424.

Bakhtin, M. M. (1981). *The Dialogic Imagination: Four Essays*. Edited by M. Holquist. University of Texas Press Slavic Series. Austin: University of Texas Press.

Beißwenger, M. and Storrer, A. (2008). Corpora of computer-mediated communication, in A. Lüdeling and M. Kytö (eds) *Corpus Linguistics: An International Handbook*. Berlin: Walter de Gruyter, 292–308.

Benson, P. (2015). YouTube as text: Spoken interaction analysis and digital discourse, in R. H. Jones, A. Chik and C. A. Hafner (eds) *Discourse and Digital Practices: Doing Discourse Analysis in the Digital Age*. London: Routledge, 81–96.

Biber, D., Conrad, S., Reppen, R., Byrd, P. and Helt, M. (2007). Speaking and writing in the university: A multi-dimensional comparison, in W. Teubert and R. Krishnamurthy (eds) *Corpus Linguistics: Critical Concepts in Linguistics*. London: Routledge, 3–41.

Biber, D., Egbert, J. and Zhang, M. (2018). Using corpus-based analysis to study register and dialect variation on the searchable web, in E. Friginal (ed.) *Studies in Corpus-based Sociolinguistics*. London: Routledge, 83–111.

Bourlai, E. E. and Herring, S. C. (2014). Multimodal communication on Tumblr: "I have so many feels!". *Proceedings of WebSci '14: The 6th Annual ACM Web Science Conference*. 23–26 June 2014. Bloomington, Indiana, U.S.A., 171–175.

Crystal, D. (2001). *Language and the Internet*. Cambridge: Cambridge University Press.

Crystal, D. (2006). *Language and the Internet*. Second Edition. Cambridge: Cambridge University Press.

Crystal, D. (2008). *Txtng: The Gr8 Db8*. Oxford: Oxford University Press.

Davis, M. and Edberg, P. (eds) (2017). Unicode Emoji – Unicode ® Technical Standard #51. Available at: http://www.unicode.org/reports/tr51/tr51-12.html, accessed 29 April 2018.

Dawkins, R. (2006). *The Selfish Gene*. Third Edition. Oxford: Oxford University Press.

Dresner, E. and Herring, S. C. (2010). Functions of the nonverbal in CMC: Emoticons and illocutionary force. *Communication Theory*, 20, 3, 249–268.

Frehner, C. (2008). *Email, SMS, MMS: The Linguistic Creativity of Asynchronous Discourse in the New Media Age*. Bern: Peter Lang.

Friginal, E., Waugh, O. and Titak, A. (2018). Linguistic variation in Facebook and Twitter posts, in E. Friginal (ed.) *Studies in Corpus-based Sociolinguistics*. London: Routledge, 342–362.

Gibson, J. J. ([1979] 1986). *The Ecological Approach to Perception*. Hillsdale: Lawrence Erlbaum Associates.

Grieve, J., Biber, D., Friginal, E. and Nekrasova, T. (2010). Variation among blogs: A multi-dimensional analysis, in A. Mehler, S. Sharoff and M. Santini (eds) *Genres on the Web*. Dordrecht: Springer, 303–322.

Hardaker, C. (2010). Trolling in asynchronous computer mediated communication: From user discussions to academic definitions. *Journal of Politeness Research*, 6, 2, 215–242.

Hardaker, C. (2013). "Uh....not to be nitpicky,,,,,but...the past tense of drag is dragged, not drug." An overview of trolling strategies. *Journal of Language Aggression and Conflict*, 1, 1, 58–86.

Hardaker, C. (2015). 'I refuse to respond to this obvious troll': An overview of responses to (perceived) trolling. *Corpora*, 10, 2, 201–229.

Hardaker, C. and McGlashan, M. (2016). 'Real men don't hate women': Twitter rape threats and group identity. *Journal of Pragmatics*, 91, 80–93.

Hardy, J. A. and Friginal, E. (2012). Filipino and American online communication and linguistic variation. *World Englishes*, 31, 2, 143–161.

Herring, S. C. (2007). A faceted classification scheme for computer-mediated discourse. *Language@internet4*, 4, 1. Available at: http://www.languageatinternet.org/articles/2007/761/, accessed 23 April 2018.

Herring, S. C. (2014). Language and the Internet, in W. Donsbach (ed.) *The Concise Encyclopedia of Communication*. Oxford: Wiley-Blackwell, 321.

Herring, S. C. and Androutsopoulos, J. (2015). Computer-mediated discourse 2.0, in D. Tannen, H. E. Hamilton and D. Schiffrin (eds) *The Handbook of Discourse Analysis*. Second Edition. Oxford: Wiley-Blackwell, 127–151.

Herring, S. C. and Dainas, A. (2017). "Nice picture comment!" Graphicons in Facebook comment threads. *Proceedings of the Fiftieth Hawaii International Conference on System Sciences*. 4–7 January 2017. Los Alamitos, California, U.S.A., 2185–2194.

Hunt, D. and Harvey, K. (2015). Health communication and corpus linguistics: Using corpus tools to analyse eating disorder discourse online, in P. Baker and T. McEnery (eds) *Corpora and Discourse Studies: Integrating Discourse and Corpora*. Basingstoke: Palgrave Macmillan, 134–154.

Jones, R. H., Chick, A. and Hafner, C. A. (2015). Introduction: Discourse analysis and digital practices, in R. H. Jones, A. Chik and C. A. Hafner (eds) *Discourse and Digital Practices: Doing Discourse Analysis in the Digital Age*. London: Routledge, 1–17.

Knight, D. (2015). e-Language: Communication in the digital age, in P. Baker, and T. McEnery (eds) *Corpora and Discourse Studies: Integrating Discourse and Corpora*. Basingstoke: Palgrave Macmillan, 20–40.

Knight, D., Adolphs, S. and Carter, R. (2014). CANELC: Constructing an e-language corpus. *Corpora*, 9, 1, 29–56.

Knobel, M. and Lankshear, C. (2007). *A New Literacies Sampler*. New York: Peter Lang.

Kramer, J., Boon, B., Schotanus-Dijkstra, M., van Ballegooijen, W., Kerkhof, A., and Van Der Poel, A. (2015). The mental health of visitors of web-based support forums for bereaved by suicide. *Crisis*, 36, 1, 38–45.

Kress, G. R. (2001). *Multimodal Discourse: The Modes and Media of Contemporary Communication*. London: Arnold.

Lankshear, C. and Knobel, M. (2006). *New Literacies: Everyday Practices and Classroom Learning*. Second Edition. Maidenhead: Open University Press.

Leech, G. (1983). *Principles of Pragmatics*. London: Longman.

Ling, R. (2003). The sociolinguistics of SMS: an analysis of SMS use by a random sample of Norwegians, in R. Ling and P. Pedersen (eds) *Mobile Communications: Renegotiation of the Social Sphere*. London: Springer, 335–349.

Loiacono, E. T. (2014). Self-disclosure behavior on social networking web sites. *International Journal of Electronic Commerce*, 19, 2, 66–94.

Martin, J. R. (2000). Beyond exchange: APPRAISAL systems in English, in S. Hunston and G. Thompson (eds) *Evaluation in Text: Authorial Stance and the Construction of Discourse*. Oxford: Oxford University Press, 142–175.

Marwick, A. (2010). *Status Update: Celebrity, Publicity, and Self-branding in Web 2.0*. New Haven: Yale University Press.

Miller, H., Thebault-Spieker, J., Chang, S., Johnson, L., Terveen, L. and Hecht, B. (2016). Blissfully happy or ready to fight: Varying interpretations of emoji. *Proceedings of the Tenth International Conference on Web and Social Media*. 17–20 May 2016. Cologne, Germany, 259–268.

Milner, R. M. (2013). Pop polyvocality: Internet memes, public participation, and the Occupy Wall Street movement. *International Journal of Communication*, 7, 2357–2390.

Miltner, K. M. and Highfield, T. (2017). Never gonna GIF you up: Analyzing the cultural significance of the animated GIF. *Social Media + Society*, 1–11. Available at: http://journals.sagepub.com/doi/pdf/10.1177/2056305117725223, accessed 22 April 2018.

Montero-Fleta, B., Montesinos-López, A., Pérez-Sabater, C. and Turney, E. (2009). Computer mediated communication and informalization of discourse: The influence of culture and subject matter. *Journal of Pragmatics*, 41, 4, 770–779.

Ooi, V. B. Y. (2009). Computer-mediated language and corpus linguistics, in Y. Kawaguchi, M. Minegishi and J. Durand (eds) *Corpus Analysis and Variation in Linguistics*. Amsterdam: John Benjamins, 103–120.

Ooi, V. B. Y., Tan, P. K. W. and Chiang, A. K. L. (2007). Analyzing personal weblogs in Singapore English: the WMatrix approach, in P. Pahta, I. Taavitsainen, T. Nevalainen and J. Tyrkkö (eds) *Studies in Variation, Contacts and Change in English 2L Towards Multimedia in Corpus Studies*. Available at: http://www.helsinki.fi/varieng/series/volumes/02/ooi_et_al/, accessed 29 April 2018.

Provine, R. R., Spencer, R. J. and Mandell, D. L. (2007). Emotional expression online: Emoticons punctuate website text messages. *Journal of Language and Social Psychology*, 26, 3, 299–307.

Puniyani, K., Eisenstein, J., Cohen, S. and Xing, E. P. (2010). Social links from latent topics in microblogs. *Proceedings of the NAACL HLT 2010 Workshop on Computational Linguistics in a World of Social Media*. 6 June 2010. Los Angeles, California, U.S.A., 19–20.

Riordan, M. A. and Kreuz, R. J. (2010). Cues in computer-mediated communication: A corpus analysis. *Computers in Human Behaviour*, 26, 6, 1806–1817.

Saxton, G. D., Neely, D. G. and Guo, C. (2014). Web disclosure and the market for charitable contributions. *Journal of Accounting and Public Policy*, 33, 2, 127–144.

Seedhouse, P. (2005). Conversation analysis and language learning. *Language Teaching*, 38, 4, 165–187.

Shifman, L. (2013). Memes in a digital world: Reconciling with a conceptual troublemaker. *Journal of Computer-Mediated Communication*, 18, 3, 362–377.

Shortis, T. (2007). Gr8 txtpectations: the creativity of text spelling. *English Drama Media Journal*, 8, 21–26.

Sindoni, M. G. (2013). *Spoken and Written Discourse in Online Interactions: A Multimodal Approach*. London: Routledge.

Skovholt, K. Grønning, A. and Kankaanranta, A. (2014). The communicative functions of emoticons in workplace emails: :-). *Journal of Computer-Mediated Communication*, 19, 4, 780–797.

Smadja, F. (1993). Retrieving collocations from text: Xtract. *Computational Linguistics*, 19, 1, 143–177.

Suler, J. (2004). The online disinhibition effect. *Cyber Psychology & Behavior*, 7, 3, 321–326.

Taddicken, M. (2014). The 'privacy paradox' in the social web: The impact of privacy concerns, individual characteristics, and the perceived social relevance on different forms of self-disclosure. *Journal of Computer-Mediated Communication*, 19, 2, 248–273.

Tagg, C. (2009). A Corpus Linguistics Study of SMS Text Messaging. PhD Thesis. University of Birmingham. Available at: http://etheses.bham.ac.uk/253/1/Tagg09PhD.pdf, accessed 28 April 2018.

Thompson, D. and Filik, R. (2016). Sarcasm in written communication: emoticons are efficient markers of intention. *Journal of Computer-Mediated Communication*, 21, 2, 105–120.

Titak, A. and Roberson, A. (2013). Dimensions of web registers: an exploratory multi-dimensional comparison. *Corpora*, 8, 2, 235–260.

Walther, J. B. and D'Addario, K. P. (2001). The impacts of emoticons on message interpretation in computer-mediated communication. *Social Science Computer Review*, 19, 3, 324–347.

Weng, J., Lim, E. P., Jiang, J. and He, Q. (2010). TwitterRank: Finding topic-sensitive influential twitterers. *Proceedings of the Third ACM International Conference on Web Search and Data Mining*. 3–6 February 2010. New York City, New York, U.S.A., 261–270.

Xu, W., Wang, J., Wang, Z., Li, Y., Yu, W., Xie, Q., He, L. and Maercker, A. (2015). Web-based intervention improves social acknowledgement and disclosure of trauma, leading to a reduction in posttraumatic stress disorder symptoms. *Journal of Health Psychology*, 21, 11, 2695–2708.

Zappavigna, M. (2012). *Discourses of Twitter and Social Media*. London: Continuum.

Zappavigna, M. (2015). Searchable talk: the linguistic functions of hashtags. *Social Semiotics*, 25, 3, 274–291.

Zappavigna, M. (2016). Social media photography: Constructing subjectivity in Instagram images. *Visual Communication*, 15, 3, 271–292.

Zappavigna, M. (2018). *Searchable Talk: Hashtags and Social Media Metadiscourse*. Sydney: Bloomsbury.

Chapter 5

Business and organisational communication online
The Dukki Facebook corpus

Social media encapsulate the connectivity and creativity of the contemporary Web, facilitating user-generated content and realising the associated features of 'Web 2.0'. Businesses engaging with social media face the challenge of distinguishing themselves through a clear and coherent brand identity. This chapter presents a case study of how the Nottingham-based independent business 'Dukki' uses Facebook to establish a brand identity that is firmly rooted in the local community and manifest in the appropriation of the Nottinghamshire dialect. This case study demonstrates how researchers can use corpus approaches to investigate highly stylised forms of online communication as well as how businesses construct their own identity and that of their customer base.

> **Task 5.1**
>
> How have social media changed the way you interact with businesses?
>
> - What opportunities are there for, in particular, smaller businesses operating through social media?
> - In what ways do you get a different perspective on business practices through their use of social media?
> - How might we expect the way businesses communicate through social media to be different from other forms of communication?
> - Can you think of any examples of businesses using social media 'well'? Are there any notable examples of 'bad practice'?

5.1 Business and social media

Through a synthesis of the various definitions of social media available, Obar and Wildman (2015: 745) report the following commonalities among social media services:

1   Social media services are (currently) Web 2.0 internet-based applications
2   User-generated content is the lifeblood of social media

3   Individuals and groups create user-specific profiles for a site or app designed and maintained by a social media service
4   Social media services facilitate the development of social networks online by connecting a profile with those of other individuals and/or groups.

Social media have impacted not only on marketing landscapes, but also on processes internal to organisations, "such as HR functions, recruitment, organisational behaviour, and training and development" (Devereux et al., 2017: 113). Social media have particular value to small and medium enterprises (SMEs) as a vehicle for developing and managing brand identity (McCann and Barlow, 2015). For companies that have limited time and resources for marketing, social media provide a ready-made architecture and online store functionality that enables smaller businesses to establish a Web presence alongside other 'larger' companies. Facebook provides pages, designed for commercial profiles and enterprises, "that let artists, public figures, businesses, brands, organizations and non-profits create a presence on Facebook and connect with the Facebook community" (Facebook, 2018) and there are a reported 80 million small businesses on Facebook (https://newsroom.fb.com/news/2018/05/community-boost-small-business-week/). Indeed, online spaces are not as strictly determined by the 'real estate' of the high street, though larger budgets and staffing can improve the production values and co-ordination of large-scale, intensive social media campaigns. This emphasises the need for businesses to clearly articulate their brand, their unique personality and tone of voice through their social media content (Darics and Koller, 2018). Although social media have facilitated a 'conversationalisation' of business discourse (Dijkmans et al., 2015: 635), "most branded social content can be categorised as functional" (Ashley and Tuten, 2015: 15). Businesses that host Facebook pages still have commercial objectives and to a large extent, rely on strategies that have long been established in advertising discourse to generate engagement with potential customers as a means of sales promotion.

5.1.1 The discourse of advertising

The 'conversationalisation' of business discourse associated with social media is, in fact, an advertising strategy that predates the Web: "Copywriters have been taught since the beginning of the profession that advertising should sound like conversation", which can "evoke a kind of ordinariness, of everyday life, that is paradoxically effective in persuasion" (Myers, 1996: 105). One of the features of advertising discourse that contributes to this 'conversationalisation' is what Fairclough (1989) termed 'synthetic personalisation', referring to "the instrumental use of linguistic features that minimise social distance and effect solidarity between participants so that discourse intended for a large audience is contrived as personal communication" (Hunt and Koteyko, 2015: 448). Examples of such features include interrogative (question) and imperative forms, as well as the emulation of spoken grammar (e.g. through exclamations).

Exclamations, Myers (1996: 50) argues, are proportionately over-represented in ads. They are seen as "an attempt to recreate the intonation and facial expression that go with face to face interaction" (Myers, 1996: 51) and often convey positivity and spontaneity, even marked by the use of exclamation marks. Questions, he writes, "imply a direct address to the reader – they require someone to answer" (Myers, 1996: 49). Furthermore, the parameters of the question help to establish the relevance of the ad, but also tell us something about what the business 'presupposes' of its customers. In other words, businesses use the ad to outline a problem they presume their audience to have and which they can solve (for example, trivago N.V. asks its customers: "Have you ever looked for a hotel online?"). Finally, Myers (1996: 47) writes that "the generic sentence type for the ad is the command, or imperative, because all ads are urging us to some action". Imperatives are rife in advertising discourse, whether the texts are compelling us to 'Have a break, have a Kit Kat', 'Just do it' (Nike), 'Buy one, get one free' or 'Click on the link'. The imperative form lacks a grammatical Subject, so the hearer/reader does not need to be singled out; if you are privy to the command, you are the addressee. Myers (1996: 47) argues that the use of commands helps to establish a more intimate type of interaction, "not because telling you to do something really makes you do what they say, but because it will create a personal effect, a sense of one person talking to another" (47). Furthermore, imperatives are used in speech when there is a presumed benefit to the hearer (e.g. 'have a seat', 'let me get you something'), which overrides any offence the hearer might otherwise feel. In this sense, businesses show their confidence in their presumed relationship, addressing (potential) customers without the politeness markers that might be more indicative of a relationship in which the participants do not necessarily know each other. The implication is that the business does know its customers and what they are telling them to do is for their own benefit.

Arguably, 'synthetic personalisation' is most explicitly manifest in the use of pronouns. Pennycook (1994) argues that the selection of pronouns can reflect power relations and pronouns can be rich with connotational meaning, as in the alienating sense of 'they', or the sexually euphemistic sense of 'it', for example (Wales, 1996: 8–9). 'We' can operate exclusively, i.e. in reference to the business and "personalises huge and impersonal corporations" (Myers, 1996: 82); or 'we' can be more inclusive, positioning the business alongside customers, as say, 'the British people', 'women', 'people who eat breakfast cereal'. This inclusive positioning is also a way in which the business can establish shared values and experiences. Timmis (2015) has shown that dialect forms of pronouns also capture shared culture and knowledge and that by referring to, for example, the wider historical context, we can understand more about how pronouns reflect social class relations. Understanding how such referents are used, for example by analysing collocates and concordance lines for 'you' and 'we', can provide insights into what a business expects and presupposes of its customers, as well as how it constructs its brand identity with respect to a local and/or global community.

> **Task 5.2**
>
> Look closely at some examples of advertising – be it on television, as posters or billboards, or online (you probably do not have to look far). What types of pronouns are used in the ads?
>
> - Is there a 'you'? What presuppositions are there about you as an addressee?
> - Is there a 'we'? Is this an inclusive or an exclusive we? Is it easy to tell?
> - Can you find any examples on an 'I'? What is the significance of the inclusion of that person? Is it a celebrity, for example? What virtues or qualities are associated with them?

5.1.2 Social actor representation

Pronouns offer a starting point for exploring how particular participants (businesses, customers etc.) are depicted in texts. To extend this inquiry, we can draw on the principles of social actor representation (van Leeuwen, 1996), which is predicated on the idea that "in naming and describing social actors, [text producers] select some aspects of reality which propagates a vision that is aligned with their ideological stance" (Jaworska, 2016: 104). Van Leeuwen (1996) provides an extensive taxonomy of the ways in which social actors can be variously grouped and labelled, typically in the use of particular nouns. In addition, Jaworska (2016: 93) explains that "words occurring in the vicinity of nouns, that is, their collocations, can tell us a great deal about the physical, evaluative, and affective attributes". This offers a means of applying corpus analysis to explore the following questions:

- **How does Dukki represent itself (i.e. through nouns and their collocates) as a business in its Facebook posts?**
- **How does Dukki characterise its customer base in its Facebook posts?**

5.2 The (commercial) value of local dialect

Dukki Gifts and Souvenirs (Dukki) provides the following description of itself and its services via its website:

> WHO THE DUCK ARE WE?
>
> Winner of the Inspiring Retail Award 2014, and finalist in the Nottingham Independent Business of the Year 2016 & 2017
>
> DUKKI is an independent gift store on St James' St, Nottingham. We design fabulous products to be enjoyed by locals and visitors alike, using the rich heritage, wonderful local dialect and beautiful landmarks of Nottingham and

its surrounding counties. Our exclusive products celebrate the East Midlands. If you're unable to pop into our shop, then you'll find everything you need right here on our website. If you're looking for a bespoke item, or personalisation on any of our products, then please get in touch via our contacts page. We pride ourselves in offering a flexible service, and welcome any suggestions you might have. (https://www.dukkigifts.co.uk/pages/abaht-us).

Task 5.3

Look closely at the 'Who the Duck are We?' text that appears on the Dukki website.

- What are your impressions of Dukki's branding strategy here?
- What qualities does the business show through this text?
- What particular language choices contribute to the brand identity presented here?

Dukki's business is to sell products that celebrate the history of Nottingham, which take the form of homeware (cushions, tableware, clocks); clothing, bags and accessories; kitchenware (mugs, lunchboxes, tea-towels), jewellery, stationery and other miscellaneous items. It is managed and run by local Nottingham residents Heidi Hargreaves (Creative Director) and her partner Ian Jones, an artist and illustrator who creates prints that celebrate landmarks and iconic figures of the local history for purchase through Dukki alongside pieces available through his personal website. Though they work with other local artists and manufacturers to produce their items, Heidi and Ian manage the store operations on their own and Heidi curates the entirety of Dukki's social media content (though Ian does often feature). One of the very explicit ways in which Dukki celebrates local identity and history is through the dialect, which is often the feature of the products that they sell. Heidi also constructs the business's Facebook posts through an approximation of the dialect, which is what has prompted the focus of this study.

The name 'Dukki' refers to arguably the most oft-cited example of the Nottinghamshire–Derbyshire dialect, the greeting 'ay up, me duck', which Dukki explains as follows:

Why do we say "Duck"?

The word "DUCK" is a term of greeting we use in NOTTINGHAM.

It dates back to SAXON times. The word 'DUCAS', a term of respect, similar to the MIDDLE ENGLISH word 'DUC' or 'DUK' which means a leader of a commander – such as the title 'DUKE'!

So don't be offended if we call you 'DUCK'! We are just being nice, and not implying that you walk with a waddle, have a beak, or even go QUACK! (https://www.facebook.com/pg/dukkigifts/posts/).

Despite these purported origins, in its current use 'duck/dukki' carries the connotations of its more 'ordinary' sense, referring to the water bird, which is reflected in the consistent use of duck symbols across Dukki's branding. What this post does indicate though, is that Dukki positions itself not only as a member of the speech community, but also as an educator of those outside of it, who may find themselves in Nottingham but unfamiliar with the dialect.

Along with some literary works, authored by the likes of D. H. Lawrence and Alan Sillitoe, the dialect of Nottingham, Derby and/or the East Midlands more broadly has been documented in a handful of dialect glossaries and these are the reference materials that guide Dukki in representing the dialect through Facebook. In 1999, John Beeton produced a pamphlet entitled *Nottingham As it is Spoke*, which has since been extended to four volumes. Beeton (1999) explains that the pamphlets were produced out of 'nostalgia' and for 'amusement' and they take the form of a glossary, interspersed with brief commentaries and anecdotes pertaining to local histories. Scollins and Titford (2000) have published a dialect glossary for the Erewash Valley (with some extrapolation to the East Midlands more broadly), a compilation of a series originating in the mid-1970s under the title, *Ey up mi Duck!*. Holland's (2008) *Words of the White Peak* is a dialect dictionary for a specific parish in the Peak District of Derbyshire (Earl Sterndale) and, on the basis of interviews with 150 people, glosses 360 dialect words from the area. Mike Smith's (2013) *Derbyshire Dialect* offers 'A Selection of Words and Anecdotes from Around Derbyshire', wherein local folk tales offer some insight into the purported origin of certain words. Finally, in 2018 Braber and Robinson (2018) published a volume dedicated to *East Midlands English* as part of the Dialects of English series (De Gruyter Mouton), providing a thorough account of phonological, morphological and lexical features associated with Derbyshire, Leicestershire and Nottinghamshire.

In sociolinguistics, the concept of 'prestige' enables us to consider how social class and formal contexts prompt (certain) speakers to adopt forms more closely aligned with the standard (e.g. Trudgill, 1974), which reiterates the notion that the standard equates with what is 'proper'. However, Labov (1966: 108) reports "an equal and opposing prestige for informal, working-class speech – a covert prestige enforcing this speech pattern" whereby lower-class speakers (particularly working-class men) persist in using non-standard forms associated with the local dialect. Furthermore, Trudgill (1972) found that working-class men would over-report their use of non-standard forms, demonstrating that this was a desirable trait for them. Regional dialect forms have a clear value, which goes beyond a demonstration of competence with language forms themselves and a sense of belonging, to tap into the qualities and values attributed to the communities who speak the dialect. They can even be monetised; as Johnstone (2009: 161) points out:

"A linguistic variety or a set of varieties is commodified when it is available for purchase and people will pay for it".

Local varieties have often been appropriated for the purposes of commercial discourse, which can point to qualities associated with geography, class or generation, alongside "ordinariness or genuineness" (Myers, 1996: 97). Jaworska (2016: 84) reports that "the tourist experience is nowadays strongly driven by the desire for 'authentic' encounters, especially with local people and their alternative or 'primitive' ways of life" and language is a key element of that. However, as Beal (2006: 82) points out:

> The main problem for any author wishing to represent a non-standard dialect is the need to strike a balance between accuracy and accessibility. If too many 'non-standard' features are used, the text may be difficult to read, especially for readers who are unfamiliar with the dialect portrayed, but the author needs to make the dialect recognisable as such.

Furthermore, there may be some disparity between what is perceived to be authentic and what features are documented by linguistic research to be indicative of a local variety (Johnstone, 2009). Often, the features associated with a variety (particularly as performed for those not part of the speech community) operate within a type of 'folklorism' (Bendix, 1988) and, rather than necessarily reflecting contemporary language use, retain old, vernacular practices, seen as 'untainted' and attesting to some degree of expertise regarding the history of the language (and by implication, the area) (Johnstone, 2009). The documentation of such language features and the transposing of these primarily spoken features to a written form can be discussed with respect to 'enregisterment'.

5.2.1 Enregisterment

'Enregisterment', according to Agha (2003), is the process by which sets of linguistic forms become established as meaningful cultural objects, such as standard languages or recognised dialects. These, in turn, index "speaker status linked to a specific scheme of cultural values" (Agha, 2003: 231). Agha (2003) discusses this in relation to Received Pronunciation (RP), a social accent in (southern) England that gained prestige through its association with the upper-middle classes (even the Queen) and is held as a standard – at least in some circles. Table 5.1 summarises some of the studies that have examined processes of 'enregisterment' around the world.

As an analytical approach, enregisterment "synthesizes history, material culture, linguistic fieldwork, folk linguistics/perceptual dialectology, discourse, style, phonology, lexis, syntax", among other disciplines (Clark, 2013: 444). In another example of a business trading on local dialect ('Pittsburghese'), Johnstone (2009: 159) makes the case that the sale of shirts bearing phrases thought to be unique to Pittsburgh "contribute to dialect enregisterment in at least four ways: they put

Table 5.1 Examples of studies of 'enregisterment'

Dialect/Community	References
'Geordie' and 'Sheffieldish', U.K.	Beal (2009)
Copper Country English/Keweenaw Peninsula, Michigan, U.S.A.	Remlinger (2009)
Putonghua/Beijing, China	Dong (2010)
'Northern'/Cleveland, Ohio, U.S.A.	Campbell-Kibler (2012)
Copenhagen, Denmark	Møller and Jørgensen (2012)
Yopno, Papua New Guinea	Slotta (2012)
Black Country, U.K.	Clark (2013)
Nineteenth-century Yorkshire	Cooper (2015)
'Yooper'/Upper Peninsula, Michigan, U.S.A.	Remlinger (2015)
North-East, U.K.	Snell (2017)

local speech on display, they imbue local speech with value, they standardize local speech, and they link local speech with particular social meanings". Similarly, Remlinger (2015: 15) asserts that "As a commodity, enregistered features not only sell things like t-shirts and ball caps, but they also sell the idea of a dialect, a sense of place, and a regional persona, but only because their meanings have become recognizable, valued and valuable". In addition to the questions outlined above relating to the representation of the brand and of customers, this case study was driven by an additional question:

- **How does Dukki contribute to the enregisterment of the Nottinghamshire dialect through its Facebook posts?**

5.3 The Dukki Facebook corpus

Dukki establishes a Web presence through its own website, Instagram, Facebook and Twitter. Given that this study was concerned with the enregisterment of dialect (and subsequently, the construction of brand and customer identity), Facebook was chosen as the site through which the sufficient amount and quality of data could be secured. Although corporate Facebook pages can be considered 'public' (and arguably would not require the consent of the subject(s)), I approached Heidi and Ian at the Dukki store to discuss their participation. This was in part motivated by the recognition that as an independent business (and given the significance of their projected identity as a personable and independent business), Heidi's and Ian's individual personae are a significant part of the brand. Rather than anonymise them, I wanted to include – and identify – them as active agents in the construction of the business identity and as such, it seemed more appropriate to notify them of the research and offer them the opportunity to approve the case study prior to publication. Heidi and Ian provided their informed consent for the study and were presented with the findings, which I had hoped would also provide them with an opportunity to reflect upon and understand what they were doing effectively. This study did not consider posts by followers/customers nor any of the interactions underneath the original posts (which do contribute to the brand identity in more collaborative ways), which would have necessitated gathering the consent of each additional user. The focus remained on Dukki as the primary brand manager.

Dukki produced 862 Facebook posts between 1 January and 31 December 2017. The distribution of these posts across the calendar months is shown in Figure 5.1. Collecting data over a calendar year allowed me to capture any seasonal variation associated with (commercial) holidays, such as Hallowe'en and Christmas, which provide opportunities for specific products and promotional strategies linked to these events.

However, Dukki's posts seem to be more directly influenced by local events. For example, in October Dukki celebrated the local Goose Fair, the Nottingham Beer Festival and their nomination in the Nottinghamshire Tourism Awards (accounting, to some degree, for the increase in posts). Indeed, Dukki is able to construct more bespoke posting events within wider seasonal trends; throughout December, Dukki posted a Nottingham Alphabet Advent Calendar, which meant that at least one post per day included a cartoon that used a sequential letter of the alphabet to celebrate a Nottingham dialect word beginning with that letter (which also appeared on a number of the products they sell). In May, Dukki adopted a similar strategy labelled '#thirtydaysofmardy'. The word 'mardy' is a local dialect term that means "childish, easily upset or cowardly" and is purportedly restricted to an area between Leicestershire and South Lancashire/South Yorkshire (Scollins and Titford, 2000: 98). Indeed, Braber and Robinson (2018: 135) discuss it as "one of the most illustrative examples of local language". This theme allowed Dukki to express mild complaints throughout the month, which ranged from Heidi and Ian's pet cat being 'mardy' because they forgot her birthday, to

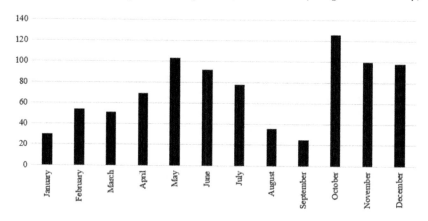

Figure 5.1 Distribution of Dukki Facebook posts across 2017.

more earnest objections; for example, in response to what they perceived to be unreasonable complaints from customers. This offers a clear example of how the business participates in (what is presented as) a dialogue around its brand identity and demonstrates that more personable, 'conversationalised' voice. There are no clear explanations as to why particular months featured fewer posts – which may simply relate to Heidi's work schedule – but it does seem that a structured theme such as #thirtydaysofmardy or the Nottingham Alphabet Advent Calendar is a way of prompting regular posts.

5.4 Features of the Dukki Facebook corpus

5.4.1 Images

Of the 862 posts collected throughout 2017, 820 included an image. The use of images is appropriate to both the conventions of social media and Dukki's commercial interests, since the images typically served to advertise the products they sell (as well as implicitly contributing to the brand identity). While the text of the posts more readily offered a means through which to explore the research questions, to dismiss the visual content would be to ignore a significant part of the branding and promotion, so it is worth briefly considering how that might be analysed alongside – and in interaction with – the written text.

For the purposes of corpus analysis, we can refer to what McGlashan (2015) has termed 'collustration', an extension of the principle of collocation to include imagery, which he explores with respect to children's picture books. For this case study, it seemed pertinent to capture a sense of the number and type of images used alongside particular language features and to mark these in a way that could be explored through corpus analysis. My observations of Dukki's images prompted a basic categorisation scheme, in that the images could be summarised as one of five types: 'candid', 'cartoon', 'postcard', 'products' and 'store'. Examples of each are represented in Figure 5.2.

'Candid' referred to photo images that were taken in situ, capturing the local surroundings for the purposes of Heidi's 'Boggercam' activity (which challenged followers to identify where the photo was taken, based on their local knowledge), for example, or as a demonstration of Dukki's connectedness with and participation in local events. Of the 820 posts that included an image, 141 had a candid photograph as the primary image. 'Cartoon' referred to an image that Heidi or Ian had drawn themselves, which typically conveyed a Nottingham dialect feature in use (as with the Nottingham Alphabet Advent Calendar) and would also be printed on one or a number of their products. Fifty-one posts used a cartoon as the primary image. The label 'postcard' was used to describe visual material that had been generated for the purposes of (social media) promotion, such as notifying customers of international shipping rates (see Figure 5.2), or the countdown of a sale period. This would also include promotional material generated by Dukki's affiliates, or other local businesses and 153 posts led with a 'postcard'

Figure 5.2 Categories of images posted on the Dukki Facebook page.

image. The largest category of images was 'products', which were often shot by Heidi holding said products in her hands, encouraging viewers to align themselves with the position of being in possession of the products. The number of posts leading with a 'product' image totalled 348 and these posts often included multiple images, as well as links to the store function of the page where the products could be purchased. Finally, the 'store' category referred to images that displayed the shop front, a display within the store (and the work involved in creating it) or a Dukki stall at an off-site commercial event. There were 127 posts where the lead image was a 'store' photo. The images – and the image categories – offered an initial examination of the ways in which Dukki promotes its products and services, as well as how it positions itself as a visible member of the Nottingham community. This simple labelling system supports an analysis of the distribution of these images, alongside features of the written text.

5.4.2 Non-standard language features

The Dukki Facebook Corpus comprised 24,329 tokens and 3,984 types, indicating that it was a reasonably focused language set (type-token ratio: 0.164). There were 3,897 non-standard tokens and 775 non-standard types (ratio: 0.199), suggesting that while there were more standard features than non-standard features, the use of non-standard features was more lexically rich. One category of non-standard features was the use of hashtags. There were 160 different hashtags used in the corpus, which related to:

- Wider events (#easterholiday, #ge2017)
- Local people and groups (#brianclough, #nffc)
- Local places (#derby, #hucknall)
- The creative industry (#craftingcommunity, #etsy)
- Dialect (#ayupduck, #regionaldialect)
- Store events (#flashsale, #openinghours) and
- Specific product items (#boxofboggers, #cocksonsticks).

The most commonly-used hashtags were #propernotts (37), #nottingham (17), #thirtydaysofmardy (16), #lovenotts (12) and #ayupmeduck (11), demonstrating Dukki's focus on its position in the wider city, the construction of a 'Nottingham' identity (#propernotts) through dialect (#ayupmeduck) and the templates that enabled regular posting, as discussed above.

The most frequently-used non-standard words are listed in Table 5.2. Since this study is concerned with social actor representation, it is significant to see that a number of pronouns are produced in non-standard orthography. This means that customers are being addressed in a way more comparable to how they would be addressed in informal speech (at least, by Nottingham locals). 'Yer' and 'yo' are

Table 5.2 The most-frequently used non-standard words in the Dukki Facebook corpus

	Word	#		Word	#		Word	#
1	yer	208	11	nah	45	21	briwyunt	30
2	boggers	206	12	frum	41	22	ta	29
3	dukki	182	13	dahn	39	23	mek	28
4	me	174	14	chrissmuss	38	24	wuz	28
5	ter	169	15	ayup	38	25	annorl	28
6	bleddeh	165	16	yersen	34	26	cob	27
7	bogger	131	17	wi'	33	27	abaht	27
8	aht	76	18	luvleh	33	28	boggercam	26
9	av	68	19	warra	32	29	gorra	23
10	fer	55	20	yo'	31	30	ee	23

forms of 'you'; 'me' appears here as a non-standard (dialect) form of the possessive determiner 'my' (distinguished from the standard use of the object pronoun 'me'); and 'ee' is a non-standard form of 'he'. These forms are reported in Scollins and Titford (2000: 31–2) and Braber and Robinson (2018: 82) and since they relate to social actors, they are discussed in more detail below.

The stylisation of the words in Table 5.2 reflects key features of the Nottingham (/East Midlands) accent. The words 'aht' ('out'), 'dahn' ('down'), 'nah' ('now') and 'abaht' ('about') reflect an accent feature whereby /aʊ/ becomes /æː/ (Braber and Robinson, 2018: 44). This is further shown in the corpus through words such as 'aahs' ('house'), 'checkaht' ('checkout'), 'discaant' ('discount') and 'thaahsund' ('thousand'). In 'aahs' we also see an example of h-dropping (Braber and Robinson, 2018: 58), which in Table 5.2 is captured in 'ee' ('he') and 'av' ('have'), and in the larger corpus in words such as 'ear' ('hear') and 'e'll' ('he'll'). 'Yer' ('you') and 'ter' ('to') demonstrate the tendency for /uː/ to become /ə/, a feature also described in Scollins and Titford (2000), alongside the vowel change whereby 'make' (/ɛɪ/) becomes 'mek' (/ɛ/) (Braber and Robinson, 2018: 44). In the words 'luvleh' ('lovely') and 'bleddeh' ('bloody') we can see how the end of such words is shortened (/ɪ/ becomes /ɛ/) (Braber and Robinson, 2018: 49). Table 5.2 also shows 'l-vocalisation' – where an 'l' sound becomes more like a vowel – in the word 'briwyunt' ('brilliant') and also reflected in the words 'coad' ('cold') and 'owd' ('old') (Scollins and Titford, 2000: 23; Braber and Robinson, 2018: 61). The words 'annorl' ('and all', meaning 'as well') and 'chrissmuss' ('Christmas') show a loss of stops (sounds like 't', 'd', 'p', 'b', 'k', 'g'). In both 'worra' ('what a') and 'gorra' ('got a') 2 words are contracted and show how a /t/ between vowels is often replaced by /r/, which Scollins and Titford (2000: 27) describe as an 'intrusive 'r''. This is also found in various forms of 'get'/'got', such as 'gerra' ('get a'), 'gerrenuff' ('get enough'), 'gerronwi-it' ('get on with it') and 'gerroverrere' ('get over here'). There is a wider pattern of contractions which seems to reflect a seamless articulation in spoken form, such as 'jigga-dahn' ('did you go down'). This presentation of the text is more conversational and follows practices established in both Beeton (1999) and Scollins and Titford (2000).

The corpus shows a pattern in which words that would otherwise have the vowel sounds /əʊ/ (like 'home', 'open'), /ɔː/ ('jaw', 'thought', 'horse') and /ɜː/ (e.g. 'dirty', 't-shirt', 'nurse') all become /ɒ/, as conveyed in their respective spellings in the corpus: 'om', 'oppen', 'jow', 'thote', 'oss', 'dotty', 't-shott' and 'noss' (see also Braber and Robinson, 2018). The 'oo' (/uː/) sound in words like 'juice', 'soon' and 'Boots' (which is celebrated as a company founded in Nottingham, where it still has its flagship store) becomes /uːə/, as reflected in the spellings 'joowus', 'soowun' and 'Boowutts'. Finally, there is a pattern in which 't' becomes 'k', as shown in the spellings 'hospickle' ('hospital'), 'kekkle' ('kettle') and 'likkle' ('little').

Table 5.2 also shows some of the dialect words used in the corpus. Arguably, the most significant of these is 'bogger', which is used as a term to address Dukki's followers. Its function in the corpus as a form of labelling and addressing potential customers is discussed below, but its meaning as a dialect term is explained in Scollins and Titford (2000: 64) as follows:

> Local version of 'bugger'. It carries no dubious sexual connotations, but is rather a mild and even affectionate term of abuse, as in: 'Yuh silly bogger!'.

Readers will likely be familiar with similar terms that are potentially offensive, yet seem to be used between close friends. This phenomenon is perhaps best captured by Leech's (1983) 'Banter principle', which describes how the use of terms that would be thought of as rude between people who were not well-acquainted can actually signal close friendship, on the basis that the speaker has confidence in the relationship enough to expect that the recipient will understand its being used ironically. Similar to the use of imperatives, it arguably demonstrates that in close friendships we do not need to provide indicators of politeness and respect, since there is a presumed familiarity and so the use of this 'mild and even affectionate term of abuse' is a demonstration of the business of setting a familiar tone, as if addressing a friend. The word 'bogger' is shown to be quite flexible, used in Dukki's unique terms 'boggercam' and 'boggertalk', as well as an all-purpose word in reference to 'things'.

Along with non-standard 'me' (see above), the corpus also provides examples of region-specific pronouns, in their reflexive form: 'mesen' ('myself'), 'yersen' ('yourself'), 'imsen'/'izsen' ('himself'/'his self'), 'ussens' ('ourselves'); in the possessive form: 'yorn' ('your'/'yours'); and in the indefinite form: 'nowt' ('nothing'), 'owt' ('anything') and 'sommat' ('something') (Braber and Robinson, 2018: 83).

5.4.3 Keywords

Keyword analysis helps us to understand which words are particularly characteristic of the data (discussed in Chapter 3). Table 5.3 shows the top keywords for the Dukki Facebook corpus when compared with the BNC1994 (sorted by LL). The significance of the images attached to the posts is reflected in the prominence of [PRODUCTS], [CANDID], [POSTCARD], [STORE] and [CARTOON] in the keyword list, as well as the inclusion of [THUMBNAIL] (which refers to the appearance of the Dukki page profile picture as part of an original post when it has been shared and thereby embedded). As noted above, the inclusion of 'product' images was typically accompanied by a link to where viewers can purchase the items and so when a product image was included, the post was also likely to include the phrase 'Products shown:' as a standard header to the hyperlinked items. Furthermore, such posts often included multiple items (or, for example, the item in a range of colours or styles) and so 'PRODUCTS' frequently appeared multiple times in quick succession, which goes some way to explaining its frequency and rank in the keyword list. Of 152 occurrences of the keyword 'store', 133 referred to the image label, with the few remaining occurrences indicating

Table 5.3 Keywords in the Dukki Facebook corpus compared with BNC1994

	Keyword	#		Keyword	#		Keyword	#
1	[PRODUCTS]	620	21	fer	55	41	Updated	38
2	boggers	206	22	photo	64	42	Warra	32
3	yer	206	23	shop	73	43	Notts	34
4	dukki	175	24	4,937	52	44	Luvleh	30
5	ter	169	25	me	212	45	Briwyunt	30
6	[CANDID]	171	26	photos	60	46	've	78
7	bleddeh	161	27	likes	59	47	Wuz	28
8	duck	151	28	nah	44	48	Annorl	28
9	[POSTCARD]	136	29	our	184	49	Yo	31
10	store/[STORE]	152	30	frum	41	50	Wi	27
11	bogger	121	31	shopping_bag	40	51	Abaht	27
12	gifts	125	32	added	80	52	Alphabet	31
13	souvenirs	111	33	dahn	39	53	Cob	26
14	Nottingham	118	34	ayup	38	54	Boggercam	26
15	aht	75	35	shared	58	55	advent_calendar	26
16	ducks	73	36	're	105	56	Ta	29
17	[THUMBNAIL]	62	37	#propernotts	37	57	Album	28
18	[CARTOON]	60	38	Ian	40	58	Ee	26
19	av	64	39	Chrissmuss	34	59	Website	23
20	we	336	40	yersen	33	60	Over	23

text references to the store. The keyword list reflects Dukki's focus on its trade (in words like 'gifts', 'souvenirs', 'shopping_bag' etc.), some of the social media functions enabled by Facebook ('added' [a] 'photo', 'likes', 'shared' and 'updated') as well as including a number of the non-standard features discussed above that reflect accent features and dialect terms. What is also shown to be prominent is a number of 'social actor' labels, through pronouns and select nouns, which is the focus of the next section.

5.4.4 Social actors

The term 'Dukki' tends only to appear in the content of the post when there is an embedded link to another part of the page (e.g. the online store), which incorporates the Dukki thumbnail and header, 'Dukki Gifts and Souvenirs'. As such, the term 'Dukki' is most explicitly linked to the sale of products and indeed, collocates highly with the use of a [PRODUCT] image and descriptors for products (e.g. 'calendar', 'coaster', 'enamel pin'). In consideration of how the business represents itself, the first-person pronouns 'we' and 'our' offer further insights. Figure 5.3 shows the collocate map for 'we', set at an MI score of 5.0 and above. The presence of 'today' as a collocate attests to Facebook's emphasis on recency (Page, 2012); given that social media activity occurs at least daily, readers can expect that 'today' still corresponds to the time at which the post is read and this creates a sense of time shared with Dukki. As with the candid photographs, the viewer is aligned, both temporally and spatially with Dukki.

Looking at the processes associated with 'we' i.e. through verb forms, the words 'do' and 'mek' suggest that Dukki positions itself as a 'maker' and otherwise active agent. Furthermore, it is an agent that 'wants' and 'loves', offering a

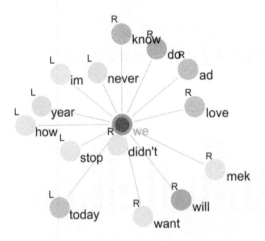

Figure 5.3 Collocates of 'we' in the Dukki Facebook corpus.

more personable representation and in fact, these material and cognitive processes are closely aligned: Dukki tells us "we love doing it", "we do this because we love it and love love mekking you boggers happy". Other objects of Dukki's 'love' include 'Nottingham' and 'our suppliers', which are effective in confirming Dukki's impetus for celebrating the local area as well as showing its affection for its work and its collaborators (including 'you boggers'). Overall, this contributes to a passionate and committed business identity. These positive affiliations are also revealed in the collocates for 'our', which include 'customers' and 'Jane', who is one of Dukki's collaborators. Referring to an individual as 'our (Jane)' is typically reserved for family members – Heidi also refers to 'our Ian' – and a feature of certain northern dialects (particularly in Yorkshire and Lancashire) (Beal, 2004), which further indicates a close affiliation. Because of this association, even references to 'our customers' carry those familial connotations, which would likely not be the case with other businesses (who do not adopt a regional dialect) when they refer to 'our customers'.

Other collocates of 'we' seem to present a more complicated picture, as with the more negative terms 'didn't' and 'never'. These examples demonstrate Dukki's adoption of a 'CHV' (see above), in that we hear about some of the challenges and setbacks associated with running an (independent) business. For example, in a post referring to the Nottinghamshire Tourism Awards, Dukki tells us "we didn't win", but this nevertheless provides an opportunity to reflect on and celebrate the successes of the business and thank followers for their role in helping the business become a finalist. Other instances further account for Heidi's and Ian's commitment and efforts, in that 'we never stop' and 'we are never late on purpose', appealing to customers' understanding when things do not quite go to plan (e.g. with a late delivery). Given the prominent representation of Heidi and Ian as a partnership entirely responsible for the management of the store, these expressions help to manage customer expectations but are also more likely to elicit empathy, since they are humanised. The success of the business is shown to be predicated on the hard work that they do, which is regularly and visually reiterated through their Facebook posts.

The pronoun 'me' is used as a first-person possessive determiner (i.e. 'my'), a documented regional variant (Scollins and Titford, 2000; Braber and Robinson, 2018). The standard first-person object pronoun 'me' is still used, presenting something of a challenge for discerning which is being used. Both forms appeared in the template for a series of posts in December, that followed the patterning of the 'Twelve Days of Christmas' as in "On the fifth day of Chrissmuss, me duck she sent ter me" where 'me duck' shows the possessive form and 'to me' the object form. A manual reading showed that 174 of the 214 instances of 'me' were in the possessive form and the collocates reveal that this was most strongly associated with terms of address directed at followers, through the words 'duck' [MI: 5.88], 'ducks' [MI: 6.30] and 'owds' [MI: 7.08]. The word 'ayup' was also a strong collocate [MI: 5.03], reflecting the frequent use of 'ayup me duck' in the corpus. Table 5.4 shows a list of concordance lines for 'me' when it is followed by 'ducks'.

Table 5.4 Concordance lines for 'me' followed by 'ducks' in the Dukki Facebook corpus

1	We're closed today,	me	ducks. Catching up on some well-earned fam..
2	merreh Chrissmus	me	ducks!
3	just clik below,	me	ducks!
4	Pick up in store today,	me	ducks!
5	Be careful aht there,	me	ducks!??
6	Ta muchly,	me	ducks!
7	open today as normal until 6pm,	me	ducks!
8	N'night,	me	ducks!
9	This weekend,	me	ducks! Free entreh
10	Comin' soowun,	me	ducks!
11	Also available from our shop,	me	ducks!
12	Highly recommended,	me	ducks!
13	We're ere,	me	ducks! Til 3pm!
14	Ay up,	me	ducks!
15	Don't miss aht,	me	ducks! #nffc [PRODUCTS]
16	click on the link,	me	ducks!
17	Back open again at 10.30am,	me	ducks! [STORE]
18	Purrit in yet diaries,	me	ducks! [CANDID] NOV 5
19	Nah we're bleddeh famous,	me	ducks!?? http://www.dailyrecord.co.uk/.../
20	This is onleh selected lines,	me	ducks! [PRODUCTS]
21	anyroad, like our page,	me	ducks!??
22	be a mad bogger ter miss aht,	me	ducks [STORE]
23	Come on then,	me	ducks!
24	thanks for tekkin part,	me	ducks!
25	Happy shopping,	me	ducks!
26	so come and find us,	me	ducks! #pride2017
27	goodies, worth over 25 paahnd,	me	ducks!
28	We can't do it wi aht yer,	me	ducks! Vote here www.itsinnottingham.com/
29	Don't forget,	me	ducks!
30	meks all the difference,	me	ducks! You can vote via this link
31	Honest opinions,	me	ducks!
32	additions before it goes ter print,	me	ducks? [PRODUCTS]
33	Little bit serious today,	me	ducks! It's always important to be nice
34	Brand new ducks in,	me	duck! Cat for scale.
35	It's starting in ten minutes,	me	ducks! Stay tuned!
36	How lucky we are,	me	ducks!
37	Ava gud'n	me	ducks!
38	should be ready in 4 weeks time,	me	ducks! [PRODUCTS]
39	this you remember frum last yeeyer,	me	ducks! [POSTCARD]
40	Frum 1888,	me	ducks! [POSTCARD]
41	Appeh sunday,	me	ducks!
42	muchly for your continuing support,	me	ducks!
43	Can yer spot Mr Heron,	me	ducks? [CANDID]

44	Warra great citeh,	me	ducks!
45	Appeh Chinese new year,	me	ducks! #rooster2017
46	Watch this space,	me	ducks!
47	Gerrin there,	me	ducks!
48	Ta muchly for your understanding,	me	ducks! #closedtoday #sorryduck #nottingham

We have seen how exclamations and imperatives are key features of advertising discourse (Myers, 1996) and in these concordance lines we find the following:

- Interjections and exclamations: 'merreh Chrissmuss', 'ta muchly' (thank you very much), 'N'night' (goodnight), 'ay up', 'happy shopping', 'Appeh Sunday', 'Appeh Chinese new year', 'ava gud'n' and 'Gerrin there' (the last two examples take the form of an imperative but in terms of pragmatics, function as an interjections)
- Imperatives: 'just clik below', 'pick up in store', 'be careful', 'Don't miss aht', 'click on the link', 'purrit in yer diaries', 'like our page', 'come on then', 'come and find us', 'Don't forget', 'Vote here', 'Stay tuned', 'Watch this space'.

The exclamations approximate a spoken register and are positive, expressing 'thanks' and 'good(ness)' and 'happiness'. The imperatives operate in establishing a more direct relationship (as discussed above) and encourage followers to engage with the business through its social media (by clicking, liking, watching) or by going into the store. Addressing followers as 'me ducks' in these instances helps to mitigate that (minor) imposition by creating affiliation and thereby appearing friendlier.

'Me ducks' is also used when delivering information that may imply some form of imposition. This can be apologetic, for example when customers are denied access to the store ('we're closed today'). Conversely, the term is used when customers are directed to go to the store (or otherwise participate e.g. calling for 'Honest opinions'), for example, given certain conditions: 'This weekend', 'We're ere', 'Back open again at 10.30am', 'Free entreh' and 'It's starting in ten minutes'. Finally, 'me ducks' is used when followers are being encouraged to buy: 'Also available from our shop', 'Highly recommended', 'This is only selected lines', 'be a mad bogger ter miss aht'. Arguably, it is the purpose of the business to try to convince followers to visit the stall/store and buy items, so it is significant to see that this promotional 'transactional voice' is so heavily embedded within the 'conversational voice', which manifests in dialect terms and affectionate forms of address ('me ducks'). This suggests that Dukki goes about its business in quite understated ways, being sure to mitigate any imposition (to visit, to spend money) through the relational work achieved through mutual identification with the regional dialect.

Followers are typically addressed as 'yer/yo boggers'. The local dialect meaning of 'bogger' is discussed above and the use of these forms of 'you' offers an interesting view on how Dukki addresses its followers and engages in 'synthetic personalisation' (Fairclough, 1989) through second-person pronouns. When used with 'boggers' this restricts the use of this form of 'you' to its plural meaning, which is likely to mitigate the sense that users are being addressed individually, however, this shows that there is an emphasis on the community. This suggests that Dukki presupposes that its followers are likely to be people who use the local dialect, otherwise they become honorary members of the community through their affiliation with Dukki. Subsequently, consistent with the brand identity that celebrates the local dialect, followers and customers of Dukki (i.e. 'boggers') are defined by their interaction with the local dialect (i.e. as people who engage in 'bogger talk') and have value as a group. Even when forms of 'you' are deployed in an unspecified single/plural sense, it is the dialect that takes precedence, as shown in the range of non-standard forms: yaht (you out), yavin (you having), yawlright (you alright?), yereart (your heart), yeroff (you off), yerup (you are up), yoav (you have), yorn/yourn (yours), yowl (you will), yud (you would), yuh (you, specifically in 'gerrit dahn yuh!').

5.5 Discussion

Returning to the proposition made by Johnstone (2009: 159) that the sale of items bearing specific regional dialect forms contributes to enregisterment, we can see how Dukki 'puts local speech on display', 'imbue[s] local speech with value', 'standardize[s] local speech' and 'link[s] local speech with particular social meanings'. The standardisation of the dialect is important for clear recognition of the dialect (and useful for the purposes of corpus analysis), though there may be some negotiation involved in determining what orthographic form spoken features take. Pearce (2015) reports a study of an online message board where the **folk linguistic** (i.e. non-specialist) perspectives of members emerged through discussion of forms associated with the dialect of the north east of England. Pearce (2015) identifies three themes from this discussion: vernacular prescriptivism and maintenance; the relationship between the north and south of England; and dialect purism, demonstrating the contrasting language ideologies but, nevertheless, the commitment to the vehement discussion of such language features within this community. Dukki bases its own enregisterment of the Nottingham dialect on previously published works, notably Beeton (1999) and Scollins and Titford (2000). As such, rather than fulfilling the role of 'prescriptivist', Dukki is able to reiterate its knowledge of the history of the local dialect and the relevant literature (which, incidentally, is also available for purchase in-store) and, as a preserver and user of the dialect, encourages dialogue with its followers about how it is enregistered in written form.

As much as there may be a tourist interest in local dialect features, as Beal (2000) remarks with respect to Geordie dialect features, Geordie writing is for Geordies: it provides a shared code that reinforces solidarity and its humour, for example, relies on insider knowledge of this shared code. As such, in assuming a 'bogger' identity and engaging with Dukki, users subscribe to a wider 'Nottingham' (/East Midlands) identity. This is a powerful, but often elusive process common to advertising (Myers, 1996), which extends beyond language to activate particular values and beliefs. Subsequently, there are risks in appropriating dialect forms as the 'inauthentic' use of such language, by implication, challenges certain belief systems. Indeed, Smokowski (2016) discusses how the appropriation of African American Vernacular English (AAVE) through stylised forms on social media serves to provide non-speakers with a means of annexing certain positive qualities associated with Black or hip-hop culture (such as toughness, coolness, an anti-establishment stance) but at the same time reproduces negative stereotypes of the people generally thought to speak AAVE, contributing to a covert racism in this instance. Indeed, the use of AAVE stylisations is thought to be intended to be humorous because of the incongruity of the characteristics of the individual using such features in an inauthentic way and the corresponding characteristics associated with the AAVE speech community (such as ethnicity, education, socioeconomic status and cultural background).

Nevertheless, if perceived to be authentic, the use of dialect features as a celebration of local history – even for commercial purposes – can be an effective tool for customer engagement, perhaps because it appeals to fundamental values and beliefs. Furthermore, enregisterment via the Web is one way in which the dialect can be documented, be it through a standardised orthography or in audio/visual form. Anduze James (2013) reports on the enregisterment of Trinidad English Creole through an online forum dedicated to news, events and social trends from Trinidad, facilitating a 'democratic grassroots' enregisterment. Anduze James (2013: 36) argues that the Internet bypasses traditional power structures and in shifting the issue of orthography "into the hands of the people", offers an alternative to previous (unsuccessful) formal enregisterment movements. The BBC Voices project (http://www.bbc.co.uk/voices/) constituted a resource for documenting various dialects from around the U.K. in both written and spoken form and in previous chapters, we have seen how mobile digital technologies are facilitating the construction of a spoken Welsh Corpus (Neale et al., 2017) by authentic users, in context.

This reflects a broader trend in social media, in which users develop a blended role as producers and consumers [or 'prosumers' (Toffler, 1980)]. Businesses can call upon social media users to contribute to their business practices, be it in relation to product development (such as the Lego Ambassador Network (https://lan.lego.com/), customer review or the self-initiated dissemination of images of its products via, for example, Instagram (Chang, 2014). Fournier and Avery (2011: 194) refer to 'open-source' branding: a practice of "participatory, collaborative, and socially linked behaviours whereby consumers serve as creators and disseminators of branded content". Users cultivate a type of personal branding, drawing prestige from their consumption of and association with recognisable brands, whereas businesses benefit from customer endorsements and constant visibility on social media platforms. The consequence of this is that businesses are not solely in control of their own brand and the input of users may affect the cohesion and the clarity of that brand identity. However, as Gensler et al. (2013: 243) point out, brand managers "are not doomed to passively watch what their consumers do to their brands. Instead, they face the challenge of integrating consumer-generated brand stories and social media into their communication mix to enable compelling brand stories". As an extension of this study, it would be fruitful to look at the ways in which Dukki interacts with its followers, how it resolves customer complaints or indeed, how the 'boggers' contribute to the enregisterment of the Nottingham dialect. The corpus approach taken here has revealed some key features of the outward-facing construction of the brand and how Dukki defines itself and its followers through text and, in a more restricted sense, images.

An expansion of the analysis of the images, which would inevitably shift away from corpus approaches, might build on Zappavigna's (2016) work on social media photography on Instagram. Zappavigna (2016) discusses 'point of view' (which has also been referred to as 'focalisation' (Painter et al., 2013)) and 'subjectification'. The former attends to how a relationship between the participants of the image and the viewer is formed, whereas the latter considers how a relationship is formed between the viewer and the image producer (Zappavigna, 2016). For example, we can say that in posting images from her point of view, Heidi encourages followers to align themselves with her perspective, which often means imagining themselves in familiar locales around Nottingham (including the Dukki store). Being associated with – and situated in – the local area is an important part of Dukki's brand identity. Furthermore, viewers are encouraged to assume Heidi's perspective in more figurative ways, as a Nottingham dialect speaker and representative of the associated values of this constructed Nottingham identity, generating a high degree of empathy and alignment with what is communicated through these posts.

Summary

This chapter offers a study of an independent business in Nottingham, whose trade is predicated on a celebration of the local history and dialect. Through an examination of frequent (non-standard) words used in a corpus of its Facebook posts, I have shown how Dukki contributes to a process of enregisterment of the Nottingham dialect. Furthermore, by looking at the collocates of terms referring to different participant groups, we were able to observe some of the characteristics and actions Dukki attributes to itself as a brand and to its followers. The prominent use of stylised forms that reflect dialect features shows it to be a core part of the brand identity, but also a way of engaging with customers. Dukki also uses strategies associated with advertising discourse more widely (such as imperatives) as well as functions associated with social media platforms (e.g. posting and sharing images, hashtags).

References

Agha, A. (2003). The social life of cultural value. *Language and Communication*, 23, 3, 231–273.

Anduze James, S. (2013). Trinidad English Creole Orthography: Language Enregisterment and Communicative Practices in a New Media Society. *Linguistics Graduate Theses & Dissertations* 29. University of Colorado, Boulder, Colorado, U.S.A. Available at: https://scholar.colorado.edu/ling_gradetds/29/, accessed 27 May 2018.

Ashley, C. and Tuten, T. (2015). Creative strategies in social media marketing: An exploratory study of branded social content and consumer engagement. *Psychology of Marketing*, 32, 1, 15–27.

Beal, J. C. (2000). From Geordie Ridley to *Viz*: Popular literature in Tyneside English. *Language and Literature*, 9, 4, 343–359.

Beal, J. C. (2004). The morphology and syntax of English dialects in the north of England, in B. Kortmann (ed.) *A Handbook of Varieties of English: Volume II*. Berlin: De Gruyter Mouton, 114–141.

Beal, J. C. (2006). *Language and Region*. London: Routledge.

Beal, J. C. (2009). Enregisterment, commodification, and historical context: 'Geordie' versus 'Sheffieldish'. *American Speech*, 84, 2, 138–156.

Beeton, J. (1999). *Nottingham As it is Spoke: Volume One*. Keyworth: Reflections of a Bygone Age.

Bendix, R. (1988). Folklorism: The challenge of a concept. *International Folklore Review*, 6, 5–15.

Braber, N. and Robinson, J. (2018). *East Midlands English*. Berlin: De Gruyter Mouton.

Campbell-Kibler, K. (2012). Contestation and enregisterment in Ohio's imagined dialects. *Journal of English Linguistics*, 40, 3, 281–305.

Chang, C. Y. (2014). Visualizing Brand Personality and Personal Branding: Case Analysis on Starbucks and Nike's Brand Value Co-creation on Instagram. MA Thesis. The University of Iowa. Available at: https://ir.uiowa.edu/cgi/viewcontent.cgi?article=5343&context=etd, accessed 28 May 2018.

Clark, U. (2013). '*Ers from off*: The indexicalization and enregisterment of Black Country dialect. *American Speech*, 88, 4, 441–466.

Cooper, P. (2015). Enregisterment in historical contexts: Nineteenth century Yorkshire dialect. *Dialectologia*, 14, 1–16.

Darics, E. and Koller, V. (2018). *Language in Business, Language at Work*. London: Palgrave Macmillan.

Devereux, L., Melewar, T. C. and Foroudi, P. (2017). Corporate identity and social media: Existence and extension of the organization. *International Studies of Management & Organization*, 47, 2, 110–134.

Dijkmans, C., Kerkhof, P., Buyukcan-Tetik, A. and Beukeboom, C. J. (2015). Online conversation and corporate reputation: A two-wave longitudinal study on the effects of exposure to the social media activities of a highly interactive company. *Journal of Computer-Mediated Communication*, 20, 6, 632–648.

Dong, J. (2010). The enregisterment of Putonghua in practice. *Language & Communication*, 30, 4, 265–275.

Facebook (2018). Newsroom – Products. Available at: https://newsroom.fb.com/products/, accessed 27 May 2018.

Fairclough, N. (1989). *Language and Power*. London: Longman.

Fournier, S. and Avery, J. (2011). The uninvited brand. *Business Horizons*, 54, 3, 193–207.

Gensler, S., Völckner, F., Liu-Thompkins, Y. and Wiertz, C. (2013). Managing brands in the social media environment. *Journal of Interactive Marketing*, 27, 4, 242–256.

Holland, F. P. (2008). *Words of the White Peak: The Disappearing Dialect of a Derbyshire Village*. Buxton: Anecdotes.

Hunt, D. and Koteyko, N. (2015). 'What was your blood sugar reading this morning?': Representing diabetes self-management on Facebook. *Discourse & Society*, 26, 4, 445–463.

Jaworska, S. (2016). A comparative corpus-assisted discourse study of the representations of hosts in promotional tourism discourse. *Corpora*, 11, 1, 83–111.

Johnstone, B. (2009). Pittsburghese shirts: Commodification and the enregisterment of an urban dialect. *American Speech*, 84, 2, 157–175.

Labov, W. (1966). *The Social Stratification of English in New York City*. Washington: Center for Applied Linguistics.

Leech, G. (1983). *The Principles of Pragmatics*. New York: Longman Group Limited.

McCann, M. and Barlow, A. (2015). Use and measurement of social media for SMEs. *Journal of Small Business and Enterprise Development*, 22, 2, 273–287.

McGlashan, M. (2015). The Representation of Same-sex Parents in Children's Picturebooks: A Corpus-assisted Multimodal Critical Discourse Analysis. PhD Thesis. Lancaster University.

Møller, J. S. and Jørgensen, J. N. (2012). Enregisterment among adolescents in superdiverse Copenhagen. *Tilburg Papers in Culture Studies* 28. Available at: https://pdfs.semanticscholar.org/67a4/278089181421bde5b1b9f1aafc55e8e22f5b.pdf, accessed 27 May 2018.

Myers, G. (1996). *Words in Ads*. London: Edward Arnold.

Neale, S., Spasić, I., Needs, J., Watkins, G., Morris, S., Fitzpatrick, T., Marshall, L. and Knight, D. (2017). The CorCenCC Crowdsourcing App: A bespoke tool for the user-driven creation of the National Corpus of Contemporary Welsh. Paper Presented at the *Corpus Linguistics Conference 2017*. 24–28 July 2017. University of Birmingham, Birmingham, U.K. Available at: https://www.birmingham.ac.uk/Documents/college-artslaw/corpus/conference-archives/2017/general/paper273.pdf, accessed 3 June 2018.

Obar, J. A. and Wildman, S. (2015). Social media definition and the governance challenge: An introduction to the special issue. *Telecommunications Policy*, 39, 9, 745–750.

Page, R. (2012). *Stories and Social Media: Identities and Interaction*. London: Routledge.

Painter, C., Martin, J. R. and Unsworth, L. (2013). *Reading Visual Narratives: Image Analysis of Children's Picture Books*. Sheffield: Equinox.

Pearce, M. (2015). Mam or mum? Sociolinguistic awareness and language-ideological debates online. *Sociolinguistic Studies*, 9, 1, 1–20. Available at: http://sure.sunderland.ac.uk/5178/1/pearce%202015b%20preprint.pdf, accessed 28 May 2018.

Pennycook, A. (1994). The politics of pronouns. *ELT Journal*, 48, 2, 173–178.

Remlinger, K. (2009). Everyone up here: Enregisterment and identity in Michigan's Keweenaw peninsula. *American Speech*, 84, 2, 118–137.

Remlinger, K. (2015). New vistas of dialect and identity in the linguistic landscape: Commodification of language, identity and place in Michigan's Upper Peninsula. Paper presented at the annual meeting of the American Anthropological Association/Society for Linguistic Anthropology. 21 November 2015. Denver, Colorado, U.S.A. Available at: http://www.academia.edu/18145340/New_Vistas_of_Dialect_and_Identity_in_the_Linguistic_Landscape_Commodification_of_Language_Identity_and_Place_in_Michigan_s_Upper_Peninsula, accessed 27 May 2018.

Scollins, R. and Titford, J. (2000). *Ey up mi Duck! Dialect of Derbyshire and the East Midlands*. Newbury: Countryside Books.

Slotta, J. (2012). Dialect, trope, and enregisterment in a Melanesian speech community. *Language & Communication*, 32, 1–13.

Smith, M. (2013). *Derbyshire Dialect*. Sheffield: Bradwell Books.

Smokowski, H. L. (2016). Voicing the Other: Mock AAVE on social media. *CUNY Academic Works*. City University of New York, New York, U.S.A. Available at: https://academicworks.cuny.edu/gc_etds/708/, accessed 27 May 2018.

Snell, J. (2017). Enregisterment, indexicality and the social meaning of 'howay': Dialect and identity in north-east England, in C. Montgomery and E. Moore (eds) *Language and a Sense of Place: Studies in Language and Region*. Cambridge: Cambridge University Press, 301–324.

Timmis, I. (2015). Pronouns and identity: A case study from a 1930s working-class community. *ICAME Journal*, 39, 1, 111–134.

Toffler, A. (1980). *The Third Wave*. New York.: Morrow.

Trudgill, P. (1972). Sex, covert prestige and linguistic change in the urban British English of Norwich. *Language in Society*, 1, 2, 179–195.

Trudgill, P. (1974). *The Social Differentiation of English in Norwich*. Cambridge: Cambridge University Press.

Van Leeuwen, T. (1996). The representation of social actors, in C. R. Caldas-Coulthard and M. Coulthard (eds) *Text and Practices: Readings in Critical Discourse Analysis*. London: Routledge, 32–70.

Wales, K. (1996). *Personal Pronouns in Present-day English*. Cambridge: Cambridge University Press.

Zappavigna, M. (2016). Social media photography: construing subjectivity in Instagram images. *Visual Communication*, 15, 3, 271–292.

Chapter 6

Online learning platforms
The Nottingham Online Business Learner English (NOBLE) corpus

In this chapter, we focus on online learning and examine a corpus of online learner comments collected from three separate deliveries of a course entitled 'How to Read Your Boss'. 'How to Read Your Boss' is a Massive Open Online Course (MOOC) generated by colleagues at the Linguistic Profiling for Professionals (LiPP) research centre at the University of Nottingham and the MOOC is hosted by The Open University Platform 'FutureLearn'. The MOOC was delivered three times: in October 2014, September 2015 and June 2016, and learner comments were collected from each iteration as a single corpus. I have labelled the corpus the 'Nottingham Online Business Learner English (NOBLE)' corpus and in the case study that follows, use methods in corpus linguistics to explore how we can evidence learning and understand more about learning processes through online forums. This chapter will also demonstrate how readers might collect and analyse their own corpus of online learner comments.

> **Task 6.1**
>
> Have you ever participated in an online learning programme?
> - What are some of the advantages of taking online courses?
> - What are some of the limitations?
> - What type of support would you look for in an online course?
> - What type of assessment would you expect to find on an online course?

6.1 Online learning

We can see how the purported virtues of the Web can be harnessed for educational purposes in that the Web brings together people from different parts of the world and from different time zones around a shared activity. That shared activity might be a niche interest or it might be a widely applicable skill or knowledge set, which can be situated and contextualised as learners work through materials in their own time and, for example, around their jobs. Online teaching can ensure that materials are up-to-date and allow learners to contact experts from around the world. Bringing together a global student cohort and a range of perspectives can promote critical thinking and reflexivity, as well as enriching discussion. Online resources can be incorporated into instructional programmes in various ways and to different degrees; courses on which all of the instruction of the content assessed by the outcome measure is delivered by the Internet are described as 'purely online' (Means et al., 2013: 6), while courses that involve a combination of online and face-to-face experiences (with 25% or more of the assessed content delivered online) can be referred to as 'blended learning' programmes. When incorporating Web-based resources into the classroom (or indeed hosting the class on the Web), educators need to consider how the technologies can support learning effectively and researchers have reiterated the importance of seeing the technology "as facilitating pedagogy, not vice-versa" (McCarthy, 2016: 3). Ally (2008: 16) points out that "it is the instructional strategy, not the technology, that influences the quality of learning" and as Clark (2001) observes, the computer is merely the vehicle that provides the processing capability and delivers the instruction to learners.

As noted above, what the Web offers is an opportunity to cultivate a diverse learning community and the expansion of online learning platforms has prompted a pedagogical shift from the transmission of knowledge towards active and interactive learning (Rudestam and Schoenholtz-Read, 2010). One important technological aspect that is influential in determining the practices of online learning and thereby the underlying pedagogy is the extent to which the activity is synchronous or asynchronous. Shotsberger (1999) argues that synchronous activity offers greater spontaneity, helps learners feel 'in sync' with others and thereby promotes collaboration. However, there is also a sense that contributors may feel under pressure to respond in a timely fashion, particularly if there is a range of language competencies (MacDonald et al., 2013; Eriksson et al., 2016). Perhaps because of time pressures, "synchronous conferences are characterized by the use of brief, rapid messages that are often superficial, socially oriented, and ambiguous, and that appear in a linear chronological rather than topical sequence" (Lapadat, 2002: 5). Asynchronous activity, on the other hand, allows for greater flexibility because learners can respond in their own time (Means et al., 2013: 9), which in turn supports more thoughtful and reflective learner participation as learners take the time to formulate their contributions clearly (Veerman and Veldhuis-Diermanse, 2001; Lapadat, 2002), leading to richer discussions involving more participants (Vonderwell et al., 2007). Lapadat (2002: 7) argues that in being able to integrate segments of the discussion into their own comments, learners can build on ideas that have been introduced in the discussion and the course more widely, "enhancing semantic cohesion across contributions and topics, and therefore potentially increasing discursive and conceptual coherence". This in turn can improve learners' engagement with and performance on the course: Sharples et al. (2016: 8) report that while "students were more satisfied with courses that had a large element of individual reading and watching of instructional videos […] students were more likely to complete courses that had more collaborative learning" and in fact, exam scores were better on courses that favoured collaborative learning. The collaborative learning approach is fundamental to the pedagogy underlying the FutureLearn platform and its MOOCs, including 'How to Read Your Boss'.

6.1.1 Massive online open courses (MOOCs)

MOOCs are defined by their size (Massive) and accessibility (Open), as well as the format (Online). Popular MOOC platforms include Coursera, edX, Udacity and FutureLearn. Coursera, edX and Udacity work closely with U.S. universities (edX with Harvard University and MIT; Udacity with Stanford University, for example) and FutureLearn is a platform owned by The Open University (U.K.) that has been hosting MOOCs in partnership with over 80 universities and other organisations since 2013. FutureLearn is a social learning platform: its approach characterised by a social constructivist pedagogy (Ferguson and Clow, 2015) that posits that learning is interactive, "technologically enhanced, distributed within a network and associated with the recognition and interpretation of patterns" (Ferguson and Clow, 2015: 51).

The MOOC design can be seen as a response to the purported shortcomings of previous distance learning approaches, such as learner isolation (Galusha, 1997), limited interaction and high dropout rates (Peters, 1992), however there have been continued concerns with dropout rates in MOOCs (Jordan, 2014; Yuan and Kim, 2014). FutureLearn reports that around a third of those who register do not actually start the course (Ferguson and Clow, 2015). The catalogue of free courses that are advertised to users may mean that enrolment operates more like bookmarking, and when it comes to the course delivery, users may have a better sense of whether they are committed to the topic or can commit the time required to participate. Initial registration therefore may not be a good indicator of who is likely to engage with and complete the course. With respect to the MOOC 'How to Read Your Boss', around 5% of those who joined the course (5.2% in 2014; 4.4% in 2015; 6.2% in 2016) unenrolled and did not actually take part. Researchers have reported that those who do post comments in the forums are far less likely to drop out than those who do not (Woodgate et al., 2015) and learners who have prior experience with online learning are more likely to post comments (Swinnerton et al., 2017). Users, it would seem, do develop an appreciation for the value of the discussion threads in enriching their learner experience.

6.1.2 How to read your boss

'How to Read Your Boss' is a FutureLearn MOOC authored by Professor Louise Mullany and delivered by her and a team of her colleagues from the University of Nottingham. It was developed to reflect the University's research interests and growing expertise in forms of business and professional communication and seen as a way to raise the profile of the University as a provider of accredited learning in these areas and in applied linguistics more generally. The development and the delivery of the MOOC coincided with the establishing of the Linguistic Profiling for Professionals (LiPP) research centre at the University of Nottingham, which offers consultancy to local SMEs alongside training packages delivered through online Continuing Professional Development (CPD) courses and practical workshops. The fundamental aim of the 'How to Read Your Boss' MOOC has been to "introduce linguistic techniques to enhance business communication" (https://www.futurelearn.com/courses/how-to-read-your-boss).

As an offering on the FutureLearn platform, the MOOC runs alongside a range of 'Business and Management' courses, including:

- a series of 'Innovation' MOOCs offered by the University of Leeds relating to specific industries alongside more transferable skills associated with starting a business such as networking, managing finances, and attracting funding (University of Leeds);
- general introductory courses such as 'Management and Leadership' (The Open University);
- more specific courses such as 'Bookkeeping for Personal and Business Accounting' (The Open University);
- language skills courses such as 'English for the Workplace' (The British Council), which is described as "for learners of English" and which helps them with "the language [they] need to find a job and successfully function in the workplace" (https://www.futurelearn.com/courses/workplace-english).

What distinguishes 'How to Read Your Boss' is the integration of findings, concepts and terminology from applied linguistics research, as generated from empirical studies of business and organisational communication. In the Introductory video to the course, author Professor Louise Mullany explains that the key aim of the course is to "provide a short introduction to some basic techniques to help raise [learners'] awareness of the language strategies that are used in [their] own workplaces", in order to help learners "enrich the communication strategies that [they] use in [their] professional lives". There are 35 units spread over a period of two weeks that cover topics such as: rapport management, face and identity, speech acts, humour and floorholding techniques (e.g. in meetings). Much of the activity across the MOOC prompts learners to reflect on their own experiences, as well as providing opportunities to apply what has been introduced on the course to practical analytical tasks. As such, it is not designed to provide instruction on the basic language skills required to participate in the world of work (as offered by the British Council, for example), but rather lends a vocabulary drawn from academic research to the experiences introduced by learners on the course as part of a toolkit to raise their awareness of their own language behaviours as well as those of their colleagues.

One of the ways through which we can evaluate the course is by looking at how learners incorporate these concepts and terms into their discussions. If learners are able to articulate or reformulate their experiences through the academic terminology introduced through the course, then we could make the case that transference and, thereby, learning has occurred. Furthermore, the discussions can provide insights into how learners process and interpret these concepts with other learners.

6.2 Evidencing learning in the NOBLE corpus

6.2.1 Technical language

'How to Read Your Boss' demonstrates the value of a 'linguistic toolkit' for understanding and discussing the importance of communication in professional contexts. The articulation of key concepts is in some part enabled by a technical vocabulary and so in this study, I examined the ways in which learners investigated this vocabulary and incorporated it into their comments. Appropriation of academic vocabulary and associated technical terms is key to demonstrating mastery and to claiming an identity as a member of a particular academic community (Li and Schmitt, 2009: 86). It is argued that a student in higher education needs to master "a core vocabulary of 2 000 high-frequency words, plus some academic words, and technical terms" (Paquot, 2010: 10). Before considering the significance of the terminology, it is first worth distinguishing between what is 'core vocabulary', what can be termed 'academic discourse' and what we might call 'technical terms'.

Paquot (2010: 9) defines academic vocabulary as "a set of lexical items that are not core words but which are relatively frequent in academic texts", though this distinction is not always clear. For example, the words 'show', 'find' and 'report' are not considered 'academic vocabulary' since they are already accounted for in 'core vocabulary', even though they feature in academic texts more frequently than the related terms 'establish', 'conclude' and 'demonstrate' (which are considered 'academic vocabulary') (Paquot, 2010: 27). 'Academic vocabulary' is distinguished from 'technical terms', since it appears "in a large proportion of academic texts, regardless of discipline". 'Technical terms' are "words whose meanings requires[sic] scientific knowledge. They are typically characterized by semantic specialization, resistance to semantic change and absence of exact synonyms" (Paquot, 2010: 13). This attests to the necessity for technical terms, since they cannot be articulated in many (if any) other ways and our creation of a technical term is with a view to provide a label for a very specific, often complex, phenomenon.

Perhaps unsurprisingly, "Technical terms occur with very high or at least moderate frequency within a very limited range of texts" (Paquot, 2010: 13), making it reasonable that speakers who do not use, engage with or produce these texts would not be familiar with such terms. In vocabulary studies, demonstrating knowledge of a word includes, for example, spelling, word parts, meaning, grammatical function and collocation (Coady, 1993; Nation, 2013), which are often tested in standard vocabulary tests. The use of vocabulary tests has raised some concerns, for example with respect to how 'deep' the learner's knowledge of the target item is and how this is indicated through such tests (Kremmel and Schmitt, 2016). Schmitt (2014) argues that to comprehend a word goes beyond recognition of the spelling and remembering its meaning. He points out that when learning a word, components such as collocation and derivative forms will be present in the learning material, but learners must know and produce all of these components independently when using the word. Schmitt (in prep.) explains that a conventional way of conceptualising vocabulary learning is from no knowledge, to receptive mastery, to productive mastery. He extends this linear process to include 'appropriacy', which involves "selecting a lexical item with the precise required semantic meaning and connotations, then being able to produce the correct form and finally being able to embed that item in context in a phraseologically-appropriate manner" (Schmitt, in prep.: 5). It would be difficult to engineer a context in which to allow learners to show this degree of vocabulary knowledge within the parameters of a MOOC, unless that was specifically one of the learning objectives of an assessment. Schmitt (in prep.: 5) suggests that testing 'appropriacy' might involve producing a scenario that constrains the lexical choice down to a single item (i.e. the piece of vocabulary we are testing) without giving it away and asking the learner to write a sentence illustrating the item for that context.

In this case study, the teaching and learning of technical vocabulary was not an explicit learning objective and no formal assessment was developed in order to test knowledge of technical terms (though an informal multiple-choice quiz allows learners to test their knowledge of key concepts introduced on the course). However, as an instructor on the course for each of its three iterations, I was aware of discussions around particular technical terms and formed an impressionistic view of some of the peer-support that emerged through the interrogation of specific vocabulary. What follows is a somewhat opportunistic inquiry of learner discussions around technical terms, through which I consider whether the corpus analysis supports my impressionistic recall of the discussion and, furthermore, what corpus analysis can reveal about the use of specific technical terms across three separate learning cohorts.

6.2.2 Compiling the NOBLE corpus

'How to Read Your Boss' was delivered over a two-week period on three separate occasions: October 2014, September 2015 and June 2016. The core learning material was the same each time but each iteration was an opportunity to work with a new cohort, who had their own perspectives on the content and their own experiences on which to draw. In 2014, there were 8,212 learners (defined by having viewed at least one learning unit on the course); with 7,369 learners in 2015 and 1,720 learners in 2016. Of these, 80% constituted what FutureLearn terms 'Active Learners', who had completed some aspect of the course; and 27% were what we can call 'Social learners', that is learners who posted at least one comment. Learners represented 182 different countries around the world and in one of the introductory units, many commenters explained that one of the reasons for participating in the course was to improve their English language competence. While this is certainly significant when considering how learners constructed their comments and perhaps adopted an academic register, it is reasonable to think that learners were equally unfamiliar with the technical terms used on the course.

Ethics

When deciding to work with learner comments it was important to revisit the ethical considerations that have been discussed in Chapter 2. Two particular aspects were of most relevance here: first, the notion of 'public versus private', since the data was only visible to those who had registered with FutureLearn and enrolled on the course. Second, it is unlikely that participants had taken part in the course primarily to be involved in research. As such, in order to treat their contributions as data, we needed to be sure that participants had an understanding of this potential use of their comments and ensure that their personal information, including their identities was protected. This was of particular concern on a course that encouraged learners to draw from their own experiences (as many MOOCs do), which could potentially implicate their colleagues or employers. On the 'How to Read Your Boss' MOOC, there was a unit that outlined expectations for participation and recommendations for getting the most out of the course; this referred to the standardised Code of Conduct outlined by FutureLearn (https://about.futurelearn.com/terms/code-of-conduct) as well as providing the following statement:

> The course will ask you to reflect upon your own experiences at work, but you must not use this as an opportunity to write down anything that could be potentially libellous, defamatory or insulting about any individual, group or organisation. You must assume that anything you write down can be read by any persons or organisations, as is the case under the Data Protection Act. Please protect the identity of all individuals, groups and organisations by not revealing their real names (https://www.futurelearn.com/courses/how-to-read-your-boss).

Learners were informed by way of the terms and conditions (https://about.futurelearn.com/terms) that MOOC activities are monitored for research purposes and through registration they provided consent for their contributions to be used in research. Learners who unregister from FutureLearn thereby withdraw their consent, however anonymised data from previous activity can still be used for research (as per the terms and conditions). FutureLearn instructs researchers to work with anonymised data. The FutureLearn policy with regard to learner comments is that it is published on the platform under a Creative Commons

License (Attribution-Non Commercial-No Derivs; BY-NC-ND), however ownership of the material remains with the author. The terms of agreement specify that learner content is licensed to the FutureLearn platform to distribute and publish the material on the site and for the purposes of research. In order to resolve the need for anonymity with recognition of the learner as producer and owner of the content, FutureLearn instructs its partners to use author IDs in citing learner content. As an example, the author's own comments on the MOOC 'How to Read Your Boss' would be cited as: https://www.futurelearn.com/courses/how-to-read-your-boss/comments/625295.

Extracting and formatting the comments

Task 6.2

Locate an online platform that enables and displays user comments. Highlight all of the comments from one page (or multiple pages if you prefer) and copy and paste them into a word processor.

- What steps would you need to take in order to produce a machine-readable corpus?
- How would you go about making any changes to the formatting? What needs to be removed? What should remain?
- How would you go about separating the content from any other meta-data or encoding?

FutureLearn provides a comments section for each learning unit, which is visible alongside the learning material for all learners. Since this is not collated as part of a larger discussion, the comments are typically related to the specific content of the unit and may even be prompted by questions introduced in that unit. The default presentation for comments is to list them in the order of most recent, though replies to specific comments appear embedded underneath the original comment. The learner is able to sort the comments to show only those that have been bookmarked; those posted by learners they are 'following', to see their own comments or to arrange by 'oldest' or 'most liked'. As this indicates, learners can Like, Bookmark and Reply to specific comments, as well as Follow other learners. This metadata, along with the learners' avatar (an image if they have uploaded one, otherwise a graphic of their initials), name and the date of the comment are visible in the comments thread. Since I was also interested in this metadata and since the comments typically only ran to a handful of pages (a page would typically display around 25 comments), I decided to simply 'copy and paste' the comments to a word processor, rather than use an automated extraction tool. Separate files were then stored for each learning unit.

Figure 6.1 demonstrates what the data from a learner comments thread might look like when copied and pasted to a word processor. Learners have already been anonymised, their user IDs provided in place of their names. From the avatars, you can see that FutureLearn displays a user's photo if provided (in this instance, the author's own) or simply provides a graphic with the user's initials (which have been changed for anonymisation). We can also see that there are a number of functions around the comment itself that we would likely want to remove prior to any corpus analysis. Some features will be hyperlinked, such as the user's avatar and username, the Follow, Like

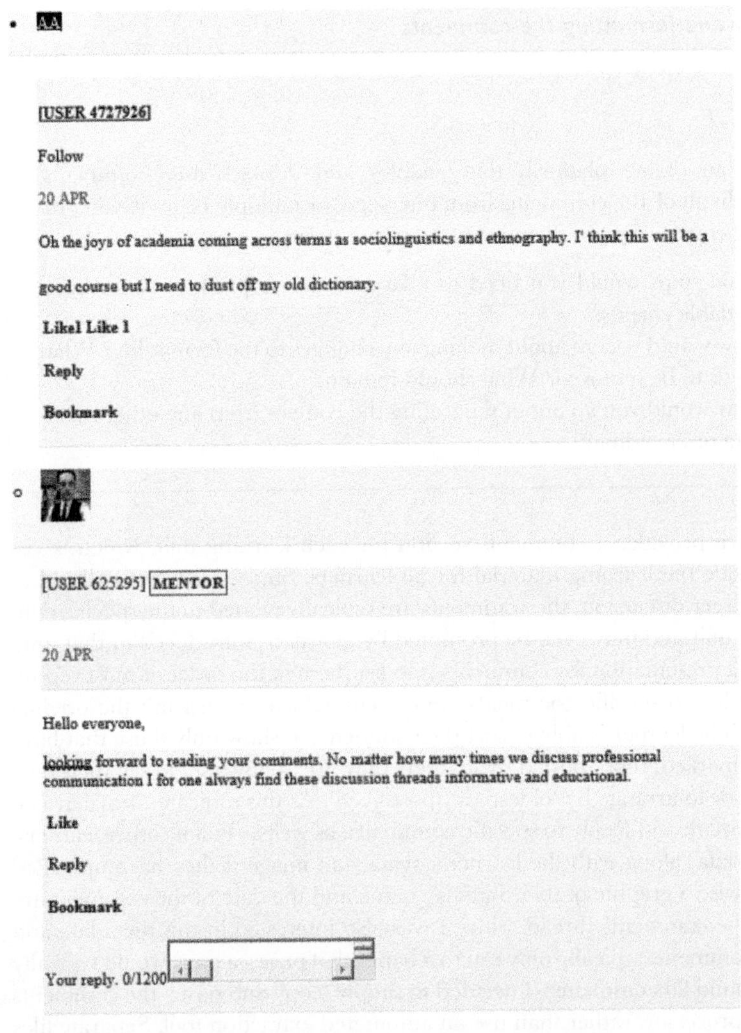

- AA

[USER 4727926]

Follow

20 APR

Oh the joys of academia coming across terms as sociolinguistics and ethnography. I' think this will be a good course but I need to dust off my old dictionary.

Like1 Like 1

Reply

Bookmark

o

[USER 625295] MENTOR

20 APR

Hello everyone,

looking forward to reading your comments. No matter how many times we discuss professional communication I for one always find these discussion threads informative and educational.

Like

Reply

Bookmark

Your reply. 0/1200

Figure 6.1 Learner comments that have been copied and pasted to a word processor.

and Bookmark functions. The 'Reply' function is hyperlinked for comments that are not already replies, otherwise the Reply text box appears for further responses. The FutureLearn discussion format only has one additional level for embedding replies; that is, comments are either originals or replies and even replies to replies are displayed at the same level as a first reply (and underneath the original comment).

Once the comment data has been copied into a word processor, it is often sensible to first click on the 'Clear all formatting' function that can be found alongside the font options in Microsoft Word. Even in a word processor, researchers can perform a number of automated 'find and replace' (Ctrl+H) procedures in order to format this type of text data for the purposes of corpus analysis. For example, by 'Selecting all' (Ctrl+A) and then pressing Ctrl+Shift+F9 the researcher can remove all hyperlinks in the document; hyperlinks can be an obstacle to the processor 'reading' the text, which is consequential for further 'find and replace' processes. It is therefore recommended that readers remove hypertext functions in their own data. Comments threads tend to follow a structural patterning, which means that even a discussion thread of hundreds or thousands of comments can be formatted semi-automatically. Pressing the pilcrow icon (¶) in Microsoft Word reveals the formatting, which can be entered into your 'find and replace' toolbar. For example, in Figure 6.1, once the formatting and hyperlinks have been cleared, everything at the bottom from 'Like' onwards can be removed (i.e. replaced with nothing) by 'finding' the following: Top of form^p Like^pBottom of Form^p Reply^pTop of Form^pBookmark^pBottom of Form. The frequent references to 'Form' indicate how the thread was structured by the host platform to support the different forms of metadata, which would change each time someone activated a Like or a Bookmark, for example. The ^p refers to paragraph breaks. This text sequence will select examples of comments that have not received any Likes and have not been Bookmarked or Replied to by the user. However, any comments that have been Liked will have a different display and the text sequence would need to be adjusted accordingly; for example, in Figure 6.1 the first comment has been Liked once and this is displayed as 'Like1 Like 1'. Researchers need to be aware of the subtle differences that are the result of user activity but nevertheless, even with minor adjustments a lot of reformatting can be completed reasonably quickly.

Researchers will need to decide if and how they want to use the metadata already attached to each comment, which can also be formatted to enable straightforward extraction. For example, as shown in Figure 6.1, a learner's username always follows an image – be it one uploaded by the user or one generated by the platform. Providing all other uses of images have been reformatted or removed (e.g. the Reply box might show up as an image), then the researcher can replace all images (by 'finding' ^g) with something like <USERNAME> to provide an initial step in annotating the data. Inserting these labels using an automated 'find and replace' can speed up the annotation process, as these can be straightforwardly separated from the message content and converted or extracted to an XML database. Through this process, I was able to compile the NOBLE Corpus comprising exclusively of comment data, as well as collating information with respect to how many comments and how often learners were posting across the three deliveries of the MOOC, which is discussed in the next section.

The content of the MOOC comments exhibited relatively few of the features associated with 'netspeak' (see Chapter 4) and, as Lapadat (2000) found, the writing in this asynchronous online learning platform largely conformed to the conventions of formal written language. This may be the result of the course being offered by a team of academics and the FutureLearn platform associating itself with university partners, thereby setting a somewhat formal tone that encouraged learners to use 'academic English'. It is also worth considering that since the course is predicated on the idea of raising learners' awareness of their language use, they might have adopted more formal (i.e. standard) language forms. This would be something to keep in mind with respect to how it might affect the social aspects of the discussion forums, particularly for those who are less confident with their language skills. As a participant in the discussions, my impression was that learners were very forthcoming and adopted a number of non-standard features that suggested a reasonably informal tone (e.g. discourse markers and contractions). Overall, relatively little standardisation was required and any normalisation seemed to be the result of typing errors or cultural variations (e.g. 'humor' and 'humour', 'organisation' and 'organization') rather than an intentional form of (online) expression.

6.3 Analysis

The NOBLE Corpus comprised 28,975 comments and 1.5 million words of data. Table 6.1 shows basic frequencies for the number of comments and number of words (tokens, as determined by WMatrix) for each delivery. Figure 6.2 shows how these comments were distributed over the 35 units, with breakdowns for each year. Figure 6.3 shows the number of words (tokens) for each comments section, which again is determined by each learning unit and broken down by year. Both graphs indicate a surge in comments in the early part of the course, with a general decline as participants moved through the learning units. There was a minor increase at the beginning of week 2, but this did not come close to the number of comments (and words) posted in the early part of week 1. This pattern held for each delivery of the MOOC.

Table 6.1 Number of comments and number of words in the NOBLE corpus

	2014	2015	2016	NOBLE
Comments	14,077	12,559	2,339	28,975
Words	741,024	629,394	128,935	1,499,353

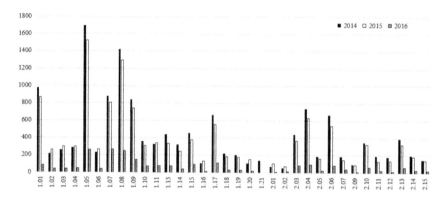

Figure 6.2 Number of comments per unit by year across the NOBLE corpus.

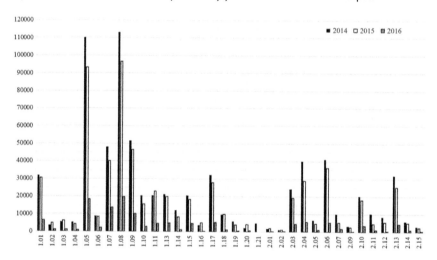

Figure 6.3 Number of words in the comments data per unit by year across the NOBLE corpus.

On the basis of the number of comments, unit 1.5 was, overall, the learning unit that elicited the largest number of comments. This unit followed the preliminaries that established how best to work with the course and introduced the teaching team; it was the first unit that attended to the topic and the first opportunity for learners to introduce themselves (beyond their names) with respect to their workplace and their position as an employee. Discussion was prompted by questions in the learning unit that asked:

- What position do you occupy in your organisation's hierarchy?
- Are you a 'boss' as well as a 'follower'?
- What terminology is adopted in your own workplace to describe job roles and how they relate to each other? Why do you think this has been adopted?

It was not surprising to see so many comments in response to these questions, since it was a straightforward way for learners to respond based on their own experience and an initial demonstration of how terminology (i.e. job titles) is important to workplace interactions. Having established a 'starting point' for learners based on personal experience, the subsequent units introduced the teaching material as generated from academic research and theory. Returning to the graphs above, unit 1.8 is of particular interest, since it consistently generated the most data in terms of number of words. This unit was concerned with the concept of 'face' and, coincidentally, was an area in which I, as a course mentor and participant in the forum, recalled particular discussions around the technical terms introduced in the unit.

Furthermore, a keyword analysis reveals that 'face' was a prominent term across the corpus, when compared with the BNC1994 Written Sampler (accessible through WMatrix). Table 6.2 shows the top 15 keywords from the NOBLE Corpus when sorted by log-likelihood (LL) and these also score highly for effect size (%DIFF). Table 6.3 shows keyword lists for the three sub-corpora from each delivery of the MOOC, demonstrating that these terms were particularly prominent across the corpus and showing the importance of 'face'. The remainder of the keywords reflect the topic of the learning materials ('boss', 'work', 'team', 'workplace') and the somewhat inevitable prominence of the first-person perspective, as shown by the high frequency of 'I' and 'my'. 'Steve', 'Michelle' and 'Matt' were characters in a role-play scenario that learners were asked to analyse.

On the basis of some preliminary corpus analysis and my own impressions of the discussion, there was a good combined rationale for investigating the term 'face' further, with specific consideration for its meaning with respect to the theoretical concepts introduced in learning unit 1.8.

Table 6.2 Keyword list for the NOBLE corpus

	Token	Occurrences	%DIFF	Log-Likelihood
1	i	54,989	417.09	**24,602.67**
2	my	21,862	641.55	**12,129.87**
3	boss	11,259	12,502.74	**10,646.54**
4	am	8,978	1,923.86	**6,954.11**
5	work	8,859	649.86	**4,942.69**
6	**face**	5,239	1,022.53	**3,456.76**
7	identity	3,743	5,070.29	**3,326.84**
8	is	28,796	89.78	**3,305.31**
9	scenario	3,159	5,1172.30	**3,107.00**
10	more	10,170	237.38	**3,106.23**
11	team	4,198	1,493.82	**3,075.88**
12	personal	3,934	1,806.00	**3,008.00**
13	think	5,139	630.05	**2,828.93**
14	workplace	2,610	1,750,001,604…	**2,611.58**
15	'm	4,558	689.11	**2,606.66**

Table 6.3 Keyword lists for the NOBLE corpus by year

2014	LL	2015	LL	2016	LL
I	18,868.92	I	18,296.36	I	5,425.27
my	912.85	my	9,446.93	boss	4,071.73
boss	8,441.95	boss	8,441.40	my	2,822.88
am	5,529.77	am	5,497.75	am	1,754.85
work	3,663.32	work	3,866.44	work	1,297.98
face	2,614.11	identity	2,774.35	workplace	1,124.37
scenario	2,570.37	**face**	2,686.72	**face**	1,032.90
identity	2,560.23	scenario	2,546.18	identity	1,000.22
team	2,546.69	personal	2,357.55	Steve	925.30
personal	2,362.56	workplace	2,300.80	team	875.05
is	2,344.47	more	2,294.10	personal	853.02
more	2,343.60	is	2,234.38	scenario	826.92
think	2,310.25	team	2,017.81	'm	793.25
Michelle	2,216.99	think	1,969.62	is	786.40
'm	2,092.28	Steve	1,869.20	Matt	756.28

6.3.1 Face

The concept of 'face' has been fundamental to studies in interactional sociolinguistics and, most explicitly, pragmatics as a core principle in (im)politeness theory. Explorations of 'face' have largely been predicated on the definition established by Goffman (1955: 307) as "the positive social value a person effectively claims for himself [sic] by the line others assume he [sic] has taken during a particular contact. Face is an image of self, delineated in terms of approved social attributes". The concept was developed as part of Brown and Levinson's (1978) 'politeness theory', which considered how our concern for 'face' influences how we construct talk. Our decision-making with respect to adopting a direct or indirect strategy for delivering messages is in part determined by our consideration for our own and others' 'face'.

As influential as Brown and Levinson's (1978) politeness theory has been, researchers have highlighted a potential Western bias (see for example: Matsumoto, 1988; Gu, 1990; Eelen, 2001). Leech (2007: 167) remarks specifically upon "their over-emphasis on face-threat and their assumptions of individualistic and egalitarian motivations, as opposed to the more group-centred hierarchy-based ethos of Eastern societies". Indeed, Matsumoto (1988: 405) reports:

> What is of paramount concern to a Japanese is not his/her own territory, but the position in relation to the others in the group and his/her acceptance by those others. Loss of Face is associated with the perception by others that one

has not comprehended and acknowledged the structure and hierarchy of the group. [...] Acknowledgement and maintenance of the relative position of others, rather than preservation of an individual's proper territory, governs all social interaction.

Similarly, Nwoye (1992) reports that for the Igbo of Nigeria, the concept of 'individual face' is subordinate to that of 'group face'. What may be thought of as 'imposition' in a Western social dynamic would be considered to be a demonstration of one's allegiance to the group in this collectivist and egalitarian society, and thereby bolster one's group face.

This concept was explored in 'How to Read Your Boss', which outlined the 'individualist' view of face – as 'personal face' – in contrast to a collectivist view of face, which is termed 'social face' or 'social identity face'. The term 'social identity face' is part of Spencer-Oatey's (2005: 106) 'rapport management' model and is said to involve "any group that a person is a member of and is concerned about. This can include small groups like one's family, and larger groups like one's ethnic group, religious group, or nationality group". In unit 1.8, learners were asked the following questions and invited to comment in the discussion:

- Is 'personal face' or 'social identity face' more appropriate for your workplace? What public self-image do you think you have at work, either individually or collectively?
- How do you think your boss views your public self-image?
- What would you like to change about your public self-image at work, if anything?

Having established 'face' as a keyword, the collocates of 'face' also give us some indication of how it was used. Table 6.4 shows the collocates with the highest MI scores, based on a collocation span of 5 words either side of the node word and a minimum frequency threshold of seven. A number of these collocates reflect the fact that learners often copied the questions into the comments to show how and where they were addressing each bullet point; this is shown most explicitly in '1.is' which is a reproduction of point 1. Nevertheless, whether learners were reproducing the questions or adopting the same terms, their responses were oriented around what is 'appropriate' or 'suitable', which type of face is 'predominant' and that the concept was discussed in terms of 'social identity', 'social' and 'personal' face. There are also terms such as 'poker (face)', 'loss (of face)' and 'save (face)', which show that learners were bringing together the theoretical terminology with the more colloquial expressions of the concept, demonstrating how the principles are expressed in 'lay' terms. Finally, the prominence of 'overlap' and 'distinction' indicate that there was some interrogation of the concept, as learners questioned the distinction between 'personal' and 'social' face and this is explored further below.

Table 6.4 Collocates of 'face' in the NOBLE corpus

Position	Collocate	MI
L	social identity	8.594
L	I.is	8.108
L	poker	8.030
R	predominant	7.561
R	appropriate	7.456
L	social	7.434
L	personal	7.390
L	identity	6.723
L	reveal	6.585
R	paramount	6.585
R	applicable	6.568
L	expressive	6.456
L	loss	6.386
R	overlap	6.343
L	save	6.336
L	concept	6.123
R	suitable	6.083
L	losing	6.069
L	lose	6.060
L	distinction	6.044
	face	6.014
L	identify	6.010

Task 6.3

How common are the expressions relating to 'losing face', 'saving face' and 'poker face' in general English?

- Choose one of the corpora we have looked at already (e.g. BNC1994, COCA) and find out how common these expressions are
- Make sure to include the different ways of expressing this in your search e.g. 'losing face', 'save (one's) face'
- Can you determine anything else about how these expressions are used, based on this initial analysis?

Social (identity) face

We can think of 'social (identity) face' as a technical term, referring to Paquot's (2010) definition. If we refer to the BNC1994 and COCA, we can see that these terms are not part of general (British/U.S.) English (see Table 6.5).

Table 6.5 'Face' terms across the BNC1994, COCA and the NOBLE corpus

	BNC1994	COCA	NOBLE
Face	32,434	235,501	5,884
social face	0	0	626
social identity face	0	0	1,071

Furthermore, the distribution of the terms across the corpus also suggests that it was not – nor did it become – a regular feature of the learners' discourse. Figure 6.4 shows the relative frequency of the term 'face' across the learning units and by year and similarly, Figure 6.5 shows the distribution of 'social face'. The term 'social identity face' only appeared in three units for the entire corpus: the three versions of learning unit 1.8 (October 2014, September 2015, June 2016).

The fact that the terms 'social face' and 'social identity face' were generally not used in other comments sections across the MOOC offers little indication that the learners incorporated these terms into their vocabulary, or at least did not articulate the concept through these terms. Given the design of the MOOC, from an educator perspective we might expect learners to use what they have been taught in earlier units in subsequent discussions, so this also raises questions about whether learners found connections between the theoretical concepts and the more practical analytical tasks that appeared later in the MOOC. In fact, when 'social face' was applied in the analytical tasks (for example, units 2.04) it seemed to be conflated with the idea of showing friendliness (sociability) through facial expressions.

Figure 6.6 shows the collocation network for 'social' in relation to 'face' and its surrounding collocates. This shows that the 'social' aspect of face was most

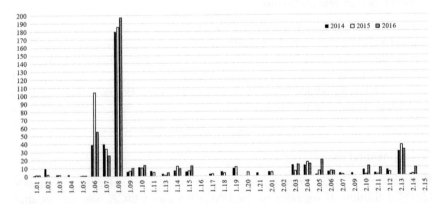

Figure 6.4 Relative frequency of 'face' by learning unit and year.

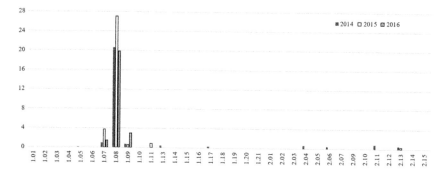

Figure 6.5 Relative frequency of 'social face' by learning unit and year.

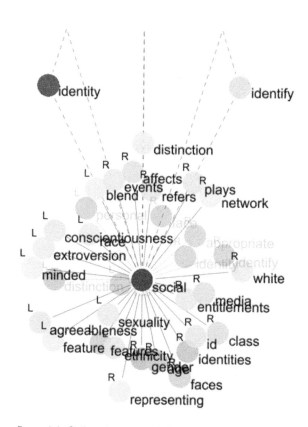

Figure 6.6 Collocation network for 'social' as extended from 'face'.

commonly articulated in relation to demographic categories such as 'sexuality', 'gender', 'ethnicity', 'white', 'age' and 'class'. What is not explicitly clear is whether learners also conceived of 'social face' operating at a more local level, relating to their workplace teams for example, as per Spencer-Oatey's (2005) definition. Figure 6.7 shows the collocates of 'social face', where 'corporate', 'clients' and 'groups' are shown to be prominent. This indicates some consideration of groups with respect to their workplace practices along with those larger social categories.

Returning to the collocates for 'face' allows us to consider how learners were 'making sense' of the concept and where there was potential for misunderstanding by looking at the collocate 'distinction'. 'Distinction' was also shown to be a strong collocate of the term 'social identity face' (MI: 7.63) and the word 'difference' collocated with 'social face' (MI: 5.24). Table 6.6 shows concordances for 'face' and 'social identity face' with the word 'distinction', along with concordances of 'social face' that included 'difference'. These examples show that there were different types of 'distinction'/'difference' that related to understanding (see examples 4, 8, 10, 11, 12, 14) and evaluation or perception (see examples 3, 7, and 9, 18). Some people rejected the distinction; others felt that their participation in the discussion was hindered by a lack of understanding, while some celebrated the distinction as an acknowledgement of culture (examples 2 and 6). There were also explicit invitations for other participants (mentors and other learners) to help in clarifying the distinction (examples 13, 14, 15) and we might read examples 1 and 10 as more implicit prompts for help. What this indicates is that learners were personalising this concept and their 'acceptance' of it was based on how it corresponded with their own worldview. As such, if it was a way to account for perceived cultural differences, it was celebrated; if there seemed little relevance in the distinction (which may be the result of being immersed in a strong individualist culture, for example), it was not accepted. For those who expressed a

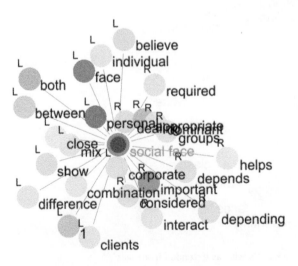

Figure 6.7 Collocation network for 'social face'.

Table 6.6 Concordances of 'social (identity) face' that include 'distinction'/'difference'

1	2014_1-07	I was just wondering whether there is a distinction between the	**Face**	one identifies him/herself with and the genuine self.
2	2015_1-07	I loved the distinction about personal and social	**face.**	Romania is more inclined towards a collectivistic approach, so the social face is
3	2014_1-08	1. I'm not sure I agree with the distinction between personal and social	**face.**	Face only exists in relation to others (that is, in a social setting),
4	2014_1-08	I'm not sure if I fully understand the distinction between personal	**face**	or social identity face at this stage, but social identity seems to require
5	2014_1-08	but a clear distinction between office and home	**face**	prevents boundaries becoming blurred. I think that it is helpful
6	2014_1-08	The distinction between "personal" and "social identity"	**"face"**	highlights how face varies across cultures.
7	2014_1-08	based on my own experience, there is not a clear distinction between personal	**face**	and social identity face since I consider myself similar to the others and
8	2015_1-08	I'm not sure I (yet) get this distinction between "personal	**face"**	and "social face" and so am hard pressed to say which of those
9	2015_1-08	I don't draw much of a distinction between personal	**face**	and social identity face. I aspire to be about the same in both
10	2014_1-08	I'm not sure on the distinction between "personal" and "social identity"	**face**	so I don't feel informed enough to answer the question set.
11	2014_1-08	hi [NAME] i also don't understand the difference between personal and	**social face.**	I would have thought that the face concept would be able to encompass both personal
12	2014_1-08	Ok, still struggling with the difference between personal and	**social face,**	but, assuming that social identity face relates to hierarchy, deference, formality
13	2014_1-08	Can someone please further explain the "personal face" and	**"social face"**	with examples and the difference

(Continued)

Table 6.6 Continued

14	2014_1-08	I don't feel I fully understand the difference between personal and	social face.	Any mentor's want to jump in?
15	2014_1-08	Would somebody explain the difference between Personal Face and	Social Face	to me? Or point me in the direction of some definitions and explanations?
16	2015_1-08	I'm glad someone else is struggling with the difference between "personal face" and	"social face".	I also like your remarks about the expectation for women to take a lot of
17	2015_1-08	If I've understood the difference between personal &	social face	correctly, then maybe personal face is more appropriate in my workplace
18	2015_1-08	I don't think there is a huge difference between my	social face	and work face- I love and live my work and would often introduce personal examples

limited comprehension of the distinction, there did at least seem to be a willingness to participate in discussion and develop their understanding, sometimes by explicit invitation. This shows that learners recognised the value of peer (and mentor) support and even found opportunities to bond through the shared 'struggle' with the technical terms (see examples 16 and 11). By pre-empting their comment with an admission of this struggle with comprehension, a learner could in effect protect their own face by instructing other learners to read their post with this in mind, thereby mitigating the level of criticism they might otherwise receive, on the basis of their perceived level of comprehension.

6.3.2 Interactivity

Exploration of the interrogation of the term 'social (identity) face' has shown that learners used the discussion to articulate and to check their level of understanding of the concepts introduced in the learning materials. This attests, to some degree, to the pedagogy of FutureLearn's approach to online learning that emphasises interactivity and discussion. Zhao et al. (2014) identify three different degrees of participation: 'participation' may involve posting independent messages; 'interaction' might involve a posting and a response from a peer, but with little or no follow-up; 'collaboration' involves a more substantial 'back-and-forth' between a learner and a peer via sequential comments. We can provide some quantitative indication of the degree of participation in discussion based on some descriptive statistics of the comments threads.

For example, looking at the number of commenters (Table 6.7) we can see how many people were involved in the discussions, at least at the level of 'participation' (Zhao et al., 2014). These findings are consistent with Swinnerton et al. (2017), who reported on learner activity across nine FutureLearn MOOCs and found that 32.1% of learners made at least one comment.

As has been shown above, unit 1.8 elicited the greatest number words across the MOOC (and the second-highest number of comments after unit 1.5). The data shows that 22.38% of comments were posted as replies (2014: 17.17%; 2015: 18.64%; 2016: 31.33%), which was consistent with the average across the MOOC (18.78%). While this is only a superficial indicator of engagement, it does at least suggest a move from 'participation' to 'interaction' (Zhao et al., 2014). In order to determine whether learners engage in 'collaboration' (Zhao et al., 2014), we might look at the comments from a more interactional perspective, drawing on principles of conversation analysis, for example, to see how learning can be observed at a turn-by-turn level.

We can get an initial sense of the qualitative aspects of the replies through a keyword analysis. Comments on the FutureLearn platform are displayed as either new responses (i.e. not replies), which we can label 'Level 1', or as replies to previous comments ('Level 2'). Table 6.8 shows the top keywords (according to LL) for Level 1 and Level 2 comments collected from unit 1.8 respectively, when compared with the BNC1994 Written Sampler. Using a third reference corpus allows

Table 6.7 Learner activity in terms of number of comments

Number of	Commenters	Learners posting only one comment	Learners posting 10+ comments
2014	2,044	739 (36.15%)	314 (15.36%)
2015	2,282	728 (31.90%)	387 (16.96%)
2016	380	118 (31.05%)	76 (20.00%)

Table 6.8 Keywords for new comments (Level 1) and replies (Level 2) compared with the BNC1994 Written Sampler

Level 1 Keyword	LL	%DIFF	Level 2 Keyword	LL	%DIFF
identity	4,129.42	12,971.58	hi	363.29	37,769.16
boss	5,061.86	12,890.17	i_agree	379.22	33,148.22
personal	6,947.87	7,946.52	personal	756.20	4,012.92
face	12,018.36	6,226.44	face	1,577.38	3,761.01
social	5,956.30	5,187.95	social	566.97	2,491.01
public	3,852.92	2,480.98	am	445.49	1,484.93
am	3,580.91	2,272.99	work	463.17	764.03
my	13,955.53	1,474.07	my	516.21	447.63
work	5,089.50	1,368.49	i	1,848.77	445.57
i	15,564.78	611.34	you	628.20	304.95

Table 6.9 A comparison of keywords for Level 1 and Level 2 comments

Level 1 Keyword	LL	%DIFF	Level 2 Keyword	LL	%DIFF
2	145.58	96.72	Sarah	51.49	9,839.38
self-image	180.01	93.72	hi	188.16	4,869.69
I	130.10	93.53	thanks	113.69	4,727.70
appropriate	117.65	87.49	thank_you	73.78	2,207.36
public	210.51	83.57	i_agree	146.93	1,451.38
image	105.22	77.29	yes	73.31	838.16
boss	121.89	66.79	're	52.83	471.05
identity	94.10	65.33	you	427.88	237.20
my	459.39	65.21	it	101.56	81.15
face	89.35	38.97	the	52.97	30.24

us to identify what is consistent between the two sub-corpora, as well as what might differ. The keywords are sorted by %DIFF i.e. in order of the difference in frequency between the data and the reference corpus.

Perhaps because of the specialisation of the topic (and because unit 1.8 elicited the most words), many of the keywords are the same and also keywords for the corpus as a whole (as shown above in Table 6.2), including: 'I', 'my', 'am', 'work', 'face' and 'personal'. In comparing Level 1 and Level 2 keywords, what stands out is the prominence of 'you', 'i_agree' and 'hi' in the Level 2 comments, which demonstrate a shift from the first person to the second person, expressions of agreement and a more dialogic approach. Table 6.9 shows the keywords for Level 1 and Level 2 comments when compared directly and this further highlights the more conversational features of replies through 'thanks', 'thank_you' and 'yes'. This shows that learners were keen to show agreement and positivity in their replies, which appear more informal since they may be addressed to specific learners. Level 1 comments more clearly adopt the terms prompted in the learning materials (and the specific question prompts) and since they are less likely to be directed at any specific other users, do not exhibit the same discursive features.

6.4 Discussion

This case study of the NOBLE Corpus was an opportunity to explore the nature of online learning and, in particular, the discussions that learners engage in as part of an online delivery platform. Through corpus analysis, there are some indications of the ways in which learners are interacting with one another and of the problem-solving that is going on as learners process technical terms introduced in the learning materials. Returning to models of vocabulary learning (e.g. Schmitt, 2014), we can see from the data that learners on the MOOC were very much in the early stages of acquisition with respect to the technical term 'social (identity) face'. It is reasonable to assume little or no knowledge of the term prior to enrolment on the course, since it is not part of a core vocabulary of general English discourse (as indicated by its absence in COCA and the BNC1994). What was shown in the data is that among the learning cohort, there was a range of mastery that extended from some challenges with receptive mastery (understanding the term as it used in context) to a reasonable demonstration of productive mastery (learners were using the term and discussing it in relation to associated concepts). This may have reflected the different degrees to which learners found the concept to be pertinent to their experiences, as it was shown that some rejected or problematised this distinction. The fact that the term was generally not used outside of the specific learning unit for which it was the topical focus offers little indication that learners would reach a level of 'appropriacy' and therefore only limited evidence that the term was 'learned'. One of the issues here might be the presentation, in that learners were introduced to a concept of social face with respect to collectivist principles and in contrast to 'personal face' (as individualist), but then asked about 'social identity face', which comes from a model in which it is not positioned within this dichotomy (Spencer-Oatey, 2005). If we want to support learners in adopting technical terms, perhaps it would be beneficial to offer a standardised vocabulary (i.e. social face or social identity face) with clear definition.

The investigation of this term and its interrogation by learners did allow us to observe some of the interactional behaviours of online learning, as participants articulated their efforts to understand the concept and even called on other learners to help them. We also saw a glimpse of how dialogue is facilitated in the replies to comments, where learners expressed agreement and gratitude, adopting a more conversational tone. Renshaw (2004) offers a comprehensive account of the development of dialogic learning, from Socrates, Freire's work in Brazil in the 1960s, Bakhtin's 'dialogism' and Vygotsky's cultural theory of learning, before introducing an analytical model for investigating learning and instruction as an inherently dialogic process. This would offer a rich theoretical perspective through which to expand this research, but it may benefit from an approach designed specifically to investigate turn-by-turn interactions and this is where corpus linguistics might operate effectively in combination with discourse analytic approaches. Guiller and Durndell (2006), for example, make some useful observations about conversational strategies with respect to gendered interactional styles in an online psychology course. Here, we were able to see some of the features of online learning that enable participants to engage with (potentially challenging) technical terms and find personal relevance in academic concepts, as well as working with their peers to develop their understanding.

Summary

One of the affordances of the Web is the capacity to bring people together around a shared interest. For educators, this relates to the dissemination of ideas and the opportunity to work with large and widespread student cohorts. For learners, the opportunity to take courses offered by experts from around the globe and work with peers from an array of backgrounds has generally been celebrated as a fundamental asset of online learning spaces. In this case study, learners were brought together to discuss their experiences of work and communication in the workplace. The analysis has shown that learners participated in discussion as a way to demonstrate their understanding and to process theoretical concepts in dialogue with their peers. The corpus analysis supported an investigation of a feature of the discussions that had been observed by the author as a participant, as well as highlighting some of the patterns associated with learner comments and replies.

References

Ally, M. (2008). Foundations of educational theory for online learning, in T. Anderson (ed.) *The Theory and Practice of Online Learning*. Second Edition. Athabasca University, Alberta: AU Press, 15–44.

Brown, P. and Levinson, S. (1978). Universals in language usage: Politeness phenomena, in E. Goody (ed.) *Questions and politeness: Strategies in social interaction*. Cambridge: Cambridge University Press, 56–311.

Clark, R. E. (2001). A summary of disagreements with the 'mere vehicles' argument, in R. E. Clark (ed.) *Learning from Media: Arguments, Analysis and Evidence*. Greenwich: Information Age Publishing, 125–136.

Coady, J. (1993). Research on ESL/EFL vocabulary acquisition: Putting it in context, in T. Huckin, M. Haynes and J. Coady (eds) *Second Language Reading and Vocabulary Learning*. Norwood: Ablex Publishing Corp., 3–23.

Eelen, G. (2001). *A Critique of Politeness Theory*. Manchester: St Jerome Publishing.

Eriksson, T., Adawi, T. and Stöhr, C. (2016) "Time is the bottleneck": A qualitative study exploring why learners drop out of MOOCs. *Journal of Computing in Higher Education*, 29, 1, 133–146.

Ferguson, R. and Clow, D. (2015). Examining engagement: analysing learner subpopulations in massive open online courses (MOOCs). *5th International Learning Analytics and Knowledge Conference (LAK15)*. 16–20 March 2015. Poughkeepsie, New York, U.S.A., 51–58.

Galusha, J. M. (1997). Barriers to learning in distance education. *Interpersonal Computing & Technology*, 5, 3–4, 6–14.

Goffman, E. (1955). On face-work: an analysis of ritual elements in social interaction. *Psychiatry: Journal for the Study of Interpersonal Processes*, 18, 3, 213–231.

Gu, Y. G. (1990). Politeness phenomena in modern Chinese. *Journal of Pragmatics*, 14, 2, 237–257.

Guiller, J. and Durndell, A. (2006). 'I totally agree with you': gender interactions in educational online discussion groups. *Journal of Computer Assisted Learning*, 22, 5, 368–381.

Jordan, K. (2014). Initial trends in enrolment and completion of Massive Open Online Courses. *The International Review of Research in Open and Distance Learning*, 15, 1, 133–160.

Kremmel, B. and Schmitt, N. (2016). Interpreting vocabulary test scores: What do various item formats tell us about learners' ability to employ words? *Language Assessment Quarterly*, 13, 4, 377–392.

Lapadat, J. C. (2000). *Teaching Online: Breaking New Ground in Collaborative Thinking*. New York: ERIC Clearinghouse on Information & Technology.

Lapadat, J. C. (2002). Written interaction: A key component in online learning. *Journal of Computer-Mediated Communication*, 7, 4, 1–16.

Leech, G. (2007). Politeness: is there an East-West divide? *Journal of Politeness Research*, 3, 2, 167–206.

Li, J. and Schmitt, N. (2009). The acquisition of lexical phrases in academic writing: A longitudinal case study. *Journal of Second Language Writing*, 18, 2, 85–102.

MacDonald, P., García-Carbonell, A. and Carot-Sierra, J. M. (2013). Computer learner corpora: Analysing interlanguage errors in synchronous and asynchronous communication. *Language Learning & Technology*, 17, 2, 36–56.

Matsumoto, Y. (1988). Re-examination of the universality of face: politeness phenomena in Japanese. *Journal of Pragmatics*, 12, 4, 403–426.

McCarthy, M. (ed.) (2016). *The Cambridge Guide to Blended Learning for Language Teaching*. Cambridge: Cambridge University Press.

Means, B., Toyama, Y., Murphy, R. and Baki, M. (2013). The effectiveness of online and blended learning: A meta-analysis of the literature. *Teachers College Record*, 115, 3, 1–47.

Nation, I. S. P. (2013). *Learning Vocabulary in Another Language*. Second Edition. Cambridge: Cambridge University Press.

Nwoye, O. (1992). Linguistic politeness and socio-cultural variations on the notion of face. *Journal of Pragmatics*, 18, 4, 309–328.

Paquot, M. (2010). *Academic Vocabulary in Learner Writing: From Extraction to Analysis*. London: Bloomsbury.

Peters, O. (1992). Some observations on dropping out in distance education. *Distance Education*, 13, 2, 234–269.

Renshaw, P. D. (2004). Dialogic teaching, learning and instruction: Theoretical roots and analytical frameworks, in van der Linden, J. and Renshaw, P. (eds) *Dialogic Learning: Shifting Perspectives to Learning, Instruction, and Teaching*. London: Kluwer Academic Publishers, 1–16.

Rudestam, K. E. and Schoenholtz-Read, J. (2010). The flourishing of adult online education: An overview, in K. E. Rudestam and J. Schoenholtz-Read (eds) *Handbook of Online Learning*. Los Angeles: Sage, 1–18.

Schmitt, N. (2014). Size and depth of vocabulary knowledge: What the research shows. *Language Learning*, 64, 4, 913–951.

Schmitt, N. (in preparation). Understanding vocabulary acquisition and instruction: A research agenda.

Sharples, M., de Roock, R., Ferguson, R., Gaved, M., Herodotou, C., Koh, E., Kukulska-Hulme, A., Looi, C.-K., McAndrew, P., Rienties, B., Weller, M. and Wong, L. H. (2016). Innovating Pedagogy 2016: Open University. *Innovation Report 5*. Milton Keynes: The Open University. Available at: https://iet.open.ac.uk/file/innovating_pedagogy_2016.pdf, accessed 5 May 2018.

Shotsberger, P. G. (1999). Forms of synchronous dialogue resulting from web-based professional development, in J. Price (ed.) *Proceedings of Society for Information Technology & Teacher Education International Conference 1999*. Chesapeake, Virginia, U.S.A.: AACE, 1777–1782.

Spencer-Oatey, H. (2005). (Im)politeness, face and perceptions of rapport: unpacking their bases and interrelationships. *Journal of Politeness Research*, 1, 1, 95–119.

Swinnerton, B., Hotchkiss, S. and Morris, N. P. (2017). Comments in MOOCs: who is doing the talking and does it help? *Journal of Computer Assisted Learning*, 33, 1, 51–64.

Veerman, A. and Veldhuis-Diermanse, E. (2001). Collaborative learning through computer-mediated communication in academic education, in P. Dillenbourg, A. Eurelings and K. Hakkarainen (eds) *European Perspectives on Computer-Supported Collaborative Learning: Proceedings of the First European Conference on CSCL.* 22–24 March 2001. McLuhan Institute, University of Maastricht, The Netherlands, 625–632.

Vonderwell, S., Liang, X. and Alderman, K. (2007). Asynchronous discussions and assessment in online learning. *Journal of Research on Technology in Education*, 39, 3, 309–328.

Woodgate, A., Macleod, H., Scott, A.-M. and Haywood, J. (2015). Differences in online study behaviour between subpopulations of MOOC learners. *Education XXI*, 18, 2, 147–163.

Yuan, J. and Kim, C. (2014). Guidelines for facilitating the development of learning communities in online courses. *Journal of Computer Assisted Learning*, 30, 3, 220–232.

Zhao, H., Sullivan, K. P. H. and Mellenius, I. (2014). Participation, interaction, and social presence; An exploratory study of collaboration in online peer review groups. *British Journal of Educational Technology*, 45, 5, 807–819.

Chapter 7

Online user comments
A corpus of the responses to news on antimicrobial resistance (AMR)

This chapter presents an application of the USAS (introduced in Chapter 3) to investigate user comments sections – also known as 'below the line' comments – discussing public health. Through a corpus analysis of groups of words of similar semantic meaning, this study captures the key themes of extended online discussions to consider the dialogue between journalists and the public in understanding complex global issues; in this instance, antimicrobial resistance (AMR). This case study offers a comparison of comments threads taken from *The Daily Mail* and *The Guardian* in response to reports of 'super-gonorrhoea' and what it means for safe sexual practices, given the lack of a treatment as a result of AMR. This allows us to consider how different publications report the news and how their readers engage in debates around the topic.

7.1 Engagement with news on the Web

The Web has undoubtedly changed the ways in which we access all kinds of information, our news being a prime example. News can be disseminated at all hours and, in theory, in all locations and the 'newness' of our news can be maximised through Rich Site Summary (RSS) feeds, for example, which collect together updates from a range of Web sources on a specified topic. There is an increased level of personalisation with news information, as users manage such feeds, as geolocation capabilities helped to identify what is local to the user and as users refer to a wider range of sources for their news, including social media (Boczkowski et al., 2016; Gottfried and Shearer, 2016). However, this move towards personalisation introduces various types of filtering (by the platform algorithms or by user preferences) that can lead to 'echo chambers' or 'filter bubbles' (Sunstein, 2001), where users are insulated from contrary perspectives and engage only with like-minded people. Furthermore, though this may elevate the frequency and amount of news we can access, because we no longer need to seek out our news, this has raised concerns for the degree to which the public engages with the news, which is purported to be more of an 'ambient journalism' (Hermida, 2010) or what Boczkowski et al. (2016) refer to as 'incidental news'. Accessing news via social media "un-differentiates news from other types of information content, such as postings from friends and family" and "young users click on news items sporadically, if at all, and engage with them only superficially on most occasions" (Boczkowski et al., 2016: 1789).

This limited engagement with the news is particularly concerning in the age of 'fake news' and 'alternative facts' (McNair, 2018). The concept of 'fake news' was articulated in a 2014 *Washington Post* article in reference to 'serial hoaxer' Paul Horner and the 'fake news industry': "a crop of Web sites dedicated solely to passing off fact as fiction, for the resulting ad revenue" (https://www.washingtonpost.com/news/the-intersect/wp/2014/10/21/this-is-not-an-interview-with-banksy/?noredirect=on&utm_term=.65599751d3c3). By December 2016, *The Guardian* was reporting on it as a global political phenomenon (https://www.theguardian.com/media/2016/dec/02/fake-news-facebook-us-election-around-the-world) and Mark Davies determined, through an analysis of the NOW Corpus, that 'fake news' was the 'Word of the Year' 2017 (https://corpus.byu.edu/now/). The initial spike in the use of the term came at the start of November 2016, during the U.S. presidential elections that saw Donald Trump lead the Republicans to victory and many will associate that particular campaign with the concretisation of the concept of 'fake news' (Allcott and Gentzkow, 2017). Trump, however, used the term not in reference to unregulated Web news services but to the likes of the BBC, the *New York Times*, the *Washington Post*, MSNBC for example, for publishing news of which he simply disapproved (McNair, 2018: 2). This has raised concerns about how members of the public come to understand the term and whether they are encouraged to be dismissive of contrary views, rather than of inaccurate news stories.

Task 7.1

Given its prominence in 2017, is the term 'fake news' still used (i.e. at the time of reading) and how is it used? Search the NOW Corpus for the use of the term 'fake news' in the last six months. How does this compare with figures for 2017? Is the use of this term still on the rise?

Look at the concordance lines for 'fake news'. Do you notice any patterns with how and where it is being used? For example, is it associated with particular individuals? Is it used in quotation marks? Does it only appear in certain types of publication?

You will find a commentary for this task at the end of the book.

Readers' awareness of the potential for 'fake news' may in turn increase their participation; Fletcher and Park (2017) found that those with low levels of trust in the news media are more likely to engage in various forms of online news participation, perhaps to authenticate the news they are reading, for example, by cross-checking various news sources (Tandoc Jr et al., 2017). There are various ways in which users can participate in the news; Jönsson and Örnebring (2011) for example, distinguish between low-participation in the form of features of personalisation (that only apply to that user e.g. RSS feeds) and polls (where contributions are aggregated); medium-participation, which is determined by existing content and actively solicited; and high-participation, where materials are not actively solicited. This, for example, would distinguish forum posts (where the topic is not pre-determined and so high-participation) from user comments following a blog post (medium-participation). It was in the early years of the Web that the potential for ordinary users to contribute to the informational content of the Web, including its news, was demonstrated. Images relating to the comet Shoemaker-Levy 9's collision with Jupiter in July 1994 were available on the Internet hours before they were broadcast through more conventional news media (Barry, 2017). This showed that users could not only participate in the discursive construction of news stories but to some extent, contribute to the production of news materials, and now it is commonplace to see images that have been taken by eye witnesses through their smartphones embedded within mainstream news articles and attributed to users by way of their social media profile (a notable example being images of a commercial aeroplane forced to land in the Hudson River in 2009).

7.1.1 User comments

In addition to providing opinions or asking questions, for example, the user comments section enables members of the public to regulate news coverage and hold journalists accountable, even providing corrections (Bode and Vraga, 2015). Graham and Wright (2015: 333) report that readers use the comments section "to both challenge and provide alternative media discourses by putting forward competing ideas and sources, thereby exposing participants, readers, and journalists to new ideas and arguments and helping to create a more inclusive news product". This, the sense of losing some authority and control over the news (Lewis, 2012), and the perception that user comments are offensive, poor in quality, untrustworthy and unrepresentative of the public (Bergström and Wadbring, 2015) have discouraged (some) journalists from fully engaging with the feature. However, user comments can be of benefit to journalists: providing opportunities to reflect on their writing, to receive feedback and to generate leads on further material (Graham and Wright, 2015). They are, therefore, a rich resource for investigating the ways in which readers contribute to the discursive construction of the news, as well as the journalistic practices behind it.

7.2 Corpus approaches to user comments

7.2.1 Examples of comments corpora

Researchers have begun to compile and analyse corpora of user comments, extending the application of corpus linguistics approaches to forms of media discourse. The Yahoo News Annotated Comments Corpus (YNACC) is a corpus of 522,000 comments, a sample of which has been annotated for sentiment, persuasiveness and tone (Napoles et al., 2017). The SENSEI Annotated Corpus is a collection of 1,845 user comments in response to articles from *The Guardian* that have been manually annotated to generate topic summaries (Barker and Gaizauskas, 2016). Baker and McGlashan (forthcoming) collected a corpus of *Daily Express* articles and user comments over a 13-year period to examine the representation of Romanians in the lead-up to the Brexit vote in the U.K. Through a keyword and cluster analysis, they report that through user comments, readers engage in 'decoding' work of the initial article, expanding on what is 'meant' at a more interpretative level and using the content to then support certain political agenda (in this instance, voting for a particular political party). They also found that comments used more inflammatory, emotive and colloquial language than the article, albeit with respect to the same topic (Baker and McGlashan, forthcoming).

The SFU Opinion and Comments Corpus (SOCC) is a substantial corpus of 10,339 opinion articles and 663,173 comments posted in response to the articles published in the Canadian newspaper *The Globe and Mail* between 2012 and 2016 (Kolhatkar et al., 2018) that is available to download as a large singular corpus or as separate sub-corpora (i.e. articles, comments or comments threads only) (https://github.com/sfu-discourse-lab/SOCC). The comments corpus alone comprises 37.6 million words and was used as a reference corpus for this study. In their own analysis of the corpus, Kolhatkar et al. (2018) annotated the comments for 'constructiveness' and 'toxicity', extending the work of Kolhatkar and Taboada (2017), who had already piloted this annotation scheme on a sample of the user comment data. 'Constructiveness' was linked to argument quality and the authors refer to the features of argumentative discourse relations as described in Joty et al. (2015) (Cause, Comparison, Condition, Contrast, Evaluation and Explanation) to identify 'constructiveness' in their comments corpus. 'Toxicity' was evaluated on a scale (Not toxic, Mildly toxic, Toxic, Very toxic), on the basis of features such as anger and frustration (Mild), sarcasm and ridicule (Toxic), or verbal abuse, offensive comments and hate speech (Very Toxic). Kolhatkar and Taboada (2017: 15) found that constructive comments were just as likely to be 'toxic' (or 'not toxic') as non-constructive comments and even that some 'toxic' comments were also deemed constructive. Kolhatkar et al.'s (2018) annotation scheme achieved 87.88% agreement for 'constructiveness' and 81.82% for 'toxicity' among the project's 'crowd annotators', though when the researchers asked a professional moderator to code the comments for 'constructiveness', they agreed with the crowd annotators 77.93% of the time. This type of manual annotation is required in order to evaluate particular qualities (in this case, 'constructiveness' and 'toxicity'), but we can also refer to automated tagging software to provide more general annotation, as with the UCREL Semantic Analysis System (USAS).

7.2.2 UCREL semantic analysis system (USAS)

The principles of USAS were introduced in Chapter 3; in short, it is a system of annotation that automatically categorises tokens of a corpus based on their semantic meaning. These categories can then be measured for keyness, following the same process for keywords that involves comparison with a reference corpus. The two main advantages of analysing keyness at the level of semantic category (as opposed to individual words) are outlined by Baker (2006), who explains that meaning might be articulated through various words (e.g. the concept of 'largeness' through the words 'big', 'huge', 'great', 'massive' etc.) such that the individual words in themselves are not used regularly enough to feature high on a keyword list and so might be overlooked. Furthermore, keyword analysis typically generates a far greater number of items than it is possible for the researcher to analyse in full and so by collating words of similar meaning, researchers can focus their efforts on a smaller set of features whilst still attending to (some of) the breadth of the phraseology.

Piao et al. (2004) found the USAS tagger to have 95.38% lexical coverage of a narrow domain corpus comprising journalistic reports from the U.K. Press Association on law/court stories from the METER Corpus and Potts (2015) uses USAS to navigate a corpus of disaster reporting (specifically, Hurricane Katrina), identifying the most frequent nomination strategies for social actors through a combined semantic tagging and collocation analysis. Potts (2015: 301) reports that "Exploring semantic preference through proportional semantic collocation offers the dual benefits of more objective categorisation of results, followed by the opportunity of various routes of down-sampling". Bednarek (2016) has explored whether USAS categories can function as 'pointers' to news values, for example how the category T1.1.2 Time: General: Present, simultaneous (which includes words such as, 'now', 'today', 'yet', 'instant') is likely to indicate 'Timeliness'. However, she concludes that the categories are a little broad to suggest any kind of equivalence and a manual reading is still required in order to draw out more nuanced meanings. As is the case with Kolhatkar et al.'s (2018) study of 'constructiveness' and 'toxicity' in SOCC discussed above, for certain research questions the USAS will not provide the requisite **granularity**; that is, the tagset will not provide the level of specificity or number of categories required to account for the nuance of this type of meaning. However, the USAS is widely applicable precisely because it operates at a more general sense of meaning, providing a level of interpretation that is likely to hold across domains and registers. Nevertheless, Lin (2017) reports that some manual checking of the semantic tagger may be required, as was the case with the use of 'like', which might automatically be tagged in the 'E2+ Like' category, even when it is used as a discourse marker (which would belong in the category Z5 Grammatical Bin). Lin (2017) still reports a 90.64% accuracy in this instance.

Collins and Nerlich (2015: 202) report that USAS "is able to objectively identify the key themes or 'topicality' of the discussion thread" and use a method outlined in Collins (2015) to examine user comments in response to news articles reporting issues around climate change. Collins (2015) demonstrates how the identification of key semantic domains can be extended to identify 'key comments' that offer some prototypical representation of the key themes of the overall discussion thread and thereby allow researchers (and journalists) to locate specific comments where those key topics are being discussed. Furthermore, Collins (2015) reports that not only did this approach highlight prominent themes, but also something of the style of the user comments discussion, such as the claim–counterclaim dyad (identified through the key semantic category 'Z6 Negative' which incorporated words that negate: 'not', 'n't', 'never' etc.). This in turn can facilitate a closer (manual) study of, say, argumentation and interactivity.

Here, the USAS was applied to examine the prominent themes of the user comments threads that followed articles that discussed AMR. The identification of key semantic categories (as indicative of prominent themes and style) supported a comparison of the user comments threads from different publications, as well as with the articles to which they were attached.

7.3 Antimicrobial resistance (AMR)

This study looked to investigate the topic of Antimicrobial Resistance (AMR) as a global health issue, one that "threatens our ability to treat common infectious diseases, resulting in prolonged illness, disability, and death" (http://www.who.int/en/news-room/fact-sheets/detail/antimicrobial-resistance). As the World Health Organisation (WHO) explains, "Antimicrobial resistance occurs when microorganisms such as bacteria, viruses, fungi and parasites change in ways that render the medications used to cure the infections they cause ineffective" (WHO, 2017). The National Institute for Health and Care Excellence (NICE) has highlighted the central role that patients have to play in an 'antimicrobial stewardship strategy' to tackle the issue (https://www.nice.org.uk/guidance/ng15). However, a systematic review of public knowledge and beliefs about AMR revealed that the public had an inadequate understanding about the causes and determinants of AMR and experienced feelings of powerlessness about the development of AMR (McCullough et al., 2016).

To "Improve awareness and understanding of antimicrobial resistance through effective communication, education and training" is one of the five key objectives of the World Health Organization's (2015: 13) *Global Action Plan on Antimicrobial Resistance* and it advises that, among other stakeholders such as civil society organisations and trade and industry bodies, the media "should help to promote public awareness and understanding of infection prevention and use of antimicrobial medicines across all sectors". It has been recognised that "[a]s a forum for the discourses of others and a speaker in their own right, the media have a key part in the production and transformation of meanings" (Carvalho, 2007: 224) and the news media are fundamental to constructing wider cultural understandings of health and disease (Briggs and Hallin, 2016). Davis et al. (2017: 4) refer to the Centre for

Disease Control and Prevention's promotional poster for their 2015 Antibiotic Awareness Week as an example of a text that "constructed dialogue between the expert knowledge provider and the concerned parent who is asked to collaborate on the use of alternatives to antibiotics". This is viewed as a more effective approach to health communication compared with what has been referred to as the 'hypodermic' model (Corcoran, 2013), whereby expert advice is simply 'transmitted' to (or injected into) the public.

The Economic and Social Research Council (ESRC) brief states that "in order to develop effective patient education and health promotion materials to reduce inappropriate antibiotic use we need to understand how people talk about, and think about, antibiotics and infection" (Wood, 2016: 3). The user comments sections following news articles offer a site of inquiry for this type of study and for a more dialogic approach to health communication, in order to consider how readers make sense of and debate the content of news on the issues around AMR.

7.4 Collecting the data

To investigate the discussion of AMR in the news, I performed a search for the terms 'AMR' or 'antibiotic resistant' or 'antibiotic resistance' in U.K. national newspapers from 2017 through Nexis®. The term 'antibiotic' resistance (referring to bacteria) was chosen over the hypernym 'antimicrobial' resistance (which refers to microbes i.e. bacteria, viruses and fungi) because, as Mendelson et al. (2017) report, despite the potential for over-extension, 'antibiotic' is favoured in the literature to address the specific challenge of maintaining effective antibiotics. Indeed, the NOW Corpus returns 4,587 hits for 'antibiotic resistance' compared with 2,530 hits for 'antimicrobial resistance'. Table 7.1 shows the highest number of articles by publication (combining, for example, the print edition of *The Daily Mail* with the online version, the *MailOnline*) to feature the search terms in 2017.

Table 7.1 Highest number of articles including the search terms 'AMR'/'antibiotic resistant'/'antibiotic resistance' by publication

Publication	Number of articles
The Daily Mail	266
The Daily Telegraph	106
The Guardian	42
The Independent	95
The Times	87
The Mirror	77
The Express	71
The Sun	36

These articles were then arranged by the highest number of comments, with the top 10 shown in Table 7.2. This list features articles from the *MailOnline* and *The Guardian* only; in fact, the top 64 ranking articles by user comments came from these 2 publications (50 for the *MailOnline*, 14 for *The Guardian*). This is consistent with Jönsson and Örnebring's (2011) work, in which they also found that *The Guardian* and *The Daily Mail* provided the most extensive comment features among their sample of Swedish and British tabloid and broadsheet newspapers online.

The search provided an opportunity to look at a substantial number of comments from two publications with vastly different readerships: *The Guardian* has largely a reported mainstream-left audience and a reputation for liberal and left-wing editorials; in contrast, *The Daily Mail* has a largely Conservative readership and a reputation for sensationalist reporting (https://web.archive.org/web/20090523104959/http://www.ipsos-mori.com/content/polls-05/voting-intention-by-newspaper-readership-quarter-1.ashx). Although item two on the list provided a far greater number of comments, item three provided an opportunity to look at two user comments sections from these two publications (comparing with item one on the list) that followed articles that had actually been prompted by the same news item and press release. The press release came from the WHO: http://www.who.int/news-room/detail/07-07-2017-antibiotic-resistant-gonorrhoea-on-the-rise-new-drugs-needed, and reported the findings of two of its papers by Wi et al. (2017) and Alirol et al. (2017). As such, the articles, 'Oral sex is causing the

Table 7.2 'AMR' articles with the highest number of user comments

	Title	Publication	Date	Comments
1	Oral sex is causing the spread of untreatable 'SUPER gonorrhoea'..	MailOnline	July 7	1,883
2	Read this and you may never eat chicken again..	The Guardian	October 13	1,465
3	What does super-gonorrhoea mean for oral sex?..	The Guardian	July 10	835
4	It isn't just halal slaughter that Britain needs to make more humane..	The Guardian	October 30	674
5	Patients infected with the plague in Madagascar are escaping from hospital..	MailOnline	November 19	671
6	Could a spoonful of SILVER make you as fit as Debbie McGee..	MailOnline	November 17	522
7	The end of antibiotics? Health chief warns..	MailOnline	May 6	460
8	You'll never guess how much bacteria is lurking in your gym!..	MailOnline	November 28	420
9	Sepsis: the truth about this hidden killer..	The Guardian	September 18	394
10	Fighting the flu can be a matter of life and death..	The Guardian	September 24	355

spread of untreatable 'SUPER gonorrhoea', World Health Organisation warns' (http://www.dailymail.co.uk/health/article-4673230/WHO-warns-imminent-spread-untreatable-superbug-gonorrhoea.html) and 'What does super-gonorrhoea mean for oral sex?' (https://www.theguardian.com/commentisfree/2017/jul/10/super-gonorrhoea-oral-sex-strain-sexually-transmitted-infection), along with their respective comments sections, were collected for further analysis.

7.5 Analysis

7.5.1 The articles

Given that AMR, as the WHO states, implicates a number of stakeholders it is an issue that is discussed in relation to a range of other topics (health, business, agriculture etc.) and so an initial starting point for the analysis of the articles was to consider what the articles were 'about', including to what extent they focused on AMR. As the headlines suggest, the articles more explicitly focused on sexual health, though they also both contextualised the problem of 'super-gonorrhoea' with respect to AMR. The *MailOnline* article was longer, comprising 1,232 tokens compared with 858 tokens for *The Guardian* article, though they demonstrated a similar degree of focus in terms of vocabulary, with 468 and 415 types, respectively. Table 7.3 presents the key semantic categories (identified through the USAS) for the article from the *MailOnline* when compared with the BNC1994 Written Sampler, along with some of the constituent tokens for each category. An LL threshold was set at 15.13 and, having established a high confidence in the keyness of these semantic categories (an LL score of 15.13 is indicative of a p-value < 0.0001), the list was sorted by effect size (LogRatio), showing which semantic

Table 7.3 Key semantic categories and constituent tokens for the *MailOnline* article

	Semantic category	Tokens (examples)
L2-	No living creatures	azithromycin, Zithromax, tetracycline
B2-	Disease	gonorrhoea, symptoms, infection
B2	Health and disease	health
B3	Medicines and medical treatment	antibiotics, antibiotic, drugs, treatment
B2+	Healthy	immune, immunity
S3.2	Relationship: Intimacy and sex	sexually, sexual, anal_sex, kissing
S8-	Hindering	resistance, resistant
B1	Anatomy and physiology	oral, chlamydia, throat, STD, urinate
S1.1.1	Social Actions, States and Processes	treated, treat, treating, contact
A2.1+	Change	become, evolve, developing, becoming
A6.2+	Comparing: Usual	common, typically, regular, normally
X2.2+	Knowledgeable	warned, experts, known, warns
L2	Living creatures, animals, birds, etc.	bacteria, superbug, bacterial

categories featured most prominently i.e. in order of the largest difference, compared with the reference corpus. Table 7.4 presents the key semantic categories for *The Guardian* article by the same criteria.

In many respects, these categories and their constituent tokens will offer no real surprise to anyone who has read the articles; they very much demonstrate that the focus of each article was on sexual health, which included references to the illness(es), treatment(s) and particular parts of the anatomy. Nevertheless, this provides some indication of the granularity of the USAS for readers, in that there are discrete categories for 'Health and disease' (B2) and 'Healthy' (B2+) and 'Disease' (B2-), for example. In the *MailOnline* article, the category of 'Comparing: Usual' included references to the advice on recognising symptoms of 'common' sexually transmitted diseases, reiterating what are 'typical' symptoms for the purposes of diagnosis (or, on the part of the reader, seeking a diagnosis from a medical professional). This category also enabled me to view some of the ways through which abnormality (with respect to news values [Bednarek, 2016], we could term this 'novelty') was created, in that while gonorrhoea is 'normally' treated with a 'simple dose of antibiotics', it has become 'increasingly resistant to common antibiotics'. To further demonstrate its 'newsworthiness', the category 'Knowledgeable' conveyed the news values 'eliteness' and 'negativity' (Bednarek, 2016) in the terms 'experts' and 'warned/warns', as well as the extent of the 'Disease' category, in that more information on symptoms was offered. This provided some indication of the evaluative, and potentially, rhetorical aspects of the piece. However, despite the 'warning' behind the article, citing oral sex as a cause and condoms a form of protection against the spread of gonorrhoea, there is no explicit instruction to the reader, so it is unclear what – if any – advice they are to take away from this. In contrast, *The Guardian* article is structured around the advice of using condoms, maintaining good health and open communication between partners. The author also calls for participation in social media activism to change the stigma around a diagnosis. These aspects of the article are not clearly reflected in the key category list in Table 7.4, however adjusting the search parameters from a LL value of 15.13 ($p<0.0001$) to a LL value of 10.83 ($p<0.001$) incorporates the categories 'X5.1+ Attentive' (including the tokens 'pay attention' and 'vigilant') and 'X2.2+ Knowledgeable' ('warning', 'awareness'), which capture some of these aspects. Researchers need to consider what thresholds provide sufficiently large,

Table 7.4 Key semantic categories and constituent tokens for *The Guardian* article

	Semantic category	Tokens (examples)
B2	Health and disease	health, infected
B2-	Disease	disease, gonorrhoea, symptoms, infections
S3.2	Relationship: Intimacy and sex	sexual, sexually, sleeping_with, lover
B3	Medicines and medical treatment	antibiotics, public_health, condoms, swab
S2	People	sex, people, population
B1	Anatomy and physiology	oral, genitals, rectum, throat, fingers, saliva

but manageable datasets for the purposes of their research question. Here, the LL threshold was kept at 15.13 simply to remain consistent with the parameters of the comments corpus (an LL value of 10.83 is still very high!).

Comparing the two lists, there are strong indications of the shared focus of the articles in that five of the six key categories for *The Guardian* article also appeared in the list for the *MailOnline* article. The only exception was the more general category for referring to 'people' (S2), which to some extent was equivalent to the *MailOnline* article's depiction of what is 'common', as with the example: 'some 78 million people in the world each year will get [gonorrhoea]'. The additional categories in the *MailOnline* list provided more specificity of the same topics in *The Guardian*, e.g. through references to 'bacteria' and 'superbugs' alongside the disease category and through specific types of antibiotics (azithromycin, Zithromax, tetracycline). Further indications of the news values of 'novelty' and 'negativity' were provided in the categories of 'Change' (A2.1+) and 'Hindering' (S8-), which referred to bacteria 'developing' and 'evolving', 'becoming' 'resistant'. Even the use of 'immune' and 'immunity' in the additional 'health' category (B2+) referred to the infection(s) being 'immune' to the treatment (i.e. antibiotics).

A keyness analysis of the articles at the level of semantic categorisation has shown the extent to which they shared a relatively narrow focus and provided an indication of what they were 'about'. The key semantic category lists also offered a basis on which to compare the articles with their respective comments threads and consider how readers responded to their themes and reporting style.

Task 7.2

Before we discuss the user comments, take a look at the first ten or so for each comments thread. You will find the links to the articles above, or you can locate them by entering the titles, 'Daily Mail 'Oral sex is causing the spread of untreatable 'SUPER gonorrhoea', World Health Organisation warns' and 'Guardian 'What does super-gonorrhoea mean for oral sex?'' into your search browser. Consider the following questions:

- What would you say the comments are 'about'? Keep a note of the key themes and topics you observe
- In what ways are the comments the same for the *MailOnline* and *The Guardian*? Are there any obvious differences?
- Referring back to your own list of key themes, would you expect the USAS to be able to categorise these? Are there any aspects of the comments that you think would not be picked up by a semantic categorisation? How, for example, would the automatic tagger capture humour?
- Would you need to edit the content of any of the comments before automatic tagging? Would you need to standardise any grammatical features, or normalise spelling, for example?

7.5.2 User comments

Table 7.2 showed us that the *MailOnline* elicited 1,883 user comments (the most of any article to feature the search terms), compared with 835 comments for *The Guardian* article. Despite this notable difference in the number of comments, the number of tokens in the comments corpora offered a closer match with 24,947 for the *MailOnline* thread and 23,355 for *The Guardian*. Furthermore, they contained a similar number of types (4,680 and 4,308, respectively). This indicates that comments in *The Guardian* thread were, on average longer but that in terms of lexical variety, the two comments corpora were similar. Twenty-nine comments in *The Guardian* thread were removed by the moderator and this is indicated by a standard error message that directs readers to the community standards page (https://www.theguardian.com/community-standards). *The Daily Mail* similarly has 'House Rules' (http://www.dailymail.co.uk/home/house_rules.html) and a means by which readers can click on a comment to report it as 'abuse' and flag it for moderation. A message at the top of the *MailOnline* comments thread indicated that it had not been moderated. The *MailOnline* comments did provide some examples of tokens that required reallocation; the word 'spread' was removed from the category 'F1 Food' and moved to 'M1 Moving, coming and going' to reflect its use as indicative of movement (i.e. spread of infection). The category 'A5.1+ Evaluation: Good' comprised 69 instances of the token 'well'; however, 52 of these were determined to be used as a discourse marker and reallocated to 'Z4 Discourse Bin'. Finally, the word 'bitter' appeared in the category 'X3.1 Sensory: Taste'; however, it was determined to be used to mean 'resentful' and so was reallocated to 'E3- Violent/Angry'. These constituted 0.3% of the tokens in the corpus. Table 7.5 represents the key semantic categories for the *MailOnline* comments thread, taking these corrections into account.

Seven of the key categories for the *MailOnline* article also featured in the 'comments' list and these covered aspects of the texts relating to sexual behaviours (S3.2), health, disease and infections (B2, B2-, L2), along with treatment (B3, L2-) and physiology (B1). What was not evident in the comments corpus was discussion of the emergent dangers of AMR and the issue of resistance to antibiotics, which in the article was articulated in the categories B2+, S8-; conveyed in the 'warnings' of 'experts' (X2.2+); and discussed with respect to what this means for treatment (A6.2+, S1.1.1) of the infections discussed. While there is some consideration for the 'risks' as represented in the semantic category A15- Danger, this seemed to reflect a reasonably flippant discussion of the trade-off between the pleasures of sexual activity (reflected in the categories E2+, E4.2+ and O4.2+) and the associated risks, in that sex was still considered 'worth the risk' by some commenters.

Conversely, the category 'S3.2- Asexual', which comprised exclusively of the tokens 'celibate' and 'celibacy', reflected the views that abstaining from sex was the only real prevention against sexually transmitted diseases. This was one of the categories that associated the transmission – and prevention – of infection with certain

Table 7.5 Top semantic categories for the *MailOnline* comments thread

		Semantic category	Tokens (examples)
1	L2-	No living creatures	antibacterial, anti-bacterial
2	S3.2-	Relationship: Asexual	celibate, celibacy
3	Q2.1-	Speech: Not communicating	keep_your_mouth_shut, shut_up, keep_quiet
4	X3.5	Sensory: Smell	smell, stinks, smelled, smells, smelling
5	B4	Cleaning and personal care	wash, gargle, shower, disinfectant, toilet
6	X3.1	Sensory: Taste	taste, flavoured, tang, stench, flavour
7	S3.2	Relationship: Intimacy and sex	love, promiscuous, kiss, sexually, sexual
8	B2-	Disease	gonorrhoea, disease, diseases, syphilis
9	E4.1+	Happy	lol, fun, funny, joke, happy, laugh, laughing
10	B1	Anatomy and physiology	mouth, swallow, sucks, suck, body, lick
11	A15+	Safe	safe, safety, guard, play_safe, conceptive
12	S3.1	Personal relationship: General	partner, partners, friend, relationship, mate
13	L2	Living creatures: animals, birds, etc.	bacteria, crabs, animals, superbug, dog, fish
14	O4.2-	Judgement of appearance: Negative	disgusting, dirty, nasty, horrible, filthy, filth
15	S4	Kin	wife, married, marriage, husband, marry
16	E4.2+	Content	glad, pleasure, proud, pleased, pleasures
17	S2.2	People: Male	men, man, guy, guys, boy, male, boys, fella
18	F1	Food	eat, eating, gobble, food, vegans, supper
19	B3	Medicines and medical treatment	antibiotics, condom, medical, Doctor, cure
20	B2	Health and disease	health, infected, endemic
21	N6+++	Frequent	always
22	A15-	Danger	risk, at_risk, danger, dangerous, dangerously
23	S2.1	People: Female	women, woman, girls, girl, female, ladies
24	S2	People	people, sex, person, kids, population
25	Z4	Discourse Bin	oh, ha, no, please, yes, sorry, right, anyway
26	A5.1+	Evaluation: Good	good, super, ok, well, great, fine, progress
27	E2+	Like	love, like, enjoy, liked, loving, loved
28	O4.2+	Judgement of appearance: Positive	nice, clean, beautiful, amazing, lovely, smart
29	A14	Exclusivizers/particularizers	just, only, especially, alone, utterly
30	A9+	Getting and possession	have, get, had, take, has, having, keep, got
31	Z8	Pronouns	you, it, I, that, your, my, they, what, this, we
32	Z6	Negative	n't, not, no, nothing, none, nor, not_really
33	A3+	Existing	is, 's, are, be, was, 'm, 're, been, were, being

lifestyle choices, to do with hygiene (B4), safe sex practices (A15+) and relationships (S3.1, S4). With respect to relationships, in the 'Personal relationship' category, the token 'partner(s)' was frequently pre-modified by words such as 'one', 'number of', 'multiple', 'many', as well as 'random', 'indiscriminate', 'casual' and 'trusted', indicating that commenters saw the number of partners, as well as the individual's level of discernment as contributing risk factors to infection. Similarly, 'monogamous' was used to determine 'relationship(s)' and this extended to the 'Kin' category, which comprised largely of 'married', 'marriage', 'wife' and 'husband'. There was a range of views expressed with respect to marriage, as commenters referred to their own experiences (and on their significant [sexual] relationships). In the article, the threat of 'super-gonorrhoea' was shown to apply to everyone, though the discussion of symptoms did discern between male and female, in terms of anatomy and physiology. Though there are a number of categories here that relate to groups of people, including separate categories for 'People: Male' and 'People: Female', the tokens 'men' and 'women' were strong collocates (with an MI score of 8.04), reflecting a tendency to refer to 'men and women' as representative of all people. However, sexual practices and relationships tended to be discussed with respect to men in relationship to women (and vice versa), indicating that it was almost exclusively heterosexual relationships that were discussed. There were some assertions that marriage, as indicative of a single and long-term sexual relationship, reduced the risk of sexual infection; however, this was met with counterclaims that marriage was no such guarantee (of avoiding disease or of fidelity) and many deriding humour from the trope of the 'sexless marriage'.

A number of the categories reflected a level of disgust expressed by readers (O4.2-), occasionally with the topic being published in the news but mostly with respect to oral sex practices and how these affected the senses (X3.1, X3.5). This also accounted for the category 'Food', which captured some of the cruder expressions and humour relating to oral sex.

Finally, the key category list also provided some indications of the interactional style used in the comments discussion. The category 'Happy' reflected the fact that there is a lot of humour in the thread, shown by the tokens 'funny', 'joke', 'laugh(ing)' and 'lol', indicating a more informal tone which was also supported by the prominence of the 'Discourse Bin' category. There were some instances where conflictual views prompted commenters to tell other users to 'keep your mouth shut' (Q2.1-), though this was also the site of anecdotal humour relating to the topic of oral sex. Words to do with negation (Z6) were applied in various ways, reflecting efforts to negate propositions that were introduced by the article, by other commenters or that were widely held as common sense. This counter-claim style was also observed in Collins and Nerlich (2015) and expected of a deliberative discussion. Conversely, the category 'Existing' tended to capture assertions (saying what 'is'), though again, the functions of such tokens are varied.

All of the key semantic categories for *The Guardian* article also appeared as key categories for the comments thread (see Table 7.6). These related to sexual behaviours (S3.2, B1), health, medicine and disease (B2, B2-, B3). Though only

Table 7.6 Top semantic categories for The Guardian comments thread

		Semantic Category	Tokens (examples)
1	X3.5	Sensory: Smell	smell, odours, odour, stinking, scented
2	S3.2	Relationship: Intimacy and sex	sexual, gay, promiscuous, sexually
3	S1.2.1+	Informal/Friendly	casual, intimate, humanity, casually
4	A1.3-	No caution	reckless, recklessly, recklessness, careless
5	B2-	Disease	gonorrhoea, HIV, diseases, disease
6	S3.1	Personal relationship: General	relationship, partners, partner, relationships
7	A15-	Danger	risk, at_risk, risks, dangerous, unsafe
8	B4	Cleaning and personal care	hygiene, mouthwash, shower, soap, wash
9	B2	Health and disease	health, infected, asymptomatic
10	G2.2	General ethics	morality, morally, objective, morals
11	B1	Anatomy and physiology	oral, promiscuity, STDs, cunnilingus
12	A15+	Safe	safe, safely, safety
13	S2.2	People: Male	men, man, male, boys, boy, guy, Viagra
14	E4.2+	Content	pleasure, pride, proud, complacent
15	S2.1	People: Female	women, woman, female, girls, vulva
16	B3	Medicines and medical treatment	condoms, antibiotics, public_health
17	Q1.1	Linguistic Actions, States and Processes: Communication	mean, means, messages, meant, said, implying, message, expressing, implied
18	L2	Living creatures: animals, birds, etc.	bacteria, virus, bacterial, superbug, chicken
19	S2	People	sex, people, children, human, person
20	E4.1+	Happy	fun, joke, happy, funny, hilarious, relief
21	E2+	Like	like, enjoy, enjoyed, love, lived_with
22	S8-	Hindering	resistance, resistant, blow, prevention
23	S4	Kin	married, marriage, husband, monogamous
24	Z4	Discourse Bin	please, oh, no, of_course, yes, you_know
25	A14	Exclusivizers/particularizers	just, only, especially, exclusively, purely
26	Z6	Negative	n't, not, no, nothing, nor, no_such
27	A9+	Getting and possession	have, get, had, has, having, catch, take
28	Z8	Pronouns	it, you, I, that, they, your, what, we, who
29	A3+	Existing	is, 's, are, be, was, were, 'm, 're, been

mentioned briefly in the article, commenters more explicitly linked the discussion back to the issue of AMR, as indicated in the categories L2 (referring to 'bacteria' and 'superbug') and S8- (referring to 'resistance'), which also included some mention of how to 'prevent' sexually transmitted diseases.

As with the *MailOnline* comments, readers discussed the 'risks' (A15-) associated with sex and the importance of safe sex practices (A15+). Contrasting with the

MailOnline discussion thread, there was more of a focus on the particular risks to sexual health for distinct social groups in *The Guardian* comments. One of the collocates of 'risk' was 'men', as commenters discussed that 'gay men'/'men who have sex with men' constitute a 'high risk' group with respect to sexually transmitted diseases ('sex workers' were also discussed as a 'high risk' group, particularly with respect to sexual violence), which was explicitly mentioned in the article. Similarly, the article provided statements relating to 'sleeping with multiple people' and 'enjoying ourselves too much', to which the commenters responded in the comments. The category 'Informal/Friendly' reflected the debate around 'casual' sex as a contributing factor to the transmission of sexual infection and the categories of 'Personal relationship' and 'Kin' reflected considerations for the (ir)relevance of types of relationship. In this thread, this aspect of the discussion developed into a debate of 'morality' (G2.2), with the castigation of those who are perceived to be 'reckless' (A1.3-). As with the *MailOnline* discussion, this also involved a debate around the pleasures and preferences associated with (oral) sex (E4.2+), though in this thread that extended to a discussion of how sexual practices related to sexual identity; for example, one commenter asked 'Are women who don't like penises gay?'. This showed that (some) readers acknowledged that sexual practices do not entail sexual identities and the significance of the journalist referring to 'men who have sex with men' as a more relevant descriptor than, say, 'gay men'.

The article also directed the content of the comments through its title, which asked "What does super-gonorrhoea mean for oral sex?" and accounted for the prominence of the category 'Linguistic Actions, States and Processes; Communication', which contained tokens pertaining to 'meaning'. Eleven of the comments in the thread started with this question and many others formulated their comments as a reply, suggesting that this was an effective way to prompt deliberation. Providing a question to direct comments sections is one of the recommendations of the Coral Project (https://coral-project.net/about/), which is an initiative of the Mozilla Foundation, in collaboration with *The New York Times* and *The Washington Post*, intended to generate more effective audience engagement through features such as user comments. There were instances where this question was treated as the set-up to a joke, for example: 'What does super-gonorrhoea mean for oral sex? … it's a blow to that job'. Nevertheless, this prompted commenters to consider the consequences for sexual practices and how this affected different social groups, as discussed above, and so seemed to be effective in facilitating contemplative discussion.

Though, as in the *MailOnline* comments thread, there was humour here expressed in puns and self-deprecation regarding sexual prowess, the tokens 'funny', 'joke', 'hilarious' etc. that made up the 'Happy' category were often used in irony, as rhetoric, or as a jumping-off point for debate, as with the example, 'this is a joke right?' and 'Jokes aside, I see where you're coming from, but..'. The 'Discourse Bin', 'Negative' and 'Existing' categories attested to a similar type of claim/counter-claim interaction as shown in the *MailOnline* comments thread.

Despite following articles that focused on different aspects of the issue, the comments threads shared 24 key semantic categories, which for the most part reflected the shared topical focus but also told us something about the interactional behaviours of each thread. Eight of those shared categories also appeared in one or both of the articles, with the comments similarly expanding the discussion to consider personal (sexual) relationships (drawing on personal experience); the importance of safe (and hygienic) sexual practices in response to associated risks; and the value of the pleasures of sex. Both comments threads also showed a relatively informal interactional style, full of humour and with some degree of debate. Where the discussions differed was, for example, in the extent and detail to which commenters discussed 'risk' (represented by the category A15- Danger). In the *MailOnline* comments, 'risk' was downplayed, in that commenters were 'not at risk' because they were denied sex (e.g. in a sexless marriage) or the risk was 'worth it'. Prompted by the article, *The Guardian* commenters discussed why different social groups might be more 'at risk', which also facilitated a conversation around the nuances between sexual behaviours and sexual identity.

More explicit differences were shown in the semantic categories that appeared as key for only one of the discussion threads. The *MailOnline* article did not introduce any explicit recommendations as to what readers could/should do in response to the issue, allowing space for commenters to suggest their own solutions, such as 'celibacy' (S3.2-), which is what prompted some debate among commenters. *MailOnline* commenters more often expressed disgust at (the sensory experience of) oral sex practices, which was dismissive of the topic and, even as a basis for humour, did not facilitate engagement with the issue since, although other commenters would express amusement (indicated by the 'Happy' category'), there was little else in the comment to build on.

While both groups discussed 'promiscuity', in *The Guardian* comments this extended to a discussion of 'morality' (indicated by the category 'General ethics'), with some users expressing disparaging views of 'casual' relationships (S1.2.1+ Informal/Friendly) and 'reckless' (A1.3- No caution) (sexual) behaviour, with others challenging such views.

The category 'Hindering' showed that *The Guardian* commenters discussed antibiotic resistance more, perhaps because it was not covered in the article. Conversely, because there was more detail on this in the *MailOnline* article, commenters may not have felt the need to provide their own information. Nevertheless, *The Guardian* commenters demonstrated that they had the knowledge and the vocabulary to refer back to the issue.

7.6 Extending the analysis

The key semantic category approach to the user comments directed the focus of this study to 33 categories for the *MailOnline* and 29 categories for *The Guardian*, amounting to hundreds of constituent tokens. By comparison, a keyword list at the same statistical thresholds would have generated 386 keywords (*MailOnline*) and 323 keywords (*The Guardian*), respectively. Drawing on semantic categories has enabled me to capture a larger sense of the datasets, with respect to key themes and interactional styles, as well as allowing us to consider how the comments threads reflect the articles above them and the contrasts between them. Though there are lots of similarities between the *MailOnline* and *The Guardian* data with respect to both the articles and the user comments, we can see with *The Guardian* comments where the article has prompted particular discussion points. This offers some evidence for the idea that user comments allow readers to respond to the journalist and demonstrate what Jönsson and Örnebring (2011) termed 'medium-participation', though we would have to look further for signs of how this constitutes an ongoing dialogue.

Similarly, there was some evidence of interaction between commenters: laughing at jokes, counter-claims and telling other users to 'shut [their] mouth'. However, in order to get a better sense of how users discussed and debated the issue amongst themselves, the study could be extended to look for, for example, 'constructiveness' and 'toxicity', following Kolhatkar et al.'s (2018) work with the SOCC. These aspects were explored through Martin and White's (2005) concept of 'appraisal', which offers a model through which we can explore interpersonal meaning, at the levels of 'attitude', 'engagement' and 'graduation'. 'Attitude' refers to emotional reactions, judgements and evaluations; 'engagement' deals with the interaction of opinions and sourcing attitudes; and through 'graduation', feelings are graded and amplified (Martin and White, 2005: 35). In order to examine the degree of deliberation in the user comments threads, we could refer to the engagement system, which allows us to demonstrate how views can be expressed in a way that opens up (expands) discussion (e.g. by acknowledging other points of view, such as 'In my opinion..') or, conversely, closes down (contracts) discussion by dismissing other voices. Since this type of analysis is based on meaning rather than form, it requires close reading and may not be possible through simple corpus queries. Nevertheless, Collins (2015) provides a demonstration of how semantic tagging can direct researchers towards a sample of 'key comments' that can be analysed along the dimensions of 'appraisal'.

Summary

The USAS is an automatic tagger that provides a form of semantic annotation and allows us to process large datasets to identify key topics and some aspects of authorial style. It has been applied here to evaluate user comments with respect to news articles and facilitated a comparison between the article and comments thread, as well as between the material from different publications. Here, the focus was on sexual health as a theme within the broader issue of AMR. Key semantic analysis demonstrated the extent to which the data shared a focus on health and disease, physiology and sexual behaviours, as well as highlighting some of the differences in how commenters expressed views about casual sexual practices and considered the implications for certain lifestyle behaviours. In providing a summary of prominent themes, key semantic category analysis facilitates a comparison of multiple datasets, for example across different publications or over time, that goes beyond what is feasible for manual types of analysis. Nevertheless, though the approach offered some initial findings relating to features of interaction with users, supplementing this with closer (manual) analysis will offer further insights into how users deliberate these key themes.

References

Alirol, E., Wi, T. E., Bala, M., Bazzo, M. L., Chen, X.-S., Deal, C., Dillon, J.-A. R., Kularatne, R., Heim, J., van Huijsduijnen, R. H., Hook, E. W., Lahra, M. M., Lewis, D. A., Ndowa, F., Shafer, W. M., Tayler, L., Workowski, K., Unemo, M. and Balasegaram, M. (2017). Multidrug-resistant gonorrhoea: A research and development roadmap to discover new medicines. *PLoS Medicine*,14, 7, e1002366. Available at: http://journals.plos.org/plosmedicine/article?id=10.1371/journal.pmed.1002366, accessed 15 July 2018.

Allcott, H. and Gentzkow, M. (2017). Social media and fake news in the 2016 election.*Journal of Economic Perspectives*, 31, 2,211–236.

Baker, P. (2006). *Using Corpora in Discourse Analysis.*London: Continuum.

Baker, P. and McGlashan, M. (forthcoming). Critical discourse analysis: a comparison of discourses around Romanians in the Daily Express with its readers' comments, in S.Adolphs and D.Knight (eds) *The Routledge Handbook of the English Language and the Digital Humanities.*London: Routledge.

Barker, E. and Gaizauskas, R. (2016). Summarizing multi-party argumentative conversations in reader comments on news. *Proceedings of the 3rd Workshop on Argument Mining (ArgMining2016).* 12 August 2016. Berlin, Germany,12–20.

Barry, M. (2017). Untangling the threads: Public discourse on the early web, in N.Brügger (ed.) *Web 25: Histories from the First 25 Years of the World Wide Web.*New York: Peter Lang,57–76.

Bednarek, M. (2016). Investigating evaluation and news values in news items that are shared through social media. *Corpora*, 11,2, 227–257.

Bergström, A. and Wadbring, I. (2015). Beneficial yet crappy: Journalists and audiences on obstacles and opportunities in reader comments. *European Journal of Communication*,30, 2,137–151.

Boczkowski, P. J., Mitchelstein, E., and Matassi, M. (2016). Incidental News: How Young People Consume News on Social Media. *50th Annual Hawaii International Conference on System Sciences (HICSS).* 4–7 January 2016. Waikoloa Village, Hawaii, U.S.A.,1785–1792.

Bode, L. and Vraga, E. K. (2015). In related news, that was wrong: The correction of misinformation through related stories functionality in social media. *Journal of Communication*, 65, 4,619–638.

Briggs, C. and Hallin, D. (2016). *Making Health Public: How News Coverage is Remaking Media, Medicine, and Contemporary Life.*London: Routledge.

Carvalho, A. (2007). Ideological cultures and media discourses on scientific knowledge: rereading news on climate change. *Public Understanding of Science*,16, 2,223–243.

Collins, L. (2015). How can semantic annotation help us to analyse the discourse of climate change in online user comments?*Linguistik Online*70, 1. Available at: https://bop.unibe.ch/linguistik-online/article/view/1743/2957, accessed 1 July 2018.

Collins, L. C. and Nerlich, B. (2015). Examining user comments for deliberative democracy: A corpus-driven analysis of the climate change debate online. *Environmental Communication*,9, 2, 189–207.

Corcoran, N. (ed.) (2013). *Communicating Health: Strategies for Health Promotion.* Second Edition. London: Sage.

Davis, M., Whittaker, A., Lindgren, M., Djerf-Pierre, M., Manderson, L. and Flowers, P. (2017). Understanding media publics and the antimicrobial resistance crisis. *Global Public Health.* Online First. Available at: https://www.tandfonline.com/doi/abs/10.10 80/17441692.2017.1336248, accessed 13 June 2018.

Fletcher, R. and Park, S. (2017). The impact of trust in the news media on online news consumption and participation. *Digital Journalism*, 5,10, 1281–1299.

Gottfried, J. and Shearer, E. (2016). News Use Across Social Media Platforms. Pew Research Center,Washington, D.C., U.S.A. Available at: http://assets.pewresearch. org/wp-content/uploads/sites/13/2016/05/PJ_2016.05.26_social-media-and-news_ FINAL-1.pdf, accessed 1 July 2018.

Graham, T. and Wright, S. (2015). A tale of two stories from "Below the line": Comment fields at the *Guardian. The International Journal of Press/Politics*, 20, 3,317–338.

Hermida, A. (2010). Twittering the news: The emergence of ambient journalism. *Journalism Practice*, 4, 3,297–308.

Jönsson, A. M. and Örnebring, H. (2011). User-generated content and the news: Empowerment of citizens or interactive illusion?*Journalism Practice*,5, 2, 127–144.

Joty, S., Carenini, G and Ng, R. (2015). CODRA: A novel discriminative framework for rhetorical analysis. *Computational Linguistics*, 41, 3,385–435.

Kolhatkar, V. and Taboada, M. (2017). Constructive Language in News Comments. *Proceedings of the 1st Workshop on Abusive Language Online.* 30 July–4 August 2017. Vancouver, Canada,11–17.

Kolhatkar, V., Wu, H., Cavasso, L., Francis, E., Shukla, K. and Taboada, M. (2018). The SFU Opinion and Comments Corpus: A Corpus for the Analysis of Online News Comments. Manuscript under review. Available at: https://www.sfu.ca/~mtaboada/ docs/publications/Kolhatkar_etal_SOCC.pdf, accessed 13 June 2018.

Lewis, S. C. (2012). The tension between professional control and open participation: journalism and its boundaries. *Information, Communication & Society*, 15, 6,836–866.

Lin, Y.L. (2017). Keywords, semantic domains and intercultural competence in the British and Taiwanese Teenage Intercultural Communication Corpus. *Corpora*,12, 2,279–305.

Martin, J. R. and White, P. R. R. (2005). *The Language of Evaluation: Appraisal in English.* New York:Palgrave Macmillan.

McCullough, A. R., Parekh, S., Rathbone, J., Del Mar, C. B., Hoffmann, T. C. (2016). A systematic review of the public's knowledge and beliefs about antibiotic resistance. *Journal of Antimicrobial Chemotherapy*,71, 1, 27–33.

McNair, B. (2018). *Fake News: Falsehood, Fabrication and Fantasy in Journalism.*London: Routledge.

Mendelson, M., Balasegaram, M.,Jinks, T., Pulcini, C. and Sharland, M. (2017). Antibiotic resistance has a language problem.*Nature*, 545, 7652. Available at: https://www.nature. com/news/antibiotic-resistance-has-a-language-problem-1.21915, accessed 15 July 2018.

Napoles, C., Tetreault, J., Pappu, A., Rosato, E. and Provenzale, B. (2017). Finding good conversations online: The Yahoo News Annotated Comments Corpus. *Proceedings of the 11th Linguistic Annotation Workshop (EACL).* 3 April 2017.Valencia, Spain, 13–23.

Piao, S. L., Rayson, P., Archer, D., and McEnery, T. (2004). Evaluating lexical resources for a semantic tagger. *Proceedings of the 4th International Language Resources and Evaluation Conference (LREC 2004).* 26–28 May 2004. Lisbon, Portugal,499–502.

Potts, A. (2015). Filtering the flood: Semantic tagging as a method of identifying salient discourse topics in a large corpus of Hurricane Katrina reportage, in P.Baker and T.McEnery (eds) *Corpora and Discourse Studies: Integrating Discourse and Corpora*. Basingstoke:Palgrave Macmillan,285–304.

Sunstein, C. R. (2001). *Echo Chambers: Bush v. Gore, Impeachment, and Beyond*. Princeton:Princeton University Press.

TandocJr, E., Ling, R., Westlund, O., Duffy, A., Goh, D. and Wei, L. Z. (2017). Audiences' acts of authentication in the age of fake news: A conceptual framework. *New Media & Society*. Online First. Available at: http://journals.sagepub.com/doi/abs/10.1177/1461444817731756, accessed 1 July 2018.

Wi, T., Lahra, M. M., Ndowa, F., Bala, M., Dillon, J.-A. R., Ramon-Pardo, P., Eremin, S. R., Bolan, G. and Unemo, M. (2017). Antimicrobial resistance in *Neisseria gonorrhoeae*: Global surveillance and a call for international collaborative action. *PLoS Medicine*, 14, 7, e1002344. Available at: http://journals.plos.org/plosmedicine/article?id=10.1371/journal.pmed.1002344, accessed 15 July 2018.

Wood, F. (2016). *Antimicrobial Resistance and Medical Sociology: Research Brief*. ESRC AMR Research Champion/University of Bristol. Available at: http://www.bristol.ac.uk/media-library/sites/social-community-medicine/documents/social-science-and-amr/MedicalSociology&AMR21092016.pdf, accessed 15 July 2018.

World Health Organization (2015). *Global Action Plan on Antimicrobial Resistance*. Available at: http://www.who.int/antimicrobial-resistance/publications/global-action-plan/en/, accessed 15 July 2018.

World Health Organization (2017). *What is Antimicrobial Resistance? Online Q&A*. Available at: http://www.who.int/features/qa/75/en, accessed 13 June 2018.

Chapter 8

Dating apps
A Tinder corpus

The Internet has grown alongside advancements in mobile technologies and one of the fundamental aspects of the modern online experience is the mobile Internet, with access enabled through handheld devices such as smartphones, tablets and more portable laptops. Because of this, location and immediacy gain further significance, in that the location of your mobile Internet device determines what type of information is prioritised in your online interactions. For example, global positioning systems (GPS) have improved personal navigation (via maps); consumer experiences (through localised news, weather, advertising, restaurant recommendations etc.); and social interactions with other nearby mobile Internet devices (and their owners), which is the focus of this chapter. Location-Based Real-Time Dating (LBRTD) relies on mobile Internet technology and has come to define the modern dating experience, producing a market of 'proximal dating' apps that reportedly generated $2.7 billion of revenue in the U.S. alone in 2016 (https://cdn2.hubspot.net/hubfs/434414/Reports/2018%20Dating%20Apps/Liftoff_2018_Mobile_Dating_Apps_Report.pdf).

While the technology of LBRTD apps is cutting-edge, the premise and content generated by users arguably maintains the format of the personal ads that have appeared for as long as there have been newspapers (Cocks, 2010). Here, premiums on space prompted the use of jargon and abbreviations (e.g. GSOH: good sense of humour), much like those that we have seen in Chapter 4 relating to 'netspeak'. Coupland (1996) has discussed the personal ad in terms of marketability, constructing the self and others as desirable commodities. By examining these texts, we can also observe cultural ideologies about, say, particular gender characteristics and roles, or age. For example, Jagger (2001) found that men more explicitly referred to financial and occupational resources in their ads, while women referred more to their physical attractiveness and body shape.

Task 8.1

Here are some popular abbreviations associated with personal ads. Do you recognise them, or can you deduce what they mean?

- ISO
- WLTM
- 30YO
- ASL?
- DDF
- NSA
- LDR
- LTR.

Are these abbreviations still in use? How would you determine the frequency of their use through a corpus query? How would you deal with other uses of these acronyms, for example American Sign Language (ASL)?

Do you know of any terms that have emerged from LBRTD apps and users' experiences with them? How would you design and build a corpus to investigate this type of language?

While the modern personal ad, in the form of a mobile dating app profile, foregrounds photos as visual representations, users can typically provide material via an 'About Me' section in their profile, which is their opportunity to present themselves through language as desirable individuals and to communicate preferences for what they are seeking in and from a (potential) partner. Indeed, Hobbs et al. (2016: 280) report that participants "acknowledged the need to engage in self-branding activities to market themselves as desirable commodities in a crowded relationship marketplace – a process of self-stylisation for self-transformation". This provides data for examining modern dating practices and the extent to which the LBRTD app has shaped the way that users construct their desirable selves and let others know what they are looking for in their relationships. This chapter presents a corpus of Tinder profiles in order to explore such representations, looking at the regular phrasal constructs identified in the 'About Me' sections as an indicator of the regular function(s) and style of this particular text type.

8.1 Location-based real-time dating (LBRTD) apps

As a form of mobile media, LBRTD apps have been developed to cater to a range of users and to facilitate various types of social relations, with a shared emphasis on proximity enabled by Bluetooth technologies (e.g. ProxiDating) and GPS. In this market, such apps are often defined by their target audience, on the basis of, for example, sexual identity and orientation (Grindr, Fem, Chappy,

Her, PERSONALS); ethnicity (Black People Meet); faith (Christian Mingle, JSwipe for Jewish people); or age (Stitch, for people aged 50 and above). Others provide mobile app versions of popular dating websites (OkCupid, Match.com), using the location-based functionality to identify potential matches that users are more likely to come across 'in real life'. In fact, some apps are built on the premise that users may already have crossed paths with potential matches, identifying those that users have passed in close proximity that day (happn) or who 'check in' to locations that the user frequents (Huggle). By far the most popular mobile dating app is Tinder, which in April 2016 had 25.6% of the market share (https://www.statista.com/statistics/737081/popular-online-dating-market-share-users-monthly/), operates in over 190 countries, reportedly facilitates 1 million dates per week and which has generated over 20 billion matches (https://www.gotinder.com/press). Users review the profiles of other users located within a set radius, 'swiping right' to indicate that they like the profile and 'swiping left' to reject the profile. If the user behind the profile reciprocates their 'like', both users are able (and encouraged) to initiate contact via the instant messaging function. Many LBRTD apps share the design format that has been popularised by Tinder and which capitalises on the core features of mobile media.

The four key affordances of mobile media, as summarised by Schrock (2015), are: portability, availability, locatability and multimediality. Such characteristics are fundamental to LBRTD apps, which, unlike traditional desktop-based dating sites, are not restricted to private spaces (typically, the home), but operate in and even create a range of private to semi-public and public spaces. The portability of mobile media extends what we might consider 'public' spaces and LBRTD apps have improved the diffusion of online dating, reducing, to some extent, the stigma associated with it (Smith and Anderson, 2015). LBRTD apps have also generated a space that is both virtual and physical for lesbian, gay, bisexual, transgender and queer (LGBTQ) communities, for whom historically, safe public spaces have not existed. Apps such as Grindr, "the world's largest social networking app for gay, bi, trans, and queer people" (https://www.grindr.com/), represent "an important cultural shift into creating and performing a community without a shared physical place" (Lutz and Ranzini, 2017: 1). Brown et al. (2005: 67) argue that the Internet has provided a space where the online identities of gay men are less likely to be "challenged, spoiled or embarrassed" and perhaps because of this and the absence of suitable public spaces in the 'real world', Daneback et al. (2005) found that homosexual men were four times more likely, and bisexual men almost twice as likely, to have engaged in this cybersex activity compared with heterosexual men.

The 'availability' of mobile media increases the number of users, the number of uses and the spontaneity of how participants engage with LBRTD apps. It is perhaps this spontaneity that has cultivated the 'hookup culture' (Sales, 2015) associated with apps like Tinder, in that they facilitate instant gratification. However, research has shown that Tinder supports users in meeting a range of needs (Ranzini and Lutz, 2017), which we will consider below. Nevertheless, the immediacy of communication and visibility of other users' profiles may influence how they are constructed; Hess and Flores (2018: 1088) argue that "given that Tinder is perceived as a competitive space, men may feel pressured to engage in certain articulations of toxic masculinity that aid in establishing their power over women". In this sense, we can examine users' profiles to investigate normative representations of various gender and sexual identities.

The 'locatability' of LBRTD apps emphasises the potential that users who interact in online spaces will, at some point, look to meet 'in real life'. At the very least, users experience 'proximity-based co-situation' (Blackwell et al., 2015: 1131), in that they share both virtual and physical space and can draw on their knowledge and construction of this space to perform identity work. The location can serve as a shared point of reference, even a mutual interest, but this nevertheless provides the incentive and the opportunity for users to cultivate offline relationships. This is a defining feature of the LBRTD app as distinct from other types of online interaction, though this may cause tensions for people who do not wish to be identified as a user of the app (Blackwell et al., 2015), for example by people with whom they are already acquainted, but whom they would not consider a potential match. The potential for meeting in person is thought to influence the type of (self-)representation provided by users of LBRTD apps, in that while users "stretch the truth a bit" (Yurchisin et al., 2005: 742) on Internet dating sites (for example, disguising what they perceive to be undesirable physical traits, writing descriptions that appear more confident and socially proficient, taking the time to cultivate more considered interactional responses [Gibbs et al., 2006]), the anticipation of face-to-face encounters arguably prompts a more 'realistic' and 'honest' online self-presentation (Ellison et al., 2012). Since the starting point for the interaction is online (through the app), the user can engage in a form of identity production that might not necessarily be considered 'inaccurate', but nevertheless foregrounds select characteristics and manages expectations in and of their potential matches.

Finally, LBRTD apps utilise the 'multimediality' of mobile media and on Tinder, this is enabled by its 'converganceability' (Marcus, 2016). Tinder profiles are most typically generated from existing Facebook profiles, which means that users can set up an account very quickly since key information is instantly transferred. However, this may introduce a tension between the types of self-presentation users may cultivate on Facebook, where they are more likely to have a range of relationships (family members, friends, colleagues etc.) and the relationships they are looking to foster through a dating app like Tinder and editing them separately is not entirely straightforward. Tinder's interoperability does mean that it can make use of the functions of other apps and on their profiles, users are encouraged to provide links to their photo archive on Instagram, along with their favourite artists on the music streaming platform Spotify, even selecting an 'anthem' for their profile. As such, while Tinder allows users to post nine photos, linking to Instagram means that the number of images the user can provide is (in theory) limitless. While it is possible to create a Tinder profile without a Facebook account, the default mode relies upon Facebook's own measures for profile verification, meaning that the opportunities for deception are minimised (Ranzini and Lutz, 2017). Given the emphasis on online interactions designed to facilitate face-to-face encounters, users have identified concerns with personal safety in this context, recognising the potential for other users to deceive them (Gibbs et al., 2011). Facebook verification is a feature of a number of LBRTD apps, such as Bumble and Coffee Meets Bagel and while Tinder offers its own verification for notable individuals and public figures, its recommendation for 'ordinary' users is to use other platforms (e.g. Facebook, Instagram) as verification.

8.1.1 Functions

Tinder markets itself as an app for 'meeting people' and succinctly describes its process in its tagline 'Swipe. Match. Chat.' (https://tinder.com/?lang=en-GB). While it may foster a range of social and sexual relationships, Ranzini and Lutz (2017: 88) conducted a self-report survey in which they explored motivations for use and found that "Entertainment is the most pronounced motivation for the respondents". Similarly, in the Netherlands, users reported using Tinder for 'entertainment' or for an ego-boost (Ward, 2017). This indicates that there is some 'sensation seeking' (Carpenter and McEwan, 2016: 2) in viewing the profiles of other users, as well as a form of self-validation in having other users 'Like' your own profile (users are not notified of those who rejected their profile). However, it has also been shown that the longer individuals used Tinder, the more they would be motivated by seriously searching for a partner (Ward, 2017) and older users reported being motivated more by friendship-seeking and significantly less by self-validation than younger users (Ranzini and Lutz, 2017: 88).

Given the proportion of users who may be looking for 'entertainment' and not seriously interested in meeting their matches in person, LBRTD apps can variously be described as 'flirting apps' and for those looking for instant gratification, 'hookup apps'. But the different motivations for using the apps "may represent a disconnect between those who wish to kill time and those who are seeking sexual partners" (Carpenter and McEwan, 2016: 1), long-term relationships or friendship. Given the LBRTD market, it may be that a user's motivations may even determine which app is chosen; for instance, MacKee (2016: 9) reports that "gay men in London have appropriated Tinder as a space suitable for romantic quests, while maintaining more traditionally hyper-sexualized online platforms, such as Grindr, as venues appropriate for the exploration of their sexual desires". In fact, given the perceived sexualisation of Grindr, many users who genuinely sought other types of relationships report being judged, ignored or blocked by other users, ultimately unable to establish interpersonal relationships because of their 'non-normative' behaviour on the app (Jaspal, 2017: 195). This shows that LBRTD apps serve different purposes (for different users) and that, ultimately, users may need to be explicit about their motivations and expectations, either in their profiles or through their interactions, in order to meet with success.

> **Task 8.2**
>
> What is your impression of LBRTD apps and how people use them? Do they still use them?
>
> Consider how one of the popular LBRTD apps (e.g. Tinder) is discussed online. Go to https://corpus.byu.edu and search the iWeb Corpus for references to the app. Searching by 'Word' (rather than the default 'List') will provide data on related topics, collocates, clusters and concordance lines. What types of views are conveyed through references to the app? Are commentators positive about the app, or cynical? How are users of the app described?

8.2 The language of dating profiles

The modern LBRTD app profile has its origins in personal ads that have long appeared in newspapers and magazines, as well as online dating websites. Content focused on the marketing of the self, motivations for posting and expectations about a prospective relationship have been found across personal ads, online dating profiles and in modern LBRTD apps such as Grindr (Birnholtz et al., 2014), attesting to their shared function. Researchers have documented some key features of the language and structure of such texts; for example, Coupland (1996: 193–195) explains that in the traditional printed personal ad, first comes the advertiser's information (sex, age, marital status, characteristics, sexual orientation, profession); second, the desired match is described through similar attributes; third, the goals of the potential relationship are defined; sometimes the ad contains special comments such as the reason for advertising; and finally, the ad includes contact information. Often, the attributes of the poster align closely with those sought in a match; Shalom (1997) and Baker (2005) both report that the word 'similar' is prominent in this type of text, though those attributes that the poster claims both of themselves and calls for in their prospective partner tended to be fairly generic, i.e. 'sincere', 'genuine' and 'attractive' (Baker, 2005: 139).

Furthermore, the range of characteristics and attributes listed in a personal ad is relatively confined and researchers often report patterns relating to gender roles and identities. Hamid and Bakar (2011) looked at frequency lists and word collocations in a combined corpus linguistics and CDA study of the written discourse of Malaysian adolescents in the personal ads in the magazine, *Galaxie*. They found that salient features of the ads could be summarised through the following categories: gender identity; ethnic/racial identity; social–relational characteristics, affective behaviour and psychological traits; and personal interests and hobbies. Key semantic categorisation using the USAS (see Chapter 3 for an introduction and Chapter 7 for an application) highlighted some key differences on the basis of the gender of the poster in a corpus of classified ads posted by individuals over 50 years of age to the Telegraph.co.uk dating website *KindredSpirits* (Mudraya and Rayson, 2011). For example, in the profiles of men looking for women, the categories 'Education', 'Unselfish' and 'In power' (bossy, control, dominant, leading on etc.) were more prominent, suggesting some adherence to dominant masculine stereotypes.

In an examination of online discourses, Baker (2018) conducted a keyword analysis of corpora of posts to the classified advertisements website *Craigslist*, comparing the language of two different sexual identity groups seeking partners online. Baker (2018: 165) reports 'me' as a keyword across the data and for both women-seeking-men and women-seeking-women, this reflected a tendency for the poster to position themselves as the (passive) recipient of a prospective partner's action (albeit more frequently used by women-seeking-men). Interestingly, in the women-seeking-women data, the keyword 'we' indicated that posters more often referred to the imagined pairing (of themselves and their match) and what they would do together.

Offering a more nuanced examination of representations of gender intersecting with religion, Marcus (2014) conducted a study of the faith-based online dating sites *JDate*, *ChristianMingle* and, as a comparison, *OkCupid*. Marcus (2014: 10) found that while across the data, male posters emphasised their careers, along with activity and sports-related words, "In the standpoint of *ChristianMingle* members, an ideal male partner is someone who is highly religious, rather than athletic", with "a higher frequency of care related words in the male profiles to the amount in the female profiles". Marcus (2014: 11) reports that religious values as expressed by the users of *ChristianMingle* relate to "service, sensitivity, and empathy".

Comparing online dating profiles with the reported features of personal ads, Mäntymäki (2010: 188) reports that "the basic elements remain the same on datingireland.com, although the amount of information is greater, and it is no longer presented in linear order because it can be accessed by clicking the links randomly". This shows that the format of dating sites and LBRTD apps can determine what information is included (and where), which may be informed by the reported observations of personal ads (e.g. Coupland, 1996). For example, Tinder provides an 'About Me' section with a limit of 500 characters, but also has entries for name, age and profession, such is the expectation that these details are fundamental to a user's self-presentation; these are automatically filled using information from the user's Facebook profile (if they have one). Since the app provides 'basic' information about the user as a matter of course, the 'About Me' section offers a rich resource for investigating if and how users take the opportunity to expand and elaborate on this as a representation of their self and their goals for using the app.

8.3 The Tinder corpus

8.3.1 Collecting the data

The collection of a corpus of LBRTD app profiles prompted ethical considerations at each of the levels outlined by Townsend and Wallace (2016) and discussed in Chapter 2: private versus public; informed consent; anonymity; and risk of harm. Tinder users can expect (and, in fact, rely upon) their profiles being visible to other users of the app, with some degree of control over their visibility based on the parameters of location and 'looking for', based on their gender and sexual identities. However, users can reasonably expect that their profiles will not appear outside of the app, despite the 'naming and shaming', or occasionally celebratory practices of certain media outlets highlighting the 'worst' (or alternatively, the 'best') Tinder profiles. Anonymity is a key concern for many users of LBRTD apps, who may be presenting particular aspects of their identity for a more closely defined and private audience that they would not share on the basis of other types of (familial, professional etc.) relationship. Particularly when such apps have an explicitly defined target audience (e.g. Grindr for LGBTQ people), users might refrain from having photos of their face for fear of being identified and 'outed' (Jaspal, 2017), or associated with 'hookup culture' (Blackwell et al., 2015; Jaspal, 2017; Ward, 2017). For some, this presents very real risks of, for example, homophobic violence (Jaspal, 2017) and for many, there is the risk of the potential psychological threat of maintaining coherence between online and offline identities (Jaspal, 2017). Given these considerations, it was of utmost importance for this study that participants self-identify and volunteer their information, rather than being recruited on the basis of them being known users of the app.

As part of their recruitment process, Blackwell et al. (2015) set up a profile on Grindr (that explicitly communicated their research objectives) as a way of directly targeting authentic users. However, I had decided that the advantages in terms of access gained by setting up a profile were mitigated by the fact that users would be 'visible' to me as someone who was not part of the app community in the 'right' spirit, according to its widely accepted function as an app for fostering social relationships. I preferred to allow participants the opportunity to decide for themselves whether their profiles would be visible to someone (i.e. me) outside of this community, which was also a key consideration in protecting users' anonymity. At the time of data collection, I was working as a Teaching Associate at the University of Nottingham, so if I were to recruit participants via the app itself, this would inevitably prioritise users who were based in my local area and since the vast majority of my interactions with people in the Nottingham area operated within a lecturer–student dynamic, there was a high probability that I might gain access to information about students relating more explicitly to their personal characteristics, their social lives, their sexual orientation and desires: information they would be unlikely to share with me on the basis of our offline relationship. Again, I wanted the decision to share this information to remain with the user and so recruiting participants through the app itself did not seem appropriate.

Instead, I devised an online questionnaire that allowed participants to reproduce the information that appeared on their Tinder profiles anonymously and to make their own decisions about what to include (even if this diverged from the 'authentic' version on Tinder). Furthermore, I was named as the contact for the study, which meant that should potential respondents be acquainted with me from some other context, they could decide to participate (or not) with the knowledge that I would see this information. The first 'page' of the questionnaire presented potential participants with the terms of the research, which was reviewed by the University of Nottingham's Research Ethics Committee, constituting the basis on which participants could indicate their informed consent. The second part of the survey was the data collection, which included four items: free text responses for 'Age', 'Gender', 'Sexual orientation' and 'About Me'. I deliberately offered free text boxes for 'Gender' and 'Sexual orientation' in order to allow participants to provide their own terms, since while Tinder reports being committed to inclusivity (https://blog.gotinder.com/genders/) and allows users to change their default gender assignation, much of its operationality is based on a binary gender distinction. This is, to some extent, prompted by the information that is transferred over from Facebook and designed to simplify the search algorithm ('man' or 'woman' looking for 'men' and/or 'women'). It was anticipated that users might use the 'About Me' section to clarify or elaborate on the more restricted definitions provided by Tinder. In order to complete the questionnaire, participants had to enter something (i.e. at least one text character) in the 'About Me' text box. Because of this, I was able to determine when users had intentionally left this blank on their Tinder profile (for example, they would write 'I have left this blank' on the questionnaire), as opposed to simply omitting this from the survey.

The final part of the survey gave participants the opportunity to provide an e-mail address, which would be entered into a prize draw to win a gift voucher as a reward (and incentive) for their participation. Given the potential for e-mail addresses to identify participants, these were stored separately from the survey responses and in accordance with the GDPR guidelines. Access to this survey was provided by a URL and this was distributed through my own online social networks, as well as flyers posted around Nottingham. This approach did largely favour the recruitment of university students, both in terms of the distribution of flyers and through my own social media network (which is largely made up of academics), with a particular focus on people in Nottingham. Nevertheless, given the mobility of students, who often live and study in different locations, along with the fact that the demographics of university students broadly align with those of Tinder users (http://www.businessofapps.com/data/tinder-statistics/), this seemed the best alternative strategy to creating a profile on the app itself for targeting users.

The questionnaire (and the research) focused only on the text of the profiles and not the images, despite the overt emphasis on photos in the presentation of the app. On the one hand, this was decided on the basis of my own research skills and interest in the linguistic content of the material and I have discussed in previous chapters how corpus approaches are not best suited to image-based analysis. In addition, my expectation was that there would be reluctance from participants to provide photo material that would compromise their anonymity, as well as potentially presenting them in a more overtly sexualised or eroticised presentation. Other studies have examined the use of images in the context of dating profiles; for example, Marcus (2014) examined photos used on *JDate*, *ChristianMingle* and *OkCupid* profiles and identified seven categories of photographs relevant to her focus on portrayals of gender and of religion: Headshot; "Sexy" body shot; Regular body shot; Professional attire shot; Shot with family/friends; Silly/Miscellaneous shot; Religious-affiliated shot. The use of images is an important aspect of self-presentation and may be restricted to particular functions and categories in the same way as the text content. Nevertheless, for the reasons relating to recruitment and anonymity discussed above, this study reports only on the recurring phrasal constructs in the text of the Tinder 'About Me' sections.

8.3.2 Respondents

There were 365 respondents to the survey, with two-thirds (66.3%) of participants identifying as male and homosexual (almost exclusively articulated as 'gay'). Table 8.1 shows the number of respondents by gender and sexual orientation and almost half (48.8%) of participants were aged 18–24 (25.8% aged 25–30; 15.9% aged 31–40; 7.9% aged 41+). The distribution of responses across gender, sexual orientation and age did not support a systematic comparison between groups so the observations discussed below are of the corpus as a whole, which is based largely on a gay male population. Ninety of the respondents indicated that their 'About Me' section was blank and although Tinder permits users 500 characters of free text (as did the questionnaire), 78.5% of responses used fewer than 40 words. In fact, 34.7% of responses included 10 or fewer words and only 12 responses used 80 or more words, approaching anywhere near the character limit. This attests to the significance of the profile photos as an important basis on which potential matches are encouraged to make their decisions, however it also places significance on the small number of words that are included in the profile, particularly if there are any recurring patterns relating to the type of content, or even phraseology. Overall, the Tinder Corpus comprised 7,910 words of 'About Me' data.

Table 8.1 Respondents by gender and sexual orientation

	Heterosexual	Homosexual	Bisexual	Pansexual	Queer	Asexual	Unspecified
Male	26	242	1	2	1	1	2
Female	51	6	8	3	2	0	4
Unknown	0	1	0	0	0	0	14
Non-binary	0	0	0	1	1	0	0

8.3.3 Formatting

Participants were encouraged to carry out their own anonymisation, with the examples of their name (substituting with '[NAME]'), their location ('[TOWN]') and workplace ('[WORKPLACE]') provided on the questionnaire. Nevertheless, further anonymisation was applied to references to names, usernames, locations (including nationalities), universities, workplaces and professions that remained within the responses. These were substituted with text following the same format as the examples above (e.g. [USERNAME]) to indicate that the respondent had included this information, without the specific details. Participants used a range of emoji in the responses and these were replaced in the corpus with their Unicode codepoint (e.g. 😂 = U+1F602) in order to enable frequency counts and corpus queries.

8.3.4 N-grams

> **Task 8.3**
>
> Collect a small corpus of between 6,000–8,000 words of your own writing (for example, a couple of essays), upload this to AntConc and carry out n-gram analysis. Try a range of n-grams (i.e. 2-grams, 3-grams, 4-grams).
>   What do the results tell you about your own writing?
>
> - Does this analysis reveal anything of your personal writing style? Do you use particular phrasal constructs?
> - Does the analysis say more about the register (i.e. academic writing)?
> - Could an analyst determine what the writing was about, based on n-grams?

In Chapter 3 I introduced the 'n-gram' as a unit of analysis: a combination of words that appears with regularity in a corpus. The occurrence and research interest in n-grams attest to the fact that phraseological units are common in English and "should be regarded as a basic linguistic construct with important functions for the construction of discourse" (Biber et al., 2004: 398). Analysis of n-grams (which might also be referred to as chunks, clusters or lexical bundles) has been used to provide evidence of the difference between modes (e.g. spoken and written English, see Carter and McCarthy, 2006), registers (Cortes, 2004) or disciplines (Hyland, 2008). AntConc supports n-gram analysis, returning the most frequent combinations on the basis of a user specifying the number (the 'n') of words in the combination, which can also incorporate a range (e.g. 2–4 word combinations). Researchers (such as Cortes, 2004; Carter and McCarthy, 2006; and Hyland, 2008) often base their analysis on 4-word combinations (4-grams) in general corpora, or 3-grams in more specialised corpora.

8.4 Analysis

8.4.1 4-grams

I initially searched the corpus for 4-grams with a minimum frequency of 5, of which there were only two: the first reflected a single respondent's use of 16 consecutive 'rainbow' emoji (🌈 U+1F308). This highlights one of the caveats of the n-gram analysis approach – which may be more of an issue in texts that use repetition for emphasis (as with emoji) – in that a sequence of 16 consecutive tokens contains 13 'sets' of four tokens. This means that such sequences are over-represented by analyses based on raw frequency, though such occurrences are quickly discerned by looking at the n-gram in context. The function of this sequence may be aesthetic, although it did follow the (straight female) user's description of themselves in politicised terms as 'feminist & socialist' and therefore is likely to connote a pro-LGBTQ rights stance.

The only other instance of a 4-gram in the corpus was the construct 'drop me a message', which occurred seven times. This simply encouraged potential matches to initiate an interaction through the apps 'chat' feature and often appeared at the end of the 'About Me' section, similar to how authors of personal ads closed with contact information as a precursor to the next phase of a prospective relationship (Coupland, 1996). Marley (2002: 94) also found that authors of personal ads would look to engage potential matches in the way they constructed their posts, where "text-initial questions, and to a lesser degree text-final challenges, invite the reader to rule themselves in as suitable for further interaction".

8.4.2 3-grams

Table 8.2 shows the most frequent 3-grams in the data (with a frequency of more than 5), alongside a list of 3-grams in the data provided by homosexual males, as the largest cohort. From this, we can see the extent to which the corpus was determined by this population, in that all of the 3-grams of the homosexual male data appear in the list for the full cohort and, for instance, 12 of the 15 occurrences of the 3-gram 'if we match' came from this group. The three additional 3-grams that appeared in the full cohort data were the sequence of rainbow emoji discussed above and the final two 3-grams 'I am a' and 'if you want'. However, 5 of the 6 occurrences of both 'I am a' and 'if you want' came from responses provided by participants identifying as gay and male. 'I am a' explicitly marks self-representation and was followed by characteristics relating to professional identity ('Senior Brand Ambassador', 'student'), personality ('friendly guy'), physicality ('chubby guy') and sexual identity ('pan sexual guy'). The 3-gram 'I have a' – which appears in both lists – offered further self-characterisation: as a pet-owner ('I have a cat called [NAME]'), as someone with tattoos/piercings or as someone living with a disability. There are some clearly perceptible implications of this (tattoos will likely be visible if users meet, matches may come across these pets if they meet with the user), but readers may also draw inferences on the associated lifestyle

182 Dating apps

Table 8.2 Most frequent 3-grams in the Tinder corpus

All respondents			Homosexual male respondents		
	Frequency	3-gram		Frequency	3-gram
1	15	if we match	1	12	if we match
2	14	(u+1f308) (u+1f308) (u+1f308)	2	8	looking for a
3	10	snapchat - [username]	3	8	looking to meet
4	8	looking for a	4	7	drop me a
5	8	looking to meet	5	7	I'm looking for
6	7	drop me a	6	7	me a message
7	7	I'm looking for	7	6	i have a
8	7	me a message	8	6	snapchat – [username]
9	7	i have a			
10	6	i am a			
11	6	if you want			

or personal qualities of pet-ownership (e.g. as generally caring, particularly for animals) or having tattoos (e.g. 'alternative' to the mainstream). In this context, the poster can stick to simple facts (e.g. I have a cat) and allow other users to discover implications that are relevant to them and their decision as to whether the poster is a suitable match or not. 'If you want' was a construct where the poster had more of a say in determining the nature of a prospective relationship ('if you want to date two ppl in a casj/not-sex-focused way'[1]), though was more often used to encourage further interaction: 'drop me a message if you want to chat', 'if you want to know anything ask away', 'swipe right if you want to know more'. Establishing some (broad) parameters for a prospective relationship and fostering interaction were also patterns indicated by the shared 3-grams, which we will now discuss in turn.

8.4.2.1 'if we match'

The most frequent 3-gram was 'if we match', which in every occurrence was followed by an incitement to initiate contact, be it 'drop me a message' as discussed above, 'message me', 'pop up', 'please text', 'start a chat', 'let's say hi' or 'please make an effort to talk'. The 3-grams 'drop me a' and 'me a message' further attest to the frequency of this construct. Given the simplicity of the platform – conveyed in its concise tagline, 'Swipe. Match. Chat.' – it seems unnecessary to instruct other users in this way, or to remind them of the conditions ('if we match'); the inclusion of this type of speculation may convey optimism, and in leading on to a (variously mitigated) directive to contact the poster, perform some initial interpersonal work by appearing welcoming. This simple reminder of the logical progression of interactions on the app may also convey a sense of frustration with the lack of such developments; the plea to 'make an effort to talk' indicates that a lack of success on the app is seen as a question of effort, since a 'match' has already been established. Reminding other users of these simple terms (following a 'match', users should 'chat') shows users' adherence to this premise and equally, admonishment of those who do not follow the established process.

8.4.2.2 'i'm looking for'

The 3-grams 'looking for a', 'looking to meet' and 'i'm looking for' make it clear what the user's intentions and expectations are regarding potential matches. When referring to the nature of the relationship, there seemed to be three 'types': first, there was what was labelled 'a relationship', with 'all the cliché relationship goals'. Alternatively, participants wrote that they were looking for 'the One', calling for respondents to distinguish themselves and drawing on the cultural narrative of a fated romantic relationship (one that is exclusive). Second, users referred to looking for 'new friends', 'new people', 'cool people', 'people to meet and chat over drinks', 'decent lads to hang out, have a laugh and some banter', with no reference to amorous or sexual intentions. Finally, some respondents stated that they were looking for something 'casual', 'not serious', 'fun and strings free commitment' or 'a bit of fun'. The euphemistic meaning of 'fun' was often indicated by the use of inverted commas or emoticons (☺), demonstrating an expectation that there would be a shared understanding of what this means without explicitly stating it. Occasionally, respondents articulated an interest in more than one of these types of relationship, or that they were uncertain what type of relationship they were interested in ('I'm not sure what I'm looking for') and this was conveyed as an openness to the various developments their interactions might take ('see where it goes').

Often, users expressed looking for 'friends and maybe more', indicating that friendship was positioned as an initial step in the advancement towards a more amorous relationship. Indeed, the overlap of dating and friendship was also positioned in contrast to the 'hookup culture' associated with such apps, as indicated by one respondent who was 'Looking for chats, dates, friends, not really into the other side'. Here, the 'other side' presumably refers to the more 'casual' type of (sexual) relationship and a similar intent was expressed in more colloquial terms by a respondent who was looking for 'someone decent, not just a f*ck and chuck'. Furthermore, respondents only referred to 'hookups' when they were negating their interest in this type of interaction ('I'm not looking for hookups'), suggesting this was used more as a disparaging term.

The 3-grams 'i'm looking for' and 'looking to meet' were also used to describe the characteristics of a potential match. As with Baker's (2005) observations, the qualities ascribed to the imagined suitor(s) were fairly generic, even vague and this may be a way of broadening the pool of respondents. Participants referred to 'someone nice', 'cool people', 'a decent guy' or 'an understanding person with a sense of humour'. These kinds of attributes appear desirable and not exclusive, since few (if any) users are likely to think of themselves as anything but 'nice', 'decent' or 'understanding'. Other participants stated that they were looking for 'that special someone', an attribute that would seemingly distinguish particular users (as out-of-the-ordinary), but paradoxically remains inclusive since it allows (even encourages) readers to define what is 'special' about themselves. Furthermore, much like Baker's (2005) and Shalom's (1997) findings that posters were looking for something 'similar', respondents in this study reported looking for 'a like-minded person', 'a guy who thinks on my level and has similar interests', for example. In order for other users to determine if they are 'similar', the poster needs to offer some characterisation of themselves and this key part of the dating profile is typically indicated in the 3-grams that include 'I', as discussed above.

8.4.2.3 snapchat - [username]

The final 3-gram in the list indicates what might be considered the modern equivalent of providing contact information, which as we have discussed, has been recognised as a recurring feature of the personal ad (Coupland, 1996). Snapchat is a multimedia messaging app and users can locate and connect with other users if they have their username. In addition to the 10 occurrences of 'snapchat – [username]' there were a further five instances of '[username] – snapchat', with an overall 34 references to 'snapchat'/'SC'/'snapchatty'. There were also 16 references to 'Instagram'/'IG'/'Insta', despite Tinder allowing users to link to their Instagram accounts on their profiles. Tinder users do not necessarily need to use other apps to interact, since Tinder has a private message function; however, users may prefer to use an app that is more explicitly oriented towards messaging and supports more developed exchanges (e.g. through video and image-sharing). Snapchat and Instagram may also provide a means of verification, or at least a way of 'cross-checking' the information that a user has on their Tinder profile. Furthermore, there may be implications for the type of relationship matched users on Tinder have, if there is a perception that Tinder is for 'hookups', while Snapchat and Instagram are for 'friends'. Much like the inclusion of contact information in personal ads (Coupland, 1996), Snapchat usernames were the last (or only) content in participants' responses in 30 instances of the 34 mentions of the app.

The username would, of course, be different for every respondent so without anonymisation this would not have been identified as a recurrent n-gram. This highlights that there may be some tension between the functional aspects of the content of a corpus like this and maintaining the specific expression used by the participant (along with the need for anonymisation), as it seems more useful to have observed that a number of users are performing the same function (i.e. providing their Snapchat contact information) than to have the variation of those discrete usernames. Alternatively, this is something that might be indicated in an annotation scheme, which could also ensure that the various spellings used in references to the app are captured.

8.5 Discussion

N-gram analysis of the Tinder Corpus has highlighted some of the key functions of the user 'About Me' section through recurrent phrasal constructs: defining the self; establishing the terms and parameters of a prospective relationship; and encouraging other users to get in touch. References to the self were visible in the 3-grams 'I am a' and 'I have a', but if we also look at the frequent 2-grams in the data we also find that 'I'm', 'I like', 'I love', 'I have' and 'I can' occurred more than 10 times. This would provide further data on how users characterised themselves, more explicitly in terms of their likes and dislikes. The 2-grams further showed that respondents referred to a fairly restricted set of identity categories, relating to gender ('I'm a girl'), age ('I'm a 29-year-old'), profession ('I'm a barista'), as well as personality characteristics (shy, bubbly, genuine, a dreamer). However, perhaps because the topic of the section is determined by its heading 'About Me', the 'I' as subject was often elided and respondents often did not use full clauses when listing their characteristics, e.g. 'Film snob. Gin enthusiast. Not-so-secret ABBA fan'. Because of this, it might be worth conducting a semantic analysis of the data alongside targeting the 'I like'/'I love' constructs to determine if these tended to belong to particular categories, such as food and drink (gin, cheesecake, drinks, baking), TV and cinema (horror movies, TV shows), sports (table tennis, cycling, motorsports).

It was shown that the corpus largely consisted of data from homosexual male respondents, and Table 8.2 demonstrated the influence of this group on the overall corpus data. Looking exclusively at the data provided by the remaining respondents, there were no recurrent (i.e. more than 5 occurrences) 3- or 4-grams and 2-gram analysis identified the constructs 'I'm a', 'I like', 'I am', 'I love', following the patterns discussed above, as well as '- [username]', as discussed with respect to the 3-grams. There were two additional 2-grams that came from this dataset: 'a lot' and '[location]/'. The construct 'a lot' typically intensified a user's likes and often appeared with 'I like'. '[location]/' represented a reference to where the user was based, with the oblique indicating that this might be one of multiple locations. This would explain the need to include this information in the 'About Me' section, since the user's location is indicated on the profile and is visible to other users on the basis of their proximity. If the user does not have a single, fixed location (such as a student having a term-time location and a 'home' address), this would warrant clarification. There is no obvious explanation as to why this might occur less frequently in the responses from homosexual male participants but could be explained if this related to the respondents working (or studying) in particular occupations. Unfortunately, this information was only available for those who chose to explicitly refer to it in their 'About Me' descriptions.

The profile is of course only the first step in any relationships that develop from LBRTD apps like Tinder and the marketing of the self continues in the form of the interactional exchanges – whether through the instant messaging system or face-to-face – that are intended to follow a match. This would be an interesting area of development for this study, particularly with respect to the ways in which users maintain cohesion between their 'profile' and their selves in interaction, and potentially between their online and offline selves. Much like the continuance from personal ad to LBRTD app profile, we can refer to a body of literature of chat room exchanges to inform an analysis of such instant messaging interactions, such as Subrahmanyam et al. (2006) who examine identity constructions in teen chat rooms; Mileham (2007), who explores online infidelity; and Del-Teso-Craviotto (2008), who explores the authentification of sexual identities among gay men.

8.6 Summary

In this chapter, I presented a study of user profiles on dating apps and used n-gram analysis to identify recurring phrasal constructs. The most frequent 3-grams provided evidence of users' self-presentation, setting parameters for prospective relationships and inciting others to get in touch with them. Many respondents were explicit in outlining what type of relationship they were looking for and equally, many were keen to reiterate the expected next steps following a match (i.e. initiating a conversation), suggesting that this was a strategy deemed effective, or at least necessary. The functions, types of relationships and desirable qualities (of both posters and responders) were shown to be reasonably restricted, but nevertheless consistent with previous observations of other types of personal ad. Furthermore, the analysis demonstrated that expressions of these components followed certain patterns, though the qualities that distinguished one user's profile from another might also be found in the collocates of set constructs.

Note

1 Here, 'casj' is understood as an abbreviation of 'casual', suggesting a more informal type of social relationship.

References

Baker, P. (2005). *Public Discourses of Gay Men*. London: Routledge.
Baker, P. (2018). Sexuality, in E. Friginal (ed.) *Studies in Corpus-based Sociolinguistics*. London: Routledge, 157–175.
Biber, D., Conrad, S. and Cortes, V. (2004). If you look at…: Lexical bundles in university teaching and textbooks. *Applied Linguistics*, 25, 3, 371–405.
Birnholtz, J., Fitzpatrick, C., Handel, M. and Brubaker, J. R. (2014). Identity, identification and identifiability: The language of self-presentation on a location-based mobile dating app. *Proceedings of MobileHCI 2014*. 23–26 September 2014. Toronto, Canada, 3–12.
Blackwell, C., Birnholtz, J. and Abbott, C. (2015). Seeing and being seen: Co-situation and impression formation using Grindr, a location-aware gay dating app. *New Media and Society*, 17, 7, 1117–1136.

Brown, G., Maycock, B. and Burns, S. (2005). Your picture is your bait: Use and meaning of cyberspace among gay men. *Journal of Sex Research*, 42, 1, 63–73.

Carpenter, C. J. and McEwan, B. (2016). The players of micro-dating: Individual and gender differences in goal orientations toward micro-dating apps. *First Monday*, 21, 5, 1–10. Available online at: http://firstmonday.org/ojs/index.php/fm/article/view/6187/5469, accessed 19 June 2018.

Carter, R. and McCarthy, M. (2006). *Cambridge Grammar of English*. Cambridge: Cambridge University Press.

Cocks, H. G. (2010). *Classified: The Secret History of the Personal Column*. London: Arrow Books.

Cortes, V. (2004). Lexical bundles in published and student disciplinary writing: Examples from history and biology. *English for Specific Purposes*, 23, 4, 397–423.

Coupland, J. (1996). Dating advertisements: Discourse of the commodified self. *Discourse & Society*, 7, 2, 187–207.

Daneback, K., Cooper, A. and Månsson, A. A. (2005). An Internet study of cybersex participants. *Archives of Sexual Behavior*, 34, 3, 321–328.

Del-Teso-Craviotto, M. (2008). Gender and sexual identity authentication in language use: The case of chat rooms. *Discourse Studies*, 10, 2, 251–270.

Ellison, N. B., Hancock, J. T. and Toma, C. L. (2012) Profile as promise: A framework for conceptualizing veracity in online dating self-presentations. *New Media & Society*, 14, 1, 45–62.

Gibbs, J. L., Ellison, N. B. and Heino, R. D. (2006). Self-presentation in online personals: The role of anticipated future interaction, self-disclosure, and perceived success in Internet dating. *Communication Research*, 33, 2, 152–177.

Gibbs, J. L., Ellison, N. B. and Lai, C. H. (2011). First comes love, then comes Google: An investigation of uncertainty reduction strategies and self-disclosure in online dating. *Communication Research*, 38, 1, 70–100.

Hamid, B. D. A. and Bakar, K. A. (2011). Articulating male and female adolescent identities via the language of personal advertisements: A Malaysian perspective, in A. Duszak and U. Okulska (eds) *Language, Culture and the Dynamics of Age*. Berlin: De Gruyter, 191–219.

Hess, A. and Flores, C. (2018). Simply more than swiping left: A critical analysis of toxic masculine performances on *Tinder Nightmares*. *New Media & Society*, 20, 3, 1085–1102.

Hobbs, M., Owen, S. and Gerber, L. (2016). Liquid love? Dating apps, sex, relationships and the digital transformation of intimacy. *Journal of Sociology*, 53, 2, 271–284.

Hyland, K. (2008). As can be seen: Lexical bundles and disciplinary variation. *English for Specific Purposes*, 27, 1, 4–21.

Jagger, E. (2001). Marketing Molly and Melville: Dating in a postmodern, consumer society. *Sociology* 35, 1, 39–57.

Jaspal, R. (2017). Gay men's construction and management of identity on Grindr. *Sexuality & Culture*, 21, 1, 187–204.

Lutz, C. and Ranzini, G. (2017). Where dating meets data: Investigating social and institutional privacy concerns on Tinder. *Social Media + Society* 1–12. Available at: http://journals.sagepub.com/doi/pdf/10.1177/2056305117697735, accessed 7 August 2018.

MacKee, F. (2016). Social media in gay London: Tinder as an alternative to hook-up apps. *Social Media + Society*. Available at: http://journals.sagepub.com/doi/pdf/10.1177/2056305116662186, accessed 19 June 2018.

Mäntymäki, T. (2010). Looking for Love. Construction of Gender in Self-narratives on datingireland.com. *Käännösteoria, ammattikielet ja monikielisyys. VAKKI:n julkaisut* 37,

187–198. Available at: http://www.vakki.net/publications/2010/VAKKI2010_Mantymaki.pdf, accessed 19 June 2018.

Marcus, S.-R. (2014). Online dating profile analysis: The intersection of identity, gender and religion. *Proceedings of the New York State Communication Association* 8. Available at: https://docs.rwu.edu/nyscaproceedings/vol2013/iss2013/8/, accessed 26 June 2018.

Marcus, S.-R. (2016). "Swipe to the right": Assessing self-presentation in the context of mobile dating applications. *The Annual Conference of the International Communication Association*. 9–13 June 2016. Fukuoka, Japan. Available at: https://www.alexandria.unisg.ch/248333/1/Swipe%20Right_final.pdf, accessed 7 August 2018.

Marley, C. (2002). Popping the question: questions and modality in written dating advertisements. *Discourse Studies*, 4, 1, 75–98.

Mileham, B. L. A. (2007). Online infidelity in Internet chat rooms: An ethnographic exploration. *Computers in Human Behavior*, 23, 1, 11–31.

Mudraya, O. and Rayson, P. (2011). The language of over-50s in online dating classified ads. *VARIENG – Studies in Variation, Contacts and Change in English* 6. Available at: http://www.helsinki.fi/varieng/series/volumes/06/mudraya_rayson/, accessed 26 June 2018.

Ranzini, G. and Lutz, C. (2017). Love at first swipe? Explaining Tinder self-presentation and motives. *Mobile Media & Communication*, 5, 1, 80–101.

Sales, N. (2015). Tinder and the dawn of the "dating apocalypse". Available at: https://www.vanityfair.com/culture/2015/08/tinder-hook-up-culture-end-of-dating, accessed 20 June 2018.

Schrock, A. R. (2015). Communicative affordances of mobile media: Portability, availability, locatability, and multimediality. *International Journal of Communication*, 9, 1229–1246.

Shalom, C. (1997). That great supermarket of desire: Attributes of the desired other in personal advertisements, in K. Harvey and C. Shalom (eds) *Language and Desire: Encoding Sex, Romance and Intimacy*. London: Routledge, 186–203.

Smith, A. and Anderson, M. (2015). 5 facts about online dating. Pew Research Center. Available at: https://internet.psych.wisc.edu/wp-content/uploads/532-Master/532-UnitPages/Unit-06/Smith_Pew_OnlineDating_2016a.pdf, accessed 11 August 2018.

Subrahmanyam, K., Smahel, D. and Greenfield, P. (2006). Connecting developmental constructions to the Internet: Identity presentation and sexual exploration in online teen chat rooms. *Developmental Psychology*, 42, 3, 395–406.

Townsend, L. and Wallace, C. (2016). Social Media Research: A Guide to Ethics. The University of Aberdeen. Available at: http://www.dotrural.ac.uk/socialmediaresearchethics.pdf, accessed 22 April 2018.

Ward, J. (2017). What are you doing on Tinder? Impression management on a matchmaking mobile app. *Information, Communication & Society*, 20, 11, 1644–1659.

Yurchisin, J., Watchravesringkan, K. and McCabe, D. B. (2005). An exploration of identity re-creation in the context of Internet dating. *Social Behavior and Personality*, 33, 8, 735–750.

Chapter 9

Corpus linguistics in perspective

9.1 Looking back: a recap

In this book, I have discussed the fundamentals of corpus linguistics and looked to demonstrate how the core methods can be applied to forms of online communication. As such, we have looked at basic frequency counts and keywords with respect to non-standard forms in a corpus of Facebook posts approximating the Nottinghamshire dialect; collocation networks in a corpus of online learner comments; key semantic categories in a discussion of 'super-gonorrhoea'; and n-grams in dating profiles. These are just some of the types of units that can be studied using corpus approaches and the results of word lists and keyness, for example, are just the beginning when we consider how corpus linguistics has been combined with other approaches, as discussed in Chapter 1.

These demonstrations have also shown what can be done with some of the corpus tools that are available to readers, and with an understanding of what processes are involved in the various types of analysis (see Chapter 3), readers can make informed decisions about what tools will best serve them with their research objectives. The tasks throughout the book have provided an opportunity to get acquainted with the interfaces of such tools and the hands-on approach is certainly the best way to understand the range of functions on offer. For those interested in looking specifically at forms of online communication, we have considered some of the challenges of working with texts from the Web and it is important to draw on the knowledge that has already been established, both with respect to what we can say about forms of online communication and how we go about researching them. Some of the key studies were discussed in Chapter 4 and in the practical applications, I have highlighted some areas where corpus approaches might be extended or adapted in order to support us in capturing more of the online interactive experience.

We have seen here how corpus approaches can be applied to dialect studies and professional communication; vocabulary studies and online learning; health communication and citizen journalism; and the self-marketing of online dating. This attests – in a fairly modest way – to the range of discourses that operate online but also to the value of corpus methods in providing insights into what is characteristic – or not, as the case may be – of those discourses, at least in the context in which they have been studied. There are very few, if any, areas of language studies that cannot, in some way, be studied online and by extending what we have discovered about language in offline contexts to how it is manifested on the Web, we can discover more about each setting. In this way, we can begin to make some assessment of what type of impact the Internet has had on how we interact with one another and if we are going to base this on anything like the scope of language data that is generated by online interactions, corpus linguistics provides a valuable set of tools in supporting us in doing this.

9.2 Looking forward: what next for corpus linguistics?

9.2.1 Reflexivity and transparency

One of the aims of this book was to provide a clear and detailed demonstration of how corpus linguistics can be applied in a practical way, with a level of detail that would support readers in conducting their own work. This has shown that there are a number of key decisions that researchers must make in order to design, implement and report their research. Baker and McEnery (2015) remind us that processes such as keyword analysis are subject to (often, quite inconspicuous) forms of bias; deciding what statistical measure to use, at what level we set our threshold, on which words from a keyword list to investigate further, all involve some degree of subjectivity. In their edited collection exploring the combination of corpus linguistics and (critical) discourse analysis, Marchi and Taylor (2018) emphasise the need for accountability (under which they include transparency and consistency) alongside self-reflexivity. They call for researchers to become "more sensitive to the impact of decisions taken" and for research to be "presented in ways that are sufficiently clear to allow for replication" (Marchi and Taylor, 2018: 12). Reflecting upon our decision-making is key to understanding our data and transparency can facilitate more understanding when we try to convey what it 'means' to audiences. This is not always straightforward – particularly when corpus linguists work with colleagues from other disciplines, as Brookes et al. (2018: 110) demonstrate in their account of their work collaborating with health professionals and, specifically, submitting their work to health journals. They write that "Although our corpus linguistics approach has generally appealed to healthcare professionals working within clinical settings [...] reviewers not cognisant with linguistic study have treated the (corpus) linguistic approach with some degree of suspicion, a method that itself becomes the research focus at the expense of the analytical findings issuing from it" (Brookes et al., 2018: 110). Most disciplines have their established methods and cross- or inter-disciplinary work often involves applying methods that are new, at least to some colleagues (and potentially, editors). If corpus linguistics is to be established as a 'tried and tested' set of methodologies across disciplines, then institutional structures from funders, to research centres, to publishers must all work to facilitate interdisciplinary collaboration.

Reflexivity is also warranted when we make decisions about what it is that we are studying. Baker (2018) points out that there has been a tendency to favour particular types of data in corpus and discourse analyses, on the basis of their having presumed importance (such as political speeches) or the relative ease with which they can be collected and compiled (such as online news data). In addition to the type of data we look at, Marchi and Taylor (2018) refer to the 'dusty corners' of 'similarity' and 'absence' in that there is an overt emphasis on difference in corpus linguistics research. We must not be afraid to take on the challenges of more 'difficult' data, particularly as those multi-layered types of data become all-the-more ordinary for language users; in this book I have only briefly discussed the multimedia/multimodal dimensions of online communication, largely because this would not be an effective way to demonstrate corpus tools (based on their current capabilities). Again, researchers have often combined approaches in order to tackle more complex datasets and we must be willing to consider multiple methods in order to get the best from our tools. Developments in the tools themselves are unlikely to come simply from our research interests. One of the key – and very tangible – changes affecting online behaviour more generally, which will also influence user interactions and how researchers (including corpus linguists) study the Web, is the implementation of the E.U. General Data Protection Regulation (GDPR) (The European Parliament and the Council of the Europoean Union, 2016) and questions of ethics.

9.2.2 Ethics

The ethics of online communication, specifically with respect to social media, is very much a part of public discourse. In April 2018, Facebook CEO Mark Zuckerberg appeared before a congressional hearing to discuss Facebook's privacy policy, after it was discovered that data collected through the site was shared with the consulting firm Cambridge Analytica, who had also worked on Donald Trump's 2016 election campaign. This prompted a notice to all Facebook users, clarifying what the terms and data policy of the service were for the time (https://newsroom.fb.com/news/2018/04/terms-and-data-policy/), which, importantly, did not reflect any changes to the policy – it simply reminded users of what they had already signed up to. At around the same time, Internet users in the E.U. had to review the terms of service for a number of Web-based applications following the introduction of the GDPR. We looked at key ethical issues for corpus-building in Chapter 2 and now that the GDPR has come into effect, we will begin to see how this shapes research design within the field. The GDPR calls for transparency so that 'data subjects' understand how their personal data is processed and under this regulation, posts to social media sites are considered 'personal data'. The regulation states that data can only be used for the purposes and terms under which it was gathered and to which the user consented. This poses quite a challenge for corpus linguists, for whom one of the benefits of building a corpus – and a payoff for the work that it involves – is that it can be queried for a number of different (often undetermined at the time of data collection) research questions. Furthermore, the data should not be held any longer than is required to complete the research. Finally, data subjects have a 'right to erasure' (also known as a right 'to be forgotten'), by which a participant can request that their data be removed from a corpus (or database). In a corpus, where the data is likely to have undergone some form of anonymisation, finding one participant's contributions is going to be difficult, particularly if the corpus has been held and used by other researchers. These aspects, in particular, may mean that it is no longer viable to keep a centrally stored corpus if it contains any personal data and so the future of corpus linguistics is likely to be shaped by this type of challenge. Corpus linguists are, of course, not alone in this challenge and the question of ethics is one that users and researchers alike will need to consider as we become more vigilant with respect to our personal data and how it is shared online.

9.3 Corpus linguistics and the Internet

In the Introduction to this book, I demonstrated how corpus linguistics has developed alongside computing technology and the future of the field will no doubt continue to run alongside the growth of the Internet. The 12 March 2016 was celebrated as the 25th anniversary of the World Wide Web and marked with the launch of a dedicated website (https://www.w3.org/webat25/), which also outlined some of the challenges that lay ahead. The principles on which the Web was developed attest to the degree of innovation shown by its creators and they remain key concerns for the continuing development of online resources:

- Decentralisation
- Non-discrimination
- Bottom-up design
- Universality
- Consensus.

The concept of 'decentralisation' means that users do not require permission from a central authority to participate in the Web and that the existence of the Web is not contingent upon any one central controlling node. Subsequently, there is no centralised process of censorship or surveillance. The concept of 'Net Neutrality' is predicated on the principle of equity, or 'non-discrimination'. This principle argues for the consistent and equal treatment of users as far as quality of service goes. This can be difficult to maintain with an ever-increasing degree of personalisation on the Web and there have been questions raised in instances where Web platforms have interfered with the functionality of, say, services offered by competitors in favour of equivalent services offered by companies that have the same ownership. As corpus linguists, understanding the processes that shape Web interactions and behaviour will inform our analysis of its language. The increase in user-generated content, for example, is a result of the principle of 'bottom-up' design, which encourages the participation and experimentation of everyone in developing the code and the functions of the Web and only by giving everyone a say in creating the standards for the Web can 'consensus' be achieved (https://webfoundation.org).

'Universality' reflects a drive towards diversity on the Web, enabled by the capacity for all computer devices to 'talk to one another'. This, of course, relates more explicitly to communication between the different technologies that enable Web access; however, we can also consider how the multilingual Web will shape future corpus linguistics research. In 2000, Xu (2000) estimated that 71% of the pages on the Web (453 million out of 634 million webpages indexed by the Excite engine at that time) were written in English, followed by Japanese (6.8%); German (5.1%); French (1.8%); Chinese (1.5%); Spanish (1.1%); Italian (0.9%); and Swedish (0.7%). In November 2017, W3Techs.com reported that 51.2% of Web content was in English, with 6.7% Russian; 5.6% Japanese; 5.6% German; 5.1% Spanish; and 4.1% French, (though the methods for determining this were not reported) (https://w3techs.com/technologies/history_overview/content_language). If corpus linguistics research is to be representative of the Web, then our research must attend to the range of languages used online and we must continue to develop our tools to support, for example, tokenisation and taggers for multiple languages (#LancsBox currently supports lemmatisation and automatic tagging in 21 languages).

The Internet is a site of perpetual innovation and in order to continue to make a meaningful contribution to language studies, corpus linguists will need to be conscientious of how it evolves and continue to develop the tools that facilitate corpus analysis. However, as McEnery (2018: 12) argues, "we should not always wait for the tide of technology to wash our problems away"; as much as developments in technology play a key role in how we conduct our research and what it is that we study, research drives the development of technology, as we generate knowledge about what can be done and where improvements are required. In closing, it is hoped that this book has helped readers to prepare for conducting their own research in order to contribute to these developments and their own findings to the field.

References

Baker, P. (2018). Conclusion: Reflecting on reflective research, in C. Taylor and A. Marchi (eds) *Corpus Approaches to Discourse: A Critical Review*. London: Routledge, 281–292.

Baker, P. and McEnery, A. (2015). Introduction, in P. Baker and A. McEnery (eds) *Corpora and Discourse Studies: Integrating Discourse and Corpora*. Basingstoke: Palgrave Macmillan, 1–19.

Brookes, G., Harvey, K. and Muallany, L. (2018). From corpus to clinic: Health communication research and the impact agenda, in D. McIntyre and H. Price (eds) *Applying Linguistics: Language and the Impact Agenda*. London: Routledge, 99–111.

Marchi, A. and Taylor, C. (2018). Introduction: Partiality and reflexivity, in C. Taylor and A. Marchi (eds) *Corpus Approaches to Discourse: A Critical Review*. London: Routledge, 1–15.

McEnery, T. (2018). The Spoken BNC2014: The corpus linguistic perspective, in V. Brezina, R. Love and K. Aijmer (eds) *Corpus Approaches to Contemporary British Speech: Sociolinguistic Studies of the Spoken BNC2014*. London: Routledge, 9–14.

The European Parliament and the Council of the European Union (2016). Regulation (EU) 2016/679 of the European Parliament and of the Council of 27 April 2016 on the protection of natural persons with regard to the processing of personal data and on the free movement of such data, and repealing Directive 95/46/EC (General Data Protection Regulation). *Official Journal of the European Union.* Available at: https://eur-lex.europa.eu/legal-content/EN/TXT/PDF/?uri=CELEX:32016R0679&from=EN, accessed 1 June 2018.

Xu, J. L. (2000). Multilingual search on the World Wide Web. In *Proceedings of the Hawaii International Conference on System Science (HICSS-33).* 4–7 January 2000. Maui, Hawaii. Available at: https://ieeexplore.ieee.org/stamp/stamp.jsp?tp=&arnumber=926582, accessed 16 April 2018.

Appendix

Types and examples of corpora. For References, see Chapter 1.

Corpus Category	Examples
General (Reference)	ACE, ANC, the Bank of English, BE06, BNC1994, BNC2014, COCA, CorCenCC, FLOB, FROWN, ICE, LOB
Specialised	CANBEC, CANELC, CORE, HERMES, MICASE, the Air Traffic Control Corpus, the ENRON Corpus
Parallel	The English-Norwegian Parallel Corpus, the English-Swedish Parallel Corpus, InterCorp, EUROPAL, the Canadian Hansard Corpus
Comparable	GloWBE, ICE
Diachronic	The Diachronic Corpus of Present-Day Spoken English, the TIME Magazine Corpus, COHA
Historical	The Helsinki Corpus of English Texts, A Representative Corpus of Historical English Registers
Monitor	COHA, News On the Web Corpus
Multimodal	Spoken Chinese Corpus of Situated Discourse, the Nottingham Multi-Modal Corpus, Multimodal Corpus of Intercultural Communication
Online communication	The Birmingham Blog Corpus, CANELC, CORE, the Dortmund Chat Corpus, the Edinburgh Twitter Corpus, GloWBE, HERMES, the iWeb Corpus, NOW Corpus, the NPS Chat Corpus, the TenTen Corpus Family, the Toronto Internet Corpus, the WestburyLab USENET Corpus

Glossary

annotation the interpretative linguistic information added to an electronic corpus. Annotation can relate to syntactic analysis, semantic analysis, error tagging, discourse and pragmatic analysis, for example.

balance a consideration for building a corpus that ensures that not only is the appropriate variety of texts included but they are also represented in the appropriate proportions.

boilerplate refers to features of a webpage that are external to its unique content, such as headers, footers, copyright notices and navigation links. Often, corpus analysts will want to remove this content prior to analysis to focus specifically on the content that has been created for that 'text'.

colligation the regular occurrence of a grammatical set alongside a search term.

collocation the regular co-occurrence of two words. A word that occurs with high statistical probability alongside our search term is called a **collocate**.

comparable corpus a corpus consisting of texts from the same domain in more than one language. The texts are not direct translations of each other (as with a **parallel corpus**) but do belong to the same genre or type.

concordance line represents one of a series of lines of text taken from a corpus which presents a search item together with its surrounding text. The process of generating concordance lines is called **concordancing**.

corpus a principled collection of machine-readable texts for the purposes of a specific set of research questions related to natural language use. The plural is **corpora**.

corpus linguistics a computational approach to linguistic analysis that identifies patterns, typically on the basis of frequency.

co-text the words or features surrounding a particular term, that help to determine its meaning.

diachronic corpus a corpus designed to capture representations of language over time and support our exploration of language change.

folk linguistics the study of speakers' (i.e. non-linguists') opinions and beliefs about language. Also called perceptual dialectology.

general corpus a collection of texts intended to represent the range and variety of genres within a language type, for example the Corpus of Contemporary American English (COCA), the British National Corpus (BNC), or the Corpus of Online Registers of English (CORE). A general corpus is often used as a point of comparison and because of that, referred to as a **reference** corpus. Furthermore, they are often defined in contrast to **specialised corpora**.

granularity refers to how subtle the differences are between the categories of an annotation scheme. A fine-grained annotation scheme is extremely precise and distinguishes many different categories. A coarse-grained annotation scheme is fairly rudimentary, providing only more general distinctions.

historical corpus a corpus that enable studies of languages over periods of time, particularly if it recalls data from a period that would not be classified as (near-) contemporary.

keyness a kind of corpus analysis which explores what is characteristic of a given corpus by looking at features that appear with unusual frequency (high or low) when compared with a norm as determined by a general corpus. Typically, keyness is explored through **keywords**, which are described as 'positive' is they occur with unusually high frequency and 'negative' if they occur with unusually low frequency.

key word in context (KWIC) the most common format of presenting corpus data, in which the search word is displayed in the middle of a series of concordances lines, which each show a different instance of the word being used.

lemma a base form of a word together with its inflected forms.

lemmatisation a process through which a root word (**lemma**) is identified as a means to collate its inflected forms (**lexemes**) as one unit of analysis.

lexeme an inflected form/grammatical variant of a root word (**lemma**) e.g. 'played' with respect to 'play'.

lexical bundle groups of words that tend to co-occur repeatedly in a specific type of discourse.

lexico-grammar a key notion in corpus linguistics which emphasizes the inseparability of grammar and lexis.

log-likelihood a type of corpus statistic that is used to compare differences in word frequencies between corpora. LL indicates how confident we can be that the identification of key items is not the result of chance.

(textual) markup refers to information about the physical appearance and formatting of a document, e.g. headings, paragraph breaks, sections.

metadata information about the texts in the corpus or 'data about the data'. For example, details about the speaker (age, gender, class), the mode of communication (spoken, written, online), the time and location of a social media post, etc.

monitor corpus a dynamic corpus that is continually updated and thereby supports studies of incremental language change.

multimodal corpus a corpus that supports analysis of the multiple 'modes' of communication (e.g. voice quality and gesture alongside language content) in interaction. In instances where these modes are considered separately but presented in alignment, we might refer to 'multimedia corpora'.

multi-word unit (MWU) a lexical unit which consists of two or more words but functions as a whole with a specific meaning e.g. 'of course'.

mutual information (MI) a type of corpus statistic that is used to measure the strength of a partnership between words. MI emphasises exclusivity and so has a propensity to highlight unusual combinations.

n-gram a regular sequence of words found in a text or corpus. The 'n' represents an unspecified number, since this might occur as a bi-gram (sequence of two), tri-gram (sequence of three), etc.

node a search word or phrase that is presented in the centre of a concordance line.

PoS-tagging (Part of Speech-tagging) an automated form of annotation that allocates each token to a grammatical word class.

reference corpus see **general corpus**.

representativeness refers to the extent to which a corpus includes the full range of variability in a population. When building a corpus, researchers must sample in such a way as to contain all types of text that are needed to make the contents of the corpus an accurate reflection of the whole of the language (or variety of language).

semantic preference the pattern of collocates of a node word in terms of lexical sets.

semantic prosody the implicit attitude or evaluation of the meaning of a word established through its frequent co-occurrence with particular words.

span the size of a search window that is used to observe the co-text of words as concordance lines. In collocation analysis, the span refers to the range within which the corpus analysis tool will consider words as appearing 'alongside' the search term.

specialised corpus a collection of text that focuses on a specific genre or particular variety of a language. Examples include: the Air Traffic Control Corpus, the ENRON Corpus, etc. Defined in contrast to a **general corpus**.

static corpus a corpus that is collected within a set period of time, which has a fixed set of texts and is not updated. Contrasts with a **monitor corpus**.

synchronic corpus a corpus that collects different examples of language from a single point in time. Contrasts with a **diachronic corpus**.

taggers the automated computational tools that provide linguistic information to all words in a corpus. See **PoS-tagging**.

T-score a statistical measure that expresses the certainty with which we can argue that there is an association between the words, i.e. their co-occurrence is not random. The value is affected by the frequency of the whole collocation which is why very frequent word combinations tend to reach a high value despite not being significant as collocations.

token what is determined to be a 'word' in a corpus, as identified through **tokenisation**.

tokenisation the process through which a text is segmented into words.

type the number of unique words in a corpus.

type-token ratio a type of corpus statistic which is a measure of lexical richness; this ratio is obtained by dividing the number of types by the number of tokens in a corpus.

web crawling a process by which a researcher provides a software tool with a sample of URLs associated with their research topic, from which the software collects the Web content and then 'follows' any hyperlinked data within that content to locate additional webpages.

wordlist a series of the words in a corpus typically ranked according to their frequency.

wpm 'words per million'; a way of normalising frequency to make 'like-for-like' comparisons across corpora of different sizes.

Task commentaries

Task 1.1

There are 381 instances of 'viral' in the BNC, running over four pages of concordance lines. These examples show 'viral' used exclusively as a biological term, in the context of infections, enzymes and DNA, for example. Entry 101 refers to 'viral content', though this is still in relation to illness. Returning to the Search page and clicking on 'Collocates' (rather than 'List') shows that 'viral' most frequently collocates with 'infection', 'hepatitis', 'infection' etc.

Given its rather narrow meaning, it is not surprising to see that although some examples of 'viral' come from the general press (in terms of tabloid and broadsheet newspapers, television news), as well as fictional prose, a great many come from sources labelled as 'science material' or 'medical' (academic or otherwise). Indeed, you can use the 'Chart' function on the original search page to see frequencies for these categories: 151 occurrences are categorised as 'non-academic' and by clicking on the heading for that column, you will see that 129 of those come from 'natSci' (natural sciences) publications. The category 'W_pop_lore' refers to popular magazines and, interestingly, these examples more often refer to animal (rather than human) biology, relating to keeping fish.

This exercise demonstrates how corpora can be used to show how quickly new uses and meanings for words can be established, supporting diachronic studies of changing vocabulary.

Task 3.2

Extract A: The word count here could range from anything between 28–35 words, depending on how you count punctuation, genitive forms (is 'anyone's' one or two words?) and noun phrases such as 'Leg-Locker Curse'.

Extract B: Arguably, there are anywhere between 14 and 30 words. The contracted forms ''s' and ''d' would typically be treated as separate by a tokeniser. The analyst would have to decide what to do with 'non-words' such as fillers ('erm') and false starts ('th-'), which are common in speech. There are a number of ways to count 'Wiltshire and Thamesdown Racial Equality Council', in that it has a single referent (and therefore could be considered a single noun phrase) or, alternatively, a series of pre-modifiers along with the noun 'Council'.

Extract C: This is likely to be considered 14 (at most, 16) words, depending on punctuation. It seems sensible to treat tags ('@kkwbeauty'), hashtags and URLs each as single units, given that they are defined by their uniqueness. With hashtags in particular, it seems possible that readers will simultaneously recognise the unit as a whole but also the meaning of the composite words; nevertheless, something like #MeToo clearly has meaning that is distinct from 'me', 'too' and 'me too'.

The potential variability here for what counts as a 'word' and subsequently, how many words there are, is important for understanding the outputs of frequency lists and any statistical processes carried out by corpus analysis tools. When working with a new tool, it is worth uploading a short text that you know contains the types of tokens you are likely to be working with in order to see how they are counted.

Task 3.6

In order to determine in which medium (written, spoken, online) the words are most common, the frequencies would have to be normalised by taking into account how large the respective corpora are. This could be done, for example, by calculating words-per-million (wpm), which is provided in the search outputs for the BNC1994 but would require the exact token count for the CORE.

What is provided in the table is the rank of each word in terms of frequency with respect to each corpus:

	BNC1994 Magazine (written)	BNC1994 Spoken	CORE (online)	Overall
time	1st	1st	1st	**1st**
okay	5th	2nd	5th	**4th**
however	2nd	4th	2nd	**2nd**
party	3rd	3rd	3rd	**3rd**
song	4th	5th	4th	**5th**

How does this compare with your predictions?

The results attest to the frequency of 'time' across modes. Arguably, this is a more abstract term than 'party' or 'song', both of which might be used in a smaller range of contexts.

'Okay' is a more informal term which we might associate with spoken discourse and, conversely, 'however' reflects a formal register used more commonly in written texts. The ranking would suggest that the CORE texts are more like written registers.

Task 7.1

I found 47,854 instances of 'fake news' in the NOW Corpus and used the 'Chart' function to find that there were 14,566 occurrences in the first 'half' of 2018. Though this was an increase on the two halves of 2017 in terms of raw frequency, this was slightly down in terms of words-per-million and seemed to be on the decline from April 2018 onwards (looking at the week-to-week counts), following a rise in the first few months of the year.

The frequency of the term meant that there was a lot of potential for varied usage but using the 'Collocates' search function showed that 'fake news' frequently appeared within quotation marks. This could indicate that it was still being treated as a loaded concept and that it was quoted sources using the term, rather than the journalists themselves, who might refrain from accepting or showing their agreement with this labelling. This was also suggested in that 'so-called' was a high-frequency collocate.

The collocates 'spread' and 'spreading', along with 'peddling' showed that concerns around 'fake news' were with its dissemination and this also carries a negative semantic prosody, since collocates of the verb 'to spread' include 'disease', 'virus', 'fire', 'rumours' and 'infection'; collocates of 'peddling' include 'drugs', 'lies', 'corruption' and 'falsehood'. 'Fake news' was presented as something to 'avoid', 'tackle' and 'combat'. Other descriptors that frequently appeared alongside 'fake news' included 'hate speech', 'propaganda', 'disinformation', 'misinformation', 'alternative facts', 'lies' and 'hoaxes', demonstrating that it was associated with words antonymous with quality information.

Index

Adolphs, S. 1, 13, 20, 34–5, 61
advertising discourse 64, 98–9, 115, 117, 176
affordances 76, 79, 172
annotation 11, 43–6, 53, 131, 152; images 63–4, 84; semantic 61–2, 153; *see also* tagging
anonymisation 34–6, 128–9, 130, 177–80, 184
AntConc 71, 180
Anthony, L. 43, 71
asynchronous 77, 79–80, 81, 89–90, 123, 132

balance 31, 38
Bank of English 18, 20
blogs 22, 44, 64, 78, 89–90
BNC *see* British National Corpus
boilerplate 39–40
British National Corpus: BNC1994 10, 15, 18, 29, 30–1, 43–5, 53, 57, 60, 66–8, 71, 137, 200, 202; BNC2014 9, 15, 18, 31–2, 44
Brown (family) 2–3, 15, 16–7, 19, 31, 56, 66, 70, 71

Caple, H. 20, 63–4
censorship 37–8
chat rooms *see* computer-mediated communication (CMC)
Chi-squared test 69
cluster 54, 64, 71, 88–9, 152, 180
colligation 58, 70
collocation 57–61, 69, 70, 87–9, 99, 100, 106, 112–3, 126–7, 136–40, 153, 162, 164, 175, 189, 202, 203
(user) comments 5, 122, 128, 130, 146, 149, 151–2, 154–6, 160, 164, 165–6,

comparable corpus 19
computational linguistics 2, 3–4
computer-mediated communication (CMC) 21, 42, 77; chat rooms 22, 186; e-language 21–2; netspeak 78, 81, 132, 170; SMS 21, 22, 43, 77, 78–9; online forum 35, 117, 122
concordancing 9, 52, 71; concordance lines 9–11, 16, 52, 70, 99, 113–5, 140; Key words in context (KWIC) 9, 52, 70
consent 34, 35–7, 104–5, 128, 177–8, 191
conversation analysis 45, 89, 143
corpus analysis tools 16, 51–2, 55, 56, 58, 69, 70–1, 80; *see also* #Lancsbox; AntConc; Wmatrix
Corpus of Contemporary American English (COCA) 15, 30, 58, 137
Corpus of Historical American English (COHA) 15, 19–20
Corpus of Online Registers of English (CORE) 22, 66
co-text 9, 11, 21, 52, 53, 70
crawling 38–9
crowdsourcing 33–4

de-duplication 41
diachronic corpora 19
disinhibition 90–1
dispersion 59, 68, 70

effect size 70
e-language *see* Computer Medicated Communication
emoji 38, 54, 76, 82–4, 88, 180–1
emoticons 53, 54, 76–7, 82–3, 87–8, 183
encoding 42, 45, 84
ethics 34–7, 128, 178, 191–2

Index

frequency 8–9, 58–9, 65–7, 70

general corpora 17–8, 30
General Data Protection Regulation (GDPR) 34–6, 178, 191
genre 22, 30, 44, 57, 64, 77, 78
gesture 20–1, 64, 82
Graphics Interchange Format (GIFs) 82, 84, 87

hashtag 37, 38, 54, 81, 108, 201
historical corpus 19, 31, 62
hyperlinks 33, 38–9, 53, 130–1
Hypertext Markup Language (HTML) 3, 4, 39–40

images 63, 82–4, 106–7, 110, 118, 131, 151, 179

keyness 66–8, 69–70, 71, 153
KWIC *see* concordancing

#Lancsbox 51–2, 59, 70, 193
lemmatisation 55, 193
lexical bundle 54, 71, 180
log-likelihood (LL) 69

markup 11, 43, 44–5
meme 84–7
metadata 11, 34, 43–4, 129, 131
monitor corpus 20
multilingual corpus 18–9, 93
multimodal 20–1, 63–4, 89, 191
multi-word units 53, 54, 62
mutual information (MI) 69

Natural Language Processing (NLP) 2
netspeak *see* computer-mediated communication (CMC)
n-gram 54, 80, 180
node 9–10, 11, 52, 58–61, 69, 136

orthography 21, 41–2, 43, 45, 53–4, 57, 77, 78, 108, 116, 117

paralinguistic 20–1, 41, 82, 83

parallel corpora 18–9
Part-of-Speech (PoS) tagging 56–7, 66, 71
pragmatics 13–4, 45, 77, 91, 115, 135

reference corpus 17–8, 66, 68, 143
register 22, 55, 64, 65, 77, 78, 80, 180
representative 29, 30–2, 33, 34, 35, 38, 193

sampling 9–10, 11, 20, 29–31, 38, 57, 70, 153
semantic categorisation 21, 61–3, 71, 89, 153, 154, 157–65, 166, 176,
semantic preference 61, 153
semantic prosody 60–1, 203
Short Messaging Service (SMS) *see* computer-mediated communication (CMC)
social media 3, 4, 10, 15, 22, 34, 36, 38, 71, 80–2, 84–5, 88, 97–8, 112, 117–8, 191
sociolinguistics 14–5, 43, 89, 102
span 9, 11, 58
spelling *see* orthography
statistics 68–70, 71, 190
stylistics 15–6

tagging 4, 14, 41, 44, 45–6, 53–4, 56–7, 61–3, 64, 71, 90, 152–3, 166, 193; *see also* Part-of-Speech (PoS) tagging; semantic categorisation
token 52–4, 58, 59, 153, 193
translation 18–9, 42
trolling 91–2
t-score 69
type-token ratio 54

Web as Corpus (WaC) 32–3
Wmatrix 62, 68, 71, 89
word class 56, 58, 64
wordlist 65, 80

XML 45–6, 132

Zappavigna, M. 20, 80–1, 84–5, 87, 88–9, 118

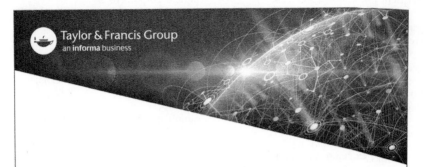